Language and the learning curve

Language and the learning curve

A new theory of syntactic development

Anat Ninio
The Hebrew University of Jerusalem

OXFORD
UNIVERSITY PRESS

OXFORD
UNIVERSITY PRESS

Great Clarendon Street, Oxford OX2 6DP

Oxford University Press is a department of the University of Oxford.
It furthers the University's objective of excellence in research, scholarship,
and education by publishing worldwide in

Oxford New York

Auckland Cape Town Dar es Salaam Hong Kong Karachi
Kuala Lumpur Madrid Melbourne Mexico City Nairobi
New Delhi Shanghai Taipei Toronto

With offices in

Argentina Austria Brazil Chile Czech Republic France Greece
Guatemala Hungary Italy Japan Poland Portugal Singapore
South Korea Switzerland Thailand Turkey Ukraine Vietnam

Oxford is a registered trade mark of Oxford University Press
in the UK and in certain other countries

Published in the United States
by Oxford University Press Inc., New York

© Oxford University Press 2006

The moral rights of the author have been asserted
Database right Oxford University Press (maker)

First published 2006

British Library Cataloguing in Publication Data

Data available

Library of Congress Cataloging in Publication Data
Ninio, Anat.
Language and the learning curve: a new theory of syntactic development/Anat Ninio.
    p. cm.
Includes bibliographical references and index.
ISBN-13: 978-0-19-929982-9 (alk. paper pbk.)
ISBN-10: 0-19-929982-X (alk. paper pbk.)
ISBN-13: 978-0-19-929981-2 (alk. paper hbk.)
ISBN-10: 0-19-929981-1 (alk. paper hbk.)
1. Language acquisition. 2. Grammar, Comparative and general–Syntax. I.   Title.
P118.N558 2006
401′.93–dc22
2006023806

Typeset by SPI Publisher Services, Pondicherry, India
Printed in Great Britain
on acid-free paper by
Biddles Ltd., King's Lynn, Norfolk

1 3 5 7 9 10 8 6 4 2

Dedication

For Shira and Uri

Acknowledgements

The work that is described here owes a great deal to people who pointed me in the direction of various research traditions that proved to be of invaluable importance for this work, and who have patiently tutored me in their intricacies. Jerry Bruner taught me to look at language in the context of social interaction, never as an abstraction. Dick Hudson spent a very generous amount of time with me discussing Dependency Grammar. Fran Poulton brought to my attention the relevance of the analogical reasoning and exemplar learning literatures, and connected my work to a long tradition in cognitive psychology. Uri Hershberg introduced me to complex systems, and Shmuel Sattath shared with me some of his vast expertise in Complexity Theory. It is difficult to give due credit to these friends and tutors—and many others I did not mention—in the shaping of the final model of syntactic development. The interdisciplinary character of the work undoubtedly owes a great deal to their different perspectives that they so generously shared with me.

Uri Hershberg, Patty Brooks, Hagit Magen, Caroline Rowland, Tamar Keren-Portnoy, and Liu Haitao read the manuscript and gave extensive comments. Michael Keren, Tali Kaufmann, and Yoram Louzoun read parts of the manuscript and made important comments. I am extremely grateful for their support as well as for their criticism, some of which I have tried to address in my text. I am sure there are many issues in which they are not satisfied with my solutions, and I am taking full responsibility for the errors that remain despite their good advice.

Thanks are due to Martin Baum, Carol Maxwell, and Bethan Lee of Oxford University Press for their help and support during the preparation of the manuscript.

Some parts of this material was presented in conference talks over the years, and in particular at the Symposium on Analogy and Cognition, Pele de Recherches en Sciences Cognitives de Toulouse (PRESCOT), Toulouse, France, May 2002; the Biennial Meeting of the Society for Research in Child Development, Tampa, Florida, April 2003; the Brown Bag Meeting of Developmental Psychology Program, The Graduate Center of the City University of New York, November 2004; the Princeton Workshop on Early Syntax, May 2005; the 30th Annual Boston University Conference on Language Development, November

2005; and the Eight Annual Gregynog/Nant Gwrtheyrn Conference on Child Language, April, 2006. Thanks to the participants of those meetings; to Edith Bavin, Jerry Bruner, Nancy Budwig, Devin Casenhiser, Gina Conti-Ramsden, Annabel Cormack, Karine Duvignau, Carol Feldman, Olivier Gasquet, Ginny Mueller Gathercole, Bruno Gaume, Adele Goldberg, Erika Hoff, Elena Lieven, Haydee Marcos, Claire Martinot, Lorraine McCune, Letty Naigles, Katherine Nelson, Matan Ninio, Julian Pine, Fran Poulton, Shmuel Sattath, Nitya Sethuraman, Anna Stetsenko, and Marilyn Vihman, for discussions, criticism, and comments.

Various aspects of the research were partly supported under United States-Israel Binational Foundation (BSF) grant nos 2467/81 and 84-00267/1; the Israeli Academy of Sciences (ISF) grant no. 27.84; grants by the Israel Foundations Trustees (Ford Foundation) (1992–1994; 1994–1996); and under grant 9500661 by the Spencer Foundation.

I am grateful to the Graduate Center of the City University of New York for having me as a Visiting Scholar between July 2004 and June 2005, and for making it possible for me to work on this manuscript in a nourishing environment. Thanks to Patty Brooks, David Bearison, Bruce Dorval, Joe Glick, Jude Kubran, Katherine Nelson, and Anna Stetsenko for making my stay highly enjoyable as well as inspiring.

Finally, I am deeply grateful to Shira Ninio and to Uri Hershberg for endless discussions, for technical help, and for support and advice throughout the preparation of the manuscript. This book is dedicated to them with much love.

Contents

Reader Quotations

Anat Ninio's new theory of language acquisition is at once compatible with recent advances in linguistic theories of lexicalist grammars, including Chomsky's most recent minimalist theory, and with social cognitivist theories of children's acquisition of syntax and vocabulary. She proposes that children follow a "third way" toward the acquisition of a first language, neither re-inventing structures already available in their heads, as nativists see it, nor internalizing language structures modeled by their parents, as social interactionists have argued. Rather, the new social cognitive theory sees children linking into the complex network of linguistic forms in their language environments, thus becoming from the beginning part of the network itself. This book is a breakthrough achievement, elegantly and logically presented, solidly based on evidence from child language research and expertise in current theoretical linguistics.

Katherine Nelson
Department of Psychology, Graduate Center, City University of New York

----

This book provides an integrated and easily understandable framework for explaining how syntax is acquired and how it develops. The proposed theory is very significant not only for first language acquisition but also for automatic acquisition of syntax by computers. The book is very interesting for researchers of language acquisition and for specialists who work on how to make computers understand language and how to link language with broader knowledge networks.

Liu Haitao
Applied and Computational Linguistics,
Communication University of China, Beijing

Anat Ninio has forged a unique role for herself in the field of language acquisition as a creative and innovative researcher. In this book she argues that children learn a lexicalist syntax and generalise on the basis of form rather than meaning. She utilises developmental learning curves to support her position and, while rejecting the notion of increasing abstraction in children's syntax, makes a rapprochement with recent developments in minimalist linguistic theory. Ninio continuously thinks across theoretical and disciplinary divides in highly constructive ways. Her book presents challenges to received wisdoms in all parts of the field and really makes one think!

Elena Lieven
Max Planck Institute for Evolutionary Anthropology,
Leipzig, Germany, and the University of Manchester, UK.

This is an ambitious undertaking that challenges dominant paradigms in developmental psycholinguistics deriving from earlier phrase-structure models of generative linguistics and from current usage-based characterizations of children's early syntax. Ninio proclaims Chomsky's Minimalist Program and the switch to a lexicalist syntax as a potential paradigm change allowing for (a non-nativist) continuity between children's earliest syntactic competence and adult grammars. Relying on ideas of predicate-argument valency and sophisticated statistical analyses of data from English and Hebrew, she argues that children's early word combinations, like all grammatical knowledge, are achieved by application of Merge/Dependency operations; that language development, like all learning, follows the Power Law of Practice; and that Complexity Theory provides a bridge between nativist and neo-behaviorist accounts of acquisition of language, as the "archetypal complex system". The monograph is bound to arouse both interest and controversy among researchers of varying persuasions.

Ruth A. Berman
Linguistics, Tel Aviv University

Ninio provides an illuminating new perspective on syntactic development, merging empirical research with up to the minute linguistic theorising and new ideas from Complexity Theory to present a compelling thesis on the nature of language and language development. This book is essential reading for researchers who welcome new ideas presenting a strong challenge to long established conventions.

Caroline Rowland
School of Psychology, University of Liverpool, UK

Ninio presents a boldly stated and provocative theory of what syntactic knowledge is and how the child achieves it. The theory is based in lexicalist accounts of syntax, and draws also on a range of linguistic theories, on learning theory, and on complexity theory. The book is valuable as a resource because Ninio's explication of the background to her proposal is comprehensive. Ninio compiles empirical support for the theory from years of her own and others' work, and she brings the evidence together in a carefully reasoned argument. Everyone who reads this book will learn from it. Some readers will be convinced of the theory and others may not be, but all readers of this work must come away convinced that Ninio's argument demands scientific attention.

Erika Hoff
Florida Atlantic University, Davie, Florida.

Language and the Learning Curve offers a provocative new account of syntactic development, neatly integrating ideas from contemporary linguistics, Complexity Theory, and the cognitive-psychological literature on skill acquisition. By demonstrating that the child's knowledge of word combinations forms an interconnected system throughout language development, Ninio debunks the established view that children acquire syntax in a piecemeal and isolated fashion, gradually acquiring abstract linguistic rules and schemas. Borrowing from observations of the behavior of users interacting with the World Wide Web, Ninio has created an alternative conceptualization of language learning that is both elegant and persuasive.

Patricia J. Brooks
The College of Staten Island and the Graduate Center,
City University of New York

Language and the learning curve is a bold attempt to integrate empirical work on children's early multi-word speech with recent developments in Linguistics, Cognitive Psychology and Complexity Theory. Particularly thought-provoking is the idea that children are learning lexically-specific semantic-syntactic mappings that form an interconnected system based on structural rather than semantic similarity.

Julian Pine
Psychology, University of Liverpool

Anat Ninio's book provides a refreshingly new perspective on the development of language. She has succeeded in weaving together a remarkably broad knowledge from areas as diverse as theoretical linguistics, cognitive psychology, and Complexity Theory to provide a synthetic view of how children learn to talk. Most importantly, she succeeded in showing that learning language takes much more than simply being subjected to social input and much more than possessing an internal 'language module.' Instead, it is the child themselves – as an agent with their own motivations and goals and a participant in social networks – who is shown to be doing the job, and not an easy one, of learning to speak. This perspective in effect shows how to unhinge syntactic development from a narrowly individualist and innatist approach that has been using this area as its showcase for too long. This book opens up new frontiers in understanding syntactic development from a dynamical, sociocultural, and situated perspective – a truly remarkable achievement.

Anna Stetsenko
Developmental Psychology, The Graduate Center, City University of New York

Introduction

This book proposes the integration of up-to-date principles of theoretical linguistics, cognitive psychology, and Complexity Theory into a model of syntactic development. The goal is to examine a few core principles developed in linguistics (about syntax), in cognitive psychology (about human learning), and in Complexity Theory (about the growth of complex systems), and to derive from them hypotheses about the possible mechanisms of syntactic development. Then, to present developmental evidence about the hypotheses, and to conclude with the best generalization about syntactic development based on theory and empirical data.

There are five principles that are presented and described in detail in the book. First, syntactic connectivity is achieved by a Merger or Dependency operation, based on individual items' predicate status and lexical valency. Second, the learning of a series of similar cognitive tasks (such as the acquisition of lexical-specific syntactic rules would be) sits on its own learning curve, earlier-learned items facilitating the learning of later ones. Third, a theoretically sound description of syntax does not require abstract syntactic rules, only lexical-specific concrete ones as detailed above. Four, syntax does not link to semantics in a systematic way for whole form-classes, only for individual predicates. Five, language is a complex system where speakers and the linguistic items they produce form a single complex network. Producing some type of linguistic item means linking into the network alongside other speakers, obeying the same rationale guiding the choice of items to link to.

These principles have important implications for first language acquisition, and these are outlined in the book in the form of hypotheses regarding the units and learning processes of syntactic development. The following claims are made regarding acquisition. First, children's word combinations—at any age—express predicate-argument relations and are generated with the use of the Merge/Dependency operation. Second, children's knowledge of producing word combinations is lexically specific but the different items are not isolated; rather, they are connected, old items facilitating new items' acquisition according to the Power Law of Practice. Third, children's combinatory rules remain item-specific throughout development, and they do not form abstract or general syntactic rules or schemas. Four, there is no role for semantic linking in learning syntax; children use similarity of form for generalization and transfer of learning, disregarding argument semantics and thematic roles. Five, a young child learning to produce some linguistic item becomes part of the language network, alongside adults producing similar kinds of items; children do not reinvent language, nor do they internalize it; they link to it. Their choice of which items to produce is guided by the same pragmatic principles as adults' choice of what to say; therefore a group of children immediately recreates the global statistical features of adults' network, without necessarily using the items most frequently used by adults.

Developmental evidence strongly supports the predictions drawn from theoretical considerations. The model of syntactic development that emerges can be summarized in terms of the growth of a complex system. Children learn lexical-specific semantics-syntactic mappings; these form an interconnected system based on similarity; the complete language system consists of various linguistic items and of speakers who produce them; children link into the system formed by adults and other speakers when they, too, produce the same type of linguistic items.

The book consists of five chapters, organized around the principles outlined above. Each of the five chapters starts with a review of the linguistic or cognitive-psychological literature on the relevant topic. This is followed by a presentation of the implications for child language acquisition, mostly in the form of an explicit hypothesis about the acquisition process. Next, empirical findings from child language research are presented, followed by a summary of the chapter's conclusions. The book gradually builds up a learning theory of syntactic development informed by theoretical linguistics, cognitive psychology, and Complexity Theory. The end-result is a view of language as a complex network that young children join during syntactic development.

Chapter 1—Valency—argues that children employ a fundamental formal syntactic operation suggested by theoretical linguistics when producing even their earliest word combinations. The chapter starts with a review of the linguistic literature concerning the Merge operation of Chomsky's Minimalist Program; the Head–Dependent relation developed in Dependency Grammars, which is shown to be identical with the Merger operation. At this point the chapter introduces syntactic trees and the tree-representation in general. It continues with an exposition of logical/semantic and syntactic valency and the concept of predicate words. The implications for first language acquisition are that adult syntax is simple; in fact, there is little reason not to assume that young children can start acquisition by right away learning to combine two words in a Merge/Dependency combination. This prediction conflicts with exiting alternative hypotheses according to which children's earliest word combinations are generated using processes different from adult syntactic principles. A review of the developmental evidence indicates that the earliest word combinations are in most probability syntactic mergers.

Chapter 2—The learning curve—presents arguments in favour of considering syntactic development as a kind of cognitive skill learning, with transfer, generalization, and other practice effects demonstrating the interconnectedness of even the earliest lexical-specific syntactic formulae. The chapter presents the literature on the Power Law of Practice that states: 'The speed of performance of a task increases as a power-law function of the number of times the task is performed'. Learning curves are introduced and described, with emphasis on the quantitative aspects such as the power-law function fitting the curves. The power-function speed-up is considered in cognitive psychology to be a benchmark test of a viable learning theory. Using this principle, the implications for first language acquisition are that if syntactic acquisition is indeed like skill learning, syntax should transfer right away, the very first items learned facilitating the acquisition of all further ones. In other words, syntactic development should sit on a learning curve of its own, the facilitation taking on a power-law shape. This prediction conflicts with an exiting alternative hypothesis—the Verb Island hypothesis—according to which early syntax is not like skill learning, as children's similar lexical-specific combinatory formulae do not connect to each other but remain isolated. According to this view, children's early learning curves should not accelerate under a power-law, exponential, or any other non-linear function. Developmental evidence regarding learning curves and generalizations in early syntax shows that syntactic development is like skill-learning, with early transfer, facilitation, and generalization demonstrating that children's lexical-specific combinatory rules are interconnected as the skill-learning approach predicts.

Chapter 3—Lexicalism—reviews the lexicalist stance of present-day generative linguistics and argues that as all syntax is in the lexicon, children do not develop abstract schemas or rules but operate solely with the lexical-specific syntactic formats they start acquisition with. The chapter presents the linguistic basis to lexicalism in Chomsky's developing versions of grammar, explaining the motivations for eliminating Phrase Structure Rules from the theory. One of the reasons is that attempts to define 'linking rules' that would systematically map verb semantics to the syntactic construction that the verb forms with its dependents are doomed to be failures, as mapping from semantics to syntax is at the most semi-regular. The implications for first language acquisition are that developmental psycholinguistics does not need to account for children's acquisition of abstract syntactic schemas, as these play no part in a theory of syntax. Lexical-specific combinatory rules, item-specific syntactic schemas should be quite sufficient for the generation of grammatical sentences in children of any developmental stage. This prediction contrasts strongly with the accepted dogma of present-day developmental psycholinguistics. Developmental evidence demonstrates that the earliest word combinations are indeed lexically-specific and, most importantly, that there is no change in the form of syntactic schemas with development—they remain lexical-specific. The conclusion is that children learn a lexicalist syntax and do not form abstract rules or schemas.

Chapter 4—Similarity—examines the potential effects of semantics in the acquisition process, and demonstrates that the dimension of similarity along which children employ analogy and transfer of learning between different item-specific syntactic formulae is not semantic similarity but a formal, morphosyntactic one. Throughout the chapter it is argued that children operate with a purely formal syntax and do not construct form-meaning schemas as part of the acquisition process. The chapter reviews the literature on similarity-based transfer in cognitive psychology. Particular emphasis is placed on discussing the potential problem arising when attempting to work with unconstrained similarity, as well as its solution using the theory of Goal-Derived Learning. Next, similarity of form and meaning of grammatical relations is discussed, and it is shown that syntax does not link to semantics in a systematic fashion. The implication for first language acquisition is that there is probably no role for semantic linking in learning syntax. The hypothesis derived is that children use similarity of form for generalization and transfer of learning, disregarding argument semantics and thematic roles. There are alternative hypotheses in the literature that are presented and described. The developmental evidence demonstrates no semantic effects in generalization and transfer of learning, showing that children use similarity of form, not of meaning, when using old learning to facilitate new ones.

Finally, Chapter 5—The growth of syntax—examines the role of the environment in syntactic development, and argues for novel conceptualization derived from Complexity Theory. According to this view, language is a complex network, consisting of linguistic items (such as words with their semantic and syntactic valency) as well as speakers who produce words and sentences when they speak. Children acquiring language are just like new users linking into the World-Wide Web: by linking into the Web, users become part of it. This chapter introduces complex systems and complex networks, in particular bipartite networks, which are then used to conceptualize speakers and linguistic items. The basics of graph theory are presented and so are Zipf and Pareto curves depicting distributions of items' frequency of use in a network. The principle of Preferential Attachment is described, contrasting it with a deterministic frequency effect. The implication for first language acquisition is that learning means linking to the huge language network; children learning to produce syntactic combinations do not reinvent language, nor do they internalize it; instead, they link to network of other speakers producing similar combinations. Developmental evidence demonstrates that a group of young children starting to use some kind of syntactic combination immediately reproduces the global statistical features of the adults' network, showing that they are probably governed by the same pragmatic principles in choosing which items to learn to produce as are adults in choosing which items to say. By contrast, gross input frequency does not predict order of acquisition. The conclusion is that learners are active agents gradually connecting into a social network composed of other agents and their productions. Complexity Theory thus offers a robust formalism for dealing with language development and with other types of cognitive learning in the social context.

1

Valency

Throughout the years of the modern study of child language development, one of the most debated topics has been the nature of the internalized rules that generate young children's word combinations, especially the early ones. The answer considered in the present work is directly derived from the latest conceptualizations of syntactic structure in formal, generative linguistics. The suggestion is that adults use and children learn a lexicalist syntax, in which the syntactic structure of the sentence is 'projected' from the lexicon. This puts lexical valency at the hub of linguistic knowledge, marking it as the central concept in developmental theorizing.

Valency is not a term often employed in present-day developmental psycholinguistic texts. Nevertheless, it might turn out to be a very useful concept for developmental theorizing. In fact, as we shall see below, there are at least two different types of valency information said to be stored in lexical entries, (1) semantic valency, listing the potential of the word for semantic relations with other items, and (2) syntactic valency, listing the syntactic combinations by which the said semantic relations are to be expressed in sentences. Syntactic development seems to consist of learning ways to express each word's inherent semantic potential in the appropriate syntactic form.

The emphasis on word valency and lexical information in modern linguistics goes hand in hand with a considerable reduction in the complexity of syntactic operations assumed to take place during the generation of sentences. As we shall see below, the linguistic literature presents us with a significantly simplified view of adult syntax in which all syntax is built on a single binary combining relation between pairs of words, recursively applied. This relation—Merge or Dependency—is said to be making use of the lexical valency information of the words involved. If we accept this generative model as a valid description of how humans produce sentences, syntactic development appears to be much easier than we had assumed. Indeed, we have little reason to assume that young children cannot master the basics of it as soon as they start to combine two words.

We shall start the detailed exposition of this model of development by reviewing the relevant linguistic literature. Then, we shall derive developmental implications from the theoretical-linguistic arguments. Finally, we shall turn to developmental evidence, attempting to test the truth of the theory-derived hypothesis on empirical developmental data.

1.1 Linguistic approaches to valency and syntactic structure

1.1.1 The building block of syntactic structure: Merge or Dependency

In the Minimalist Program, Chomsky defines the major building block of syntactic structure as an operation creating a new syntactic unit from the unification of two old ones. He says: 'Narrow syntax has one operation that comes "free", in that it is required in some form for any recursive system: the operation Merge. [...] Any operation other than Merge requires empirical motivation, and is a derivation from SMT [the Strong Minimalist Thesis].' (Chomsky, 2001, p. 4).

The operation Merge combines two elements in an asymmetrical process in which one element, the Head, provides the properties for the resultant combination. The Head is also used as the label of the combination, so the same label is used both for one of the combining units and for the resulting combination. In linguistics, syntactic structure is often represented by trees in which the nodes are the units generating the structure and the edges (arcs) represent relations between units.[1] A typical tree-structure illustrating Merge is (1), representing the phrase 'saw it' as in 'The man saw it' (based on Chomsky's (1995) example (11), p. 247):

(1) saw
     saw   it

The recursive application of the operation Merge creates the complete tree-structure of the sentence. There is no limit on the number of times the operation Merge may be applied in an iterative fashion, so that potentially it can generate an infinitely large syntactic structure. Indeed, Merge is the primitive operation that is the key to the 'discrete infinity' of the language system, which is so central to Chomsky's conception of language: 'the language faculty is [...] a system of discrete infinity. Any such system is based on a primitive operation that takes n objects already constructed, and constructs from them a new object: in the simplest case, the set of n objects.' (Chomsky, 2004, p. 10).

Like Merge, Dependency is an asymmetrical operation between two syntactic elements, in which the combination shares the grammatical features of the Head and not of the Dependent unit entering the combination (Tesnière, 1959; Mel'cuk, 1979; Hudson, 1984). The tree-structure (2) represents the same phrase 'saw it' as (1), in a Dependency-type notation:[2]

(2)

In this case, too, the Head unit and the resultant combination are labelled identically by the label of the Head unit. The difference is that the Dependency tree only uses one single node to represent both: the single node labelled 'saw' is to be seen both as the Head element 'saw' and the combination of 'saw' and 'it'. It is obvious that the two-node tree in (2) is more elegant than the three-node Merge tree of (1) and it is also obvious that (1) can always be collapsed into (2). In fact, computer theorists such as Aho *et al.* (1986) who have the greatest respect for Chomskian linguistics and have adopted Chomsky's 'Rewrite Rules' as the basic method for defining the 'syntax' of programs for compilers, have quietly done exactly that for many years.[3]

Just to complete the example, (3) presents the complete Merge-tree of the sentence *The man saw it*, together with its Dependency version.

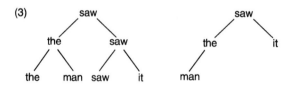

As Dependency Grammars are much less well known than the Minimalist Program, I shall give a short introduction to the Dependency approach.

Dependency Grammars are a family of linguistic theories built on the Dependency relation between two words as their building block for syntactic structure. It originated in the so-called Prague School of linguistics of which the French linguist Lucien Tesnière was a member. Among others, the grammars belonging to this family include Tesnière's (1959) original formulation of Dependency theory; Mel'cuk's Meaning-Text Theory (1979, 1988); Hudson's various versions and in particular Word Grammar (1984, 1990, see also Fraser, 1994); Sgall's Functional Generative Description (Sgall *et al.*, 1986), Starosta's Lexicase (1988), and more. These type of grammars are extremely prominent in European linguistics, but they are not very well known in the United States.

In such syntactic theories, grammatical relations such as subject and direct object are seen as subtypes of a general, asymmetrical Dependency relation: one of the words (the Head) exhibits a host of local control phenomena towards another word (the Dependent). First, Heads determine the syntactic and semantic features of the Head-dependent combination, so that in most cases the combination inherits the features of the Head word. For example, a modified noun such as 'white cat' is still a nominal just like 'cat' as far as its semantics and its syntactic combinatory behaviour are concerned. Second, Heads control the characteristics and placement of their dependents: for example, the transitive verb 'hit' in 'John hit Fred' requires a pre-verbal subject nominal complement ('John') and a postverbal direct object ('Fred'). According to theory, the syntactic structure of a sentence as a whole is built up from such pairwise Dependency relations between individual pairs of words.

Formally, the Dependency relation is an antisymmetrical, antireflexive, and antitransitive ordering relation. Two restrictions are placed on the Dependency structure of a grammatical sentence: first, every word (but one) must have a Head, and second, every word has only a single Head.[4] The exception is the root, namely, the highest word of the sentence, which does not have a Head.

Although the number of Heads per dependent is restricted to one, the converse is not true, so that a Head may have a theoretically unlimited number of dependents. For instance, a verb may take multiple adverbial adjuncts, as in 'Mary lives in London near the British Museum on the second floor of a renovated apartment house.' Another example could be a ditransitive verb such as *give* which is the Head of both its direct-object complement and its indirect-object complement. Formally, Dependency—just like Merge—is a binary operation combining two syntactic units, but a given word may function as the Head of several different Dependency/Merge operations.

The overall syntactic structure of a sentence is obtained by the putting together of the different Dependency relations existing between its elements. In mathematical terms, the Dependency relation imposes a hierarchical structure on the words of a sentence which has the characteristics of a directed tree. As we saw above, a directed tree is a completely connected, two-dimensional, directed acyclic graph with a single root. Each node of the tree represents a word and directional arcs between the nodes represent the Dependency relation, leading from Head to dependent. The tree is headed by the highest word in the sentence, the root, which is the word that does not possess a Head of its own.[5]

In summary, Dependency Grammar characterizes syntactic structure in the main in terms of Dependency relations among the words of a sentence, without resorting to units of analysis smaller or larger than the word. In particular, combinations of words are not represented formally in the grammar in the form of independent symbols on which grammatical rules are predicated. The Head of each pairwise combination represents the combination as a whole in all further Dependency relations; phrases and clauses are thought to be redundant as formal linguistic entities as all that needs to be posited about such non-terminal constituents can be posited about their highest word without loss of information. Informally, it is possible of course to speak of phrases, clauses, or sentences; it is only as formal components of syntactic rules that these are deemed redundant. The only place in the grammar when constituents larger than words are used is in coordination; but even then the conjuncting units are not phrases in their phrase-structure definitions. For details, see Hudson (1990, p. 405). In the same vein, it is possible to speak informally of words as constituents of combinations, whether of phrases, clauses, or sentences; however, the syntactic rules regulating the lawful creation of structure do not make formal use of a containment relation between larger units and their constituents. The place of 'rewrite rules' familiar from phrase-structure approaches, specifying the 'daughters' of a phrasal symbol, is taken by specifications of the direct government or Dependency relation between 'sisters'. Dependency Grammar works with horizontal, rather then vertical grammatical relations.

The convergence between Chomskian linguistics and Dependency Grammars has been noted by linguists of the two schools of thought (e.g., Hudson, 1995; Epstein *et al.*, 1998; Epstein, 1999),[6] but it is certainly not the case that the two theories are to be fused in the near future. Maybe the impetus will come from Natural Language Processing, where people building automatic parsers find a combination of Phrase Structure Grammar and word-based dependencies with labelled grammatical relations more useful than either approach separately (e.g., Collins, 1996). For our purposes, it is only necessary that we recognize the fundamental principles shared by the two kinds of theory.

1.1.2 Valency

If we wanted a term that summarized in a nutshell the main principles of lexicalist grammars, we would do very well with the concept of valency. This term refers to the two sets of lexical features that encode words' semantic and syntactic combinatory possibilities.

The concept of valency (or valence) was introduced to syntactic theory by Tesnière (1959),[7] as part of his model of a Dependency Grammar. He borrowed the term from chemistry, where it characterizes the combinatory abilities of atoms, denoting the number of atoms of hydrogen they can combine with to create a chemical compound. The chemical metaphor establishes valency as an asymmetrical relationship where the element possessing the valency is responsible for the combination. We might say that combination resides in an a priori way with the element having the valency for it.

Tesnière arrived at the concept of valency through an analysis of verb semantics. He viewed the simple sentence as a description of dramatic action, event, or scenario, in which the verb referred to the dynamic process itself, while the rest of the sentence provides details on the identity of the actors and circumstances of the action. He made a fundamental distinction among the persons and other entities with the role participants in the drama whose presence in the scene is strongly implied by the action depicted by the verb, and the more loosely connected depictors of the circumstances of action, like its time, place, and so on.

Tesnière compared the verb's ability to attract the terms for actors and circumstances with an atom's possessing the chemical valency to attract other atoms. The verb was seen as possessing 'hooks' to attach the dependent expressions to itself, thus being responsible for their number and presence in the sentence. This metaphor emphasizes the inequality of the elements combining in syntactic combinations, due to their asymmetrical semantics and the asymmetrical semantic roles they play in the sentence. Fundamentally, the valency of the verb is grounded in its lexical meaning, and hence, the sentence as a whole is retraceable to the semantics of the verb around which it is built.

Word valency is a theory-neutral construct, variously recognized in concepts such as the 'predicate-argument structure' of words as well as their 'subcategorization' (Chomsky, 1981; Goldberg, 1995; Grimshaw, 1990; Jackendoff, 1983; Levin and Rappaport Hovav, 1995; Rappaport Hovav and Levin, 1995; Williams, 1984), their 'logical-functional structure' (Bresnan, 1978; Kaplan and Bresnan, 1982), and so forth.

It is customary to distinguish between two different types of valency for each verb or other valency-bearing word: logical-semantic valency and syntactic valency. Logical-semantic valency analyses words' performance as linguistic signs bearing meaning, as contributors to a sentence's overall meaning. This is the concept equivalent to argument structure. Syntactic valency analyses words' performance as formal objects, contributors to a well-built grammatical sentence. This is the concept equivalent to subcategorization. Let us describe each in more detail.

Although logical valency and semantic valency are closely related (see below), it is best to consider them separately as a first approximation. The term 'semantic valency' refers to the fact that a valency-bearing word such as a verb only provides a partial or insufficient description of the event or scene it refers to. Ever since Frege (1967[1879], 1970[1891]) and Husserl (1970[1900]), it has been pointed out that some words 'make sense' on their own, independent of the rest of the sentence in which they occur, whereas others do not. The latter are felt to be 'unsaturated', of 'incomplete meaning', to possess 'an empty space' in them that requires completion by the meaning carried by other words. Prototypical examples of the 'complete' class are pronouns and proper names; of the latter, verbs, adjectives, and adverbs. Words possessing 'complete' meaning are of a different logical type than words of the 'unsaturated' kind; whereas the former denote entities of some sort, the latter present second-level information about entities such as their properties, states, or transformations, namely, they denote concepts defined in relation to other concepts. In consequence, words of the 'incomplete' type need to be supplemented by some other elements of the sentence, designating the entities they provide information on, in order to denote a 'complete' second-level concept. In informational terms, without a supplementary specification of the entities involved, the information encoded in these second-level words is not utilizable.

As an example, let us take the preposition *in*. This word denotes the positioning of an entity inside some space; it is impossible to define its meaning without mentioning both the entity and the space. The very concept of 'in-ness' is defined relative to these other two concepts, and not as an absolute notion that can stand on its own.

The property of having a 'complete' or 'incomplete' meaning is thus seen as word's fixed logical characteristic *qua* linguistic signs, a feature that belongs to the words as they are entered in the mental lexicon.[8] This feature bridges word-semantics and word-syntax: it is the essence of a word's use in sentences.

The acknowledgement of logically 'incomplete' words forms part of most syntactic theories. Valency-bearing words are commonly designated as *predicate words, function words* or *functors* (see Reichenbach, 1947). Predicates are also-called *predicators;* The term 'predicator' was introduced by Carnap (1947, p. 6).

Traditionally, the term 'predicate' is applied to expressions which take the subject of the sentence in order to form propositions, considered to be the semantic backbone of sentences. The predicate ascribes a property to the subject, such as some quality, characteristics, action, or involvement in some event. For example, in the sentence 'John is my friend.', John is the subject, and the property that he is my friend is predicated of him (i.e., attributed to him). The predicate of the sentence is the expression 'my friend'. When we talk of a lexical item being a (simple) predicate, we mean that it is an argument-taking word, one that can potentially serve as the sentencial predicate forming a proposition with the subject. In predicate logic, a predicate designates a property of some entity or a relation between two or more entities that are said to be its arguments. Supplying values for these arguments turns the predicate (a kind of open proposition with variables) into a full proposition. Namely, a predicate word or predicator is any argument-taking lexical item.

The term 'logical valency' (also 'arity' or 'adicity') refers to a word's characterization as a predicate with logical arguments, or, as an approximate mathematical function. In fact, it summarizes the words' semantic valency pattern in quantitative terms only. Unary predicates are like a function with one argument or $f(x)$, binary predicates are like a function with two arguments, i.e., $f(x,y)$, and so forth. Predicates' combinatory behaviour is explored in *predicate calculus*, a branch of formal logic, which serves as the basis of such linguistic systems as Montague Grammar (Montague, 1974).[9]

While arity or logical valency is a quantitative measure of how many different arguments a word takes, a predicate's semantic valency specifies the content of the arguments it takes. Semantic valency is very closely correlated with logical valency, so that some theoreticians talk about the logical-semantic valency without discriminating between the two. This practice will be followed here.

In formal linguistics, logical-semantic valency is often represented by such systems as case roles, thematic roles, or theta roles (e.g., Fillmore, 1968; Dowty, 1991; Van Valin, 1993), but of course it is possible to define for each word its own specific semantic complements without striving for a uniform set of designations for the arguments of groups of words. Thus, a word such as *like* would be marked in the lexicon as possessing two semantic arguments, one the person who does the liking and the second, the entity who is liked. Another binary predicate such as *break* would have as semantic arguments the entity who performs the act of breaking and the entity that is being broken.

The fact that a word has a logical-semantic valency for a certain kind of argument means that it is somehow incomplete unless the rest of the sentence provides the information on the 'value' of these arguments. For example, when someone hears the verb *like* in a sentence, they need also to know who is doing the liking and who is being liked. It is important to note that logical-semantic valency is for information on the identity of the argument-entities, and that means the need is for a complete referring expression that provides the information, regardless of what form that expression takes.

In most cases, single words are insufficient to specify the value of a word's semantic argument and the speaker uses a referring expression which is a phrase or a clause. For example, in the sentence *See the doll on the second shelf*, the entity seen—the second argument of the verb *see*—is specified by a complete referring expression, i.e., *the doll on the second shelf* and not by any one word of this expression, however syntactically prominent. In Chomskian linguistics, the selection of complements (or theta role assignment) is for a sister-constituent, so that the verb assigns a theta role to a noun-phrase (or a Determiner-phrase) and not to a single word heading the phrase. For example, the verb *closed* is said to assign the Patient theta role to its sister-phrase *the door* in (4), and not to the determiner-head of the phrase, namely to *the*:[10]

(4)   Mary [closed [the door]].

Logical-semantic valency clearly requires units larger than a single word; even such aggressively word-based Dependency Grammar as Word Grammar (Hudson, 1984) has a formal use of phrases in its characterization of semantics.

The second type of word valency acknowledged in formal linguistics is syntactic valency. The syntactic valency of the word is the formal character-ization of its valency arguments or complements, what is often called its *subcategorization frame* or *valency frame*. Saying that a word has its syntactic valency registered in the lexicon means that the lexicon provides not only the sound and meaning of a word but also the basic format for its use in syntactically constructed sentences, together with the expressions that it needs in order to be fully comprehensible (Bresnan, 1978; Chomsky, 1981; Allerton, 1982; Hudson, 1990; Haegeman, 1991).

When it comes to syntactic valency, all Dependency Grammars and even such an aggressively phrase-oriented approach as the Chomskian use a word-based definition of the selection of complements. The reason is that, ever since Bresnan (1970), Chomskian linguistics has assumed that selection is a Head-to-Head relation (e.g., Chomsky 1986, p. 27). Bresnan pointed out a fact often emphasized by Dependency grammarians that verbs not only select an argu-ment in general but, rather, they select an argument headed by a specific type of Head. For example, verbs requiring a clausal complement select for clauses headed by a particular complementizer and do not accept others; e.g., *wonder* accepts a clause headed by *if* but not by *that*. This is of course true for phrasal complements as well as clausal ones: the verb *rely* selects for the preposition *on* for its single object, while *trust* selects for a direct object noun-phrase without a preposition. The paradoxical situation is that semantic selection (aka theta role assignment) is a relation between phrases or other constituents that are 'maximal projections', while syntactic selection is Head-to-Head, and it involves the words at the Head of the same constituents, and not the constituents themselves. It seems that logical-semantic valency and syntactic valency are partially disparate phenomena. This topic will be taken up again in Chapter 3.

To summarize this part of the exposition, it appears that in modern theoretical approaches, verbs and other predicates are said to possess logical-semantic arguments; they also subcategorize syntactically for certain syntactic complements that express the semantic arguments in the correct interpretable form. Both types of valency information are stored in each word's lexical entry, alongside the sound, meaning, and morphological class of the word.

1.1.3 Shared principles of syntactic structure in Phrase Structure and Dependency Grammars

We have seen that despite their differences—which may turn out to be more a matter of style than of substance—Phrase Structure Grammars and Dependency Grammars appear to share many of their essential tenets. On the most basic level, Phrase Structure Grammars and Dependency Grammars share four founding principles:

- Both approaches are based on the assumption that syntax is built by the recursive application of a single primitive structure-building operation creating a new element out of existing ones. This primitive operation is Merge or Dependency (see Section 1.1.1).

- Both approaches assume that the syntactic structure of the sentence is projected from the lexicon where the differential combinatory potentials of words are stored in the form of valency or subcategorization information.

- Both approaches assume that the structure-building operation utilizes an a priori asymmetry between combining objects; this is the concept of Headhood on which Merge and the Dependency relations are built.

- Both approaches define the logical-semantic valency of verbs and other predicates as the need for information on the dependent event participants implied by the meaning of the verb, and syntactic valency as the formal specification of words to serve as Heads of syntactically dependent phrases.

There are quite a few other basic principles shared by the two types of linguistic theory that are outcomes of the principles of asymmetry and lexicality of the Dependency/Merge operation. For example, both approaches see the (finite) verb as the highest element of a clause, determining its overall structure through its regulation of the number of the other elements that have to occur in the sentence.[11] In both approaches, the distinction between complements and adjuncts is a crucial part of theory, with complements being the a priori defined dependents of verbs and other predicates, while adjuncts are dependents added on freely, their occurrence in a sentence or their form not determined by their Head.[12]

We shall take these principles as representing the consensus among the majority of linguists active today[13] and adopt them as the foundation of a model of syntactic development in children.

1.2 Implication for acquisition: syntax is simple

The review of the linguistic literature presented us with a view of adult syntax, which appears to simplify considerably the job of explaining acquisition. We are told that adult syntax is built on a binary Merge/Dependency relation between two words (recursively applied), and that this relation is 'projected' from the lexical features—the semantic and syntactic valency—of the predicate word. If this description is accurate—and even its critics do not dispute the veracity of its major thrust—we are faced with an amazingly simple basic building block of syntax. There is little reason not to assume that young children can start acquisition by right away learning to combine two words in a Merge/Dependency combination. One Merge/Dependency couple does not make for the whole of syntax—so we can expect them subsequently to learn to apply recursion, building infinitely long structures from these humble building blocks (Hauser *et al.*, 2002). But first, as a start, they should simply learn to produce the single Merge/Dependency, valency-built, two-word combination.

It has been suggested before (e.g., by MacWhinney, 1975, 1982; Robinson, 1986; Van Langendonck, 1987; Ninio, 1994, 1996; Green, 1997; Powers, 2002; and see also Radford, 1990) that children's word combinations, including even the earliest ones, are produced as syntactic Merge or Dependency couples. However, in the absence of systematic testing, this hypothesis has not yet been given much attention in the developmental literature.

1.3 Developmental evidence: the earliest word combinations are syntactic mergers

1.3.1 Children's word combinations are mostly error-free

First and foremost, it is a well-established generalization that whatever formal rules children possess, these are, with a few exceptions, correct segments of the end-state grammar. This was long ago pointed out by Brown (1973).

On the whole, children do not make grammatical mistakes (Maratsos, 1979, 1982; Chiat, 1981). This is expressed in two characteristics of their word combinations: they make correct form-class distinctions and keep to the correct word order.

The first important finding is that children from the very first word combinations very rarely make form-class errors. Thus, Brown (1973), summarizing the evidence on English-speaking children's early combinations from his own and from Leopold (1939–1949), Bloom (1970), and Schlesinger's (1971) data, concluded that such errors are very infrequent. Maratsos (1983), in a later review, reached a similar conclusion. Bowerman (1973a) found that most words in Finnish-speaking children's vocabularies that she classified to word classes according to adult syntactic privileges of occurrence, were classified similarly in adult Finnish. Category errors are also extremely rare in Hebrew (Berman, 1988; Levy, 1988). It seems that to the extent that children use some term in word combinations, they mostly do so in conformity with the combinatorial restrictions applying to such terms in the end-state grammar: different kinds of terms fit into different, and mostly appropriate, syntactic environments.

Second, the word order between combining constituents in child utterances in most cases mirrors the target grammar's word order (Brown and Fraser, 1963; Bloom, 1970; Bowerman, 1973a; Brown, 1973; Bloom, *et al.*, 1975; Braine, 1976; Pinker, 1984; Bloom, 1990; Radford, 1990). On first generating word combinations using some predicate, children may for a while 'grope' for the correct word order, but they soon settle into an order similar to the canonical adult one (Braine, 1976; Tomasello, 1992).

These findings lay the foundations for our quest for the syntactic operation that children employ for producing their word combinations. Given the similarity of form-class distinctions and word order to adult models, it seems likely that children indeed internalize the underpinning of syntax right from the beginning. It needs now to be demonstrated that children indeed employ the fundamental Merge/Dependency operation in order to map predicate-argument relations into surface structure. If we succeed, we have shown that young children's syntactic rules represent the internalization of a crucial segment of the adult system.

1.3.2 **Evidence for children using Merge/Dependency**

There are, as we know, many different descriptions of children's early word combinations, especially at the notorious 'two-word stage'. If we are correct in our prediction drawn from the linguistics literature, all these different descriptions refer to the same animal—a Merge/Dependency pair, built on the predicate word's valency for an argument. To see if this hypothesis is correct, we shall review three classical and apparently conflicting descriptions of children's word combinations at the two-word stage—telegraphic speech, semantic relations, and the pivot look—and 'deconstruct' them as crypto-Merge/Dependency descriptions.

Telegraphic speech

One of the well-known characterizations of children's early multiword utterances is that they resemble telegrams: they omit all items that are not essential for conveying the gist of the message. The term 'telegraphic speech' was coined by Brown and Fraser (1963). Brown and Fraser, as well as Brown and Bellugi (1964), Ervin-Tripp (1966), and others pointed out that children's early multiword utterances tend to omit closed-class words such as articles, auxiliary verbs, copulas, prepositions, and conjunctions, compared with the sentences adults typically say in the same circumstances.[14] Children's sentences tend to include mostly open-class or substantive words such as nouns, verbs, and adjectives. For example, Eve, one of the children observed by the Brown group said *Chair broken* when an adult would have said *The chair is broken*, or *That horsie* when an adult would have said *That is a horsie*. Despite the omissions, the sentences do not fall very far from their presumable adult models, as the order of the content-words making them up usually replicates the order in which the same words would have appeared in the fully constructed adult sentence.

Given the selective omission of closed-class items, the first possibility to be checked was that maybe children only use open-class words in their early speech but not closed-class or 'function' words. Brown (1973) searched through available child corpora and found that this hypothesis was incorrect: he found many closed-class or function words in children's two-word and early multiword speech, among them *more, no, off* and the pronouns *I, you, it*, and so forth. In fact, most of what Braine (1963) called pivot-open combinations were built on closed-class items as pivots.

It appears that children are perfectly able to produce word combinations with closed-class items—but they will not include them in utterances if they are not essential for conveying the gist of the message. The words 'missing' from the utterances may have important grammatical functions in the relevant adult sentences, but the words 'retained' are the substantive words carrying the semantic content of their respective phrases.

In the meta-language of the present monograph, 'telegraphic speech' represents an extremely elliptical method for satisfying the semantic and syntactic valency of the predicates around which the sentence is built—but satisfying them nevertheless. The word combinations correctly 'project' the lexical valency of the predicate words involved, satisfying both semantic and syntactic requirements. For example, the shortened sentence *Adam make tower* produced by another of the children observed by the Brown group satisfies the verb *make*'s semantic requirement for two logical arguments, one for the maker and one for the thing made; the child speaker even has the correct idea where to place them relative to the verb, meaning that he already has a workable syntactic valency frame established for this verb, including the SVO word order for the subject, verb, and the direct-object elements. There is some other rule that this sentence is breaking to do with the obligatory determinants heading noun phrases in English, but at the bottom line, that rule is irrelevant for satisfying the valency requirements of the verb *make*, and that's what 'telegraphic' sentences appear to take as a first priority. The 'retained' content words form obvious and recognizable Merge/Dependency couples, with predicates getting their arguments in the correct syntactic configuration (but see Lebeaux, 2000).

To summarize, the 'telegraphic speech' depiction of early word combinations easily translates to a generalization that early multiword utterances are generated on the basis of adult syntactic principles, exemplifying the saturation of lexical valency through the Merge/Dependency operation. It is possible, however, that this description is only appropriate for a slightly advanced stage in children's multiword speech (Braine, 1963), and that the earliest two-word speech might possess other features. We explore this possibility in the next two sections.

Semantic relations

The second classical description of early multiword utterances is that they are the result of the combinations of semantic categories.

Researchers such as Bowerman (1973a), Brown (1973), and Schlesinger (1971) suggested that many or maybe all of children's early word combinations can be characterized with the help of a few central case-like or thematic categories such as actor (or agent), action, object (or patient), location, and so forth, which the children combine into proposition-like utterances, mostly according to their correct word order in adult sentences. For instance, an utterance such as 'see bird' would be categorized by Brown (1973) as an instance of an action-object combination.

As thematic roles or case roles are in the first place classifications of predicates' semantic arguments, the 'semantic' description of early multiword combinations translates quite straightforwardly to the language of predicate-argument relations. The most transparent bridge between the approaches is provided by Braine (1976), who raised the possibility that the semantic categories generating children's utterances may be narrower than the maximum-width case roles proposed by the other semanticists; in the limit the relevant categories may be word-specific and include only one predicate combining with its individual logical argument, e.g., *see* + thing seen.

We shall therefore assume that the 'semantic relations' depiction of the Brown (1973) group is a valid description of early word combinations, but instead of categories, they should better be on a word by word basis. Translated to formal linguistic terms, it means that according to the semantic approach, word combinations consist of predicates and their logico-semantic arguments.

This 'appropriation' works well enough for the majority of semantic relations used by Brown and the other researchers, including agent-action, action-object, entity-attribute, entity-location, and so forth. The major obstacle to the identification of semantic relations as predicate-argument ones is the set of sentences that constitute of the combination of two nouns. It is well known that researchers and in particular Bloom (1970) drew attention to the presence of such utterances as *Mommy sock* in child language, and in fact such combinations provided much of the motivation for writing child grammars with the help of semantic categories. However, noun–noun (NN) combinations should not be given too much weight as counter-evidence to the basically predicate-argument nature of early combinations. First, it is possible that many are in fact not syntactic or semantic word combinations that the child intended to be combined into a unified semantic interpretation, but merely a vocative (e.g., *Mommy*) followed by some other word (e.g., *sock*). Campbell (1976) examined many of the relevant utterances in the Bloom (1970) corpus and found that the evidence strongly supported the vocative interpretation (see also Ewing, 1982). Second, several researchers (e.g., Braine, 1963) have pointed out that NN combinations tend to occur rather late in multiword speech, thus increasing the probability that they represent some marginal problem with the construction of longer utterances.

Whatever their explanation, it is clear that NN combinations are not characteristic of children's entry into multiword speech. That period can be accurately described as one in which children learn to express semantic relations—but the relevant semantic relations are in all probability specific ones that exist between individual predicate words and their logical arguments. This topic will be further dealt with in Chapter 3.

Pivot-look

Braine (1963) as well as, independently, Miller and Ervin (1964) claimed that early word combinations produced by English-speaking children can best described as combinations between a specific word placed in a fixed position (first or last) in the combination, and sets of words filling the complementary position. Braine defined these item-set combinations as between a small group of words belonging to the 'pivot-class' and a larger set of words belonging to an 'open class'. (Miller and Ervin referred to the former as 'operators' but otherwise provided a very similar characterization.) The discrimination between the two primitive form-classes rests on the differential distribution of the two types of words: a few (the pivots) occur with high frequency, occupy a constant position in the sentence (first or last), and appear with a varying set of complements. The large class of 'open class' items occur much less frequently, occur with different 'pivots' and in different positions in the word combination. For example, the child Andrew generated many different combinations in which the word *more* appeared in the first position, for example, *more car*, *more cereal*, and *more cookie* (Braine, 1963). This kind of distributional asymmetry provided the motivation for declaring *more* the pivot of the combinatory formula generating these and many other word combinations.

Although pivot-grammar as a formalization of early syntax was severely criticized (e.g., by Brown, 1973 and Bowerman, 1973a), the characterization of early speech corpora as having a 'pivot-look' has survived.[15] Quite a few researchers continue to hold to this very day that, if not for all children and all utterances, then for a considerable proportion of them, word combinations are pivotal in nature (e.g., Lieven *et al.*, 1997).

It appears that despite the weaknesses of the original pivot grammar, the field insists that there is something fundamentally accurate in its description of children's early sentences. Whatever the specifics of the formalization used by researchers, it is an attempt to account for the 'pivot-look', which is that in early child sentences a few words combine with many others, and that members of this set appear to serve as the pivots around which the other words rotate in the sentence. Somehow or other, the pivot words are responsible for the combination, while the words accompanying them are merely slot-fillers.

It does not take a wide leap to recognize the pivot-open type of word combinations as consisting of predicates and their logical arguments, and possibly exemplifying the Merge/Dependency syntactic relation. The great majority of words identified as pivots—e.g., *all, hi, more, no, off, other*, and *see* in the Andrew corpus—are in fact words having a valency requirement for some complement that the 'open-class' slot-fillers provide.

The suggestion that pivot-open combinations are more correctly described as predicate-argument ones has been made before, e.g., by Gentner (1978), MacWhinney (1982), and Ninio (1988), as well as Braine himself in a later publication (1976). Bloom (1970) also saw pivotal combinations as consisting of 'relational words' and their complements, though she only applied this analysis to closed-class predicates and not to verbs (see also Bloom and Lahey, 1978; McCune-Nicolich, 1981; McCune and Vihman, 1999; Deuchar and Quay, 2000). For example, Gentner (1978) says: 'The pivot/open distinction was an early formulation of the phenomenon that a small class of predicates is used broadly in early speech, while a large class of argument words, mostly simple nouns, is used more specifically (Braine 1963; also see Bloom 1970).' (pp. 995–996).

Similarly, Ninio (1988) ties pivot-open combinations to predicate-argument ones, attributing the connection to the semanticist writers:

> [S]yntactic rules are, to some extent, abstract and productive from the very beginning of combinatorial speech: Their productive abstractness consists of the possibility of predicate words to combining with all terms in children's vocabularies that are arguments of the relevant propositional function (Bloom, 1970; Braine, 1976; Brown, 1973). The earliest combinations seem to consist of such formulae with one fixed element and one variable, such as this+(object noticed], when each element is soon accorded a fixed position in the string. [. . .] Among 'predicate' words observed in early speech are forms such as 'no,' 'another,' 'up,' 'here'; determinatives such as 'this'; adjectives; and verbs. In such combinations the semantic relation between the two items is an inherent component of the meaning of the fixed element. Once a certain relational term is chosen to express whatever semantic relation the child has in mind, it restricts the choice of the other terms in the combination to such items that are legitimate arguments of the predicate.
>
> Ninio (1988, p. 111)

It is, nevertheless, impossible to equate a pivot-open characterization of early word combinations with a description in terms of predicate-argument relations. In fact, a pivot-type grammar puts no constraint on the items that will form the frames of a combinatory formula and does not restrict pivots to predicate words. The problem is easy to detect: some of the pivots identified as such by Braine (1963) and by other researchers in this tradition are most certainly not logical predicates with valency arguments. For instance, Braine, as well as Brown and Fraser (1963), Pine *et al.* (1998), Childers and Tomasello (2001), Matthews *et al.* (2005) recognize pronouns like *I* or *it*, and some proper nouns such as *Mommy* and *Daddy*, as pivots of combinations. Obviously, pronouns and proper names do not have a semantic or syntactic valency for complements, being the quintessential zero-valency items. This is not a marginal issue, as in the most recent publications suggesting pivot-open type descriptions of early word combinations (e.g., Tomasello, 2003), frames built around pronouns such as '*he* X-ed *it*' are proffered as possibly even more important for syntactic development than ones built around verbs and other true predicates.

The source of the problem is that pivot-type descriptions are based on a kind of principle that is basically alien to the predicate-argument, Merge/ Dependency, valency-based one. Pivot-open or slot-and-frame descriptions of early sentences base the identification of pivots solely on distributional facts (namely, that pivots be positionally constant and frequent items with many different 'partners' with which they are combined), and not on an a priori lexical-semantic feature we call valency that pivot words but not their arguments possess vis-à-vis the other. Given the appeal of objective criteria such as pure distributional facts, and their wide spread in contemporary theorizing, if one wishes to replace the different pivot-open, item-and-set, or slot-and-frame descriptions by one involving predicates and their logical arguments in a syntactic combination, it needs to be convincingly argued that the distributional definition is seriously flawed.

The first problem with the distributional definition is that it is based on words' mutual linear ordering in the sentence. Most languages do not employ a rigid word order when expressing syntactic relations between words. Positional formulae are based on strict positional consistency of the pivotal items relative to the variable slot-fillers and in fact that is the only criterion for identifying such formulae. In a language with free word order, most utterances would be classified as positionally inconsistent and would fall outside the descriptive power of the grammar.

Second, and more disturbingly, it is notoriously incorrect to identify syntactic structure with linear-positional regularities, and see Chomsky's publications on the matter.[16] Despite hopes to the contrary (e.g., Lieven *et al.*, 1997), such positional frames cannot lead a child to adult syntax. Nor are there good reasons to assume that children are misled into misinterpretation of adult data because of mechanistic positional regularities. For example, Lee (2004) gives some examples from child corpora in Cantonese, a language with rigid word order, which make it clear that children do not form false 'positional formats' with such items as sentence-final particles and the 'variable material' preceding them. Instead, they quite early figure out the correct function and placement rules of these items and use them correctly in their own utterances. As Lee points out, children's early word combinations show a much stronger evidence of continuity with adult grammatical rules than assumed by the theories attributing them merely distributional or positional formulae.

The decisive argument against an approach based on distributional criteria in child language is, however, that such criteria are inherently flawed in their logic. As it will be detailed below, the systematic application of the criteria for identifying pivots generates an apparent paradox: it turns all 'open-class' slot-fillers into pivots themselves.

The problem with the distributional basis of pivot grammars and other slot-and-frame approaches

Pivot-grammars or slot-and-frame type systems are built on classification of all words in utterances into two classes: the ones that are pivots (or the fixed elements of formulae) and the others that are slot-fillers. As these grammars are distributional systems, the criterion for being the pivot, or fixed element in a format is that the relevant word appears in the same position in several word combination with several different associates taking up the other sentencial position. Slot-fillers are basically undefined except for their ability to freely appear with all pivots, as slot-fillers in formulae.

There is, however, an unresolvable logical paradox in the very definition of pivot words versus slot-filler words. If the filler words can appear freely with any and all pivots, they are in fact expected to be words that appear in many word combinations in the same position, with many different words taking up the other sentencial position. Thus, the members of the slot-filler or 'open' category in positional grammars are in fact defined exactly as pivots are.

It can be objected that pivots are expected to occupy a fixed position in the sentence, occupying either the first position or the second in two-word utterances, whereas slot-filler words are expected to occur in both positions, complementary to the positioning of the pivot words—in final position with first-place pivots, and in first position with second-place pivots. However, in a seriously Head-initial language such as English, this is a moot point: most pivots are first-place pivots, and thus slot-filler words are in fact likely to appear only in second-position.

In fact, there is no procedure for blocking a word classified as a filler word (because it appears with established pivots) from being itself classified as a pivot, based on the very same utterances, in cases when it does not stray from a fixed positioning. To see how deeply this can damage a pivot-style grammar, we should return to Braine's original (1963) sample.

Steven's corpus demonstrates the phenomenon most clearly as, in Braine's words, in his corpus there is 'substantial overlap between the sets of words that follow the various first-position pivots.' (p. 8). For example, the pivot 'see' occurred with four different words following it:

see ball

see doll

see record

see Stevie

Some of these words overlapped the slot-fillers following the first-place pivot 'here':

here bed

here checker

here doll

here truck

Braine points out that the overlap involved, besides *see* and *here,* also the first-place pivots *want, it,* and *there,* all of which had the majority of their slot-fillers also following another pivot word (p. 8).

What Braine does not discuss, though, is the inevitable outcome of the large degree of overlap: that many slot-fillers will therefore answer to the criterion for being a pivot! For example, the word *doll* answers to the criterion for being a pivot better than *see* or *here,* above. It occurred seven times in the second place, each time with a different item taking up the first position:

it doll

get doll

see doll

there doll

that doll

here doll

baby doll

There is nothing in the distributional criteria for pivothood that could block *doll* from being categorized as a pivot. Calling its distributional behaviour— many different associates, consistent placement—an example of filler 'overlap' rather than 'pivothood' has no legs to stand on. Within a system totally relying on distributional evidence, there are simply no grounds for not classifying *doll* as a pivot. As we said above, the very feature that defines the 'open' class—the possibility to occur freely as fillers with various different pivots—also defines all open-class words as potential pivots! The same problem, of course, exists in the definition of slot-and-frame patterns defined by Pine and Lieven's (1993) criteria: given the set of utterances produced by Steven, above, they would have no choice but to acknowledge both *see X* and *X doll* as productive word-based formulae.

Thus, the central problem with the pivot-open type grammars is that the difference between pivots and open-class items is untenable and decisions based on it are inherently arbitrary. It is of course impossible to define all words appearing with multiple partners as pivots—if we do that, the whole system collapses. The moral is that distributional behaviour, namely, the number of different associates and the constancy of positioning, does not and cannot pick out the 'pivots' responsible for the word combination, and distinguish them from the filler words that merely serve as their arguments or dependents. Such a distinction can only be made on the basis of the words' inherent nature, namely, their valency.

1.3.3 Support for a valency-based grammar for young children from bilingual development

Support for a valency-based grammar for young children comes also from a consideration of bilingual development. Vihman (1999), in an important study of the development of early word combinations in her son Raivo who grew up bilingual in Estonian and English, presented a series of findings seriously damaging for an approach that connects early word combinations to the learning of positional formulae from the input. In his first 4 months of word combinations, Raivo produced many mixed-language utterances, joining words from English and Estonian in the same utterance.[17] Vihman carefully tested these constructions for productivity, and identified a few that were undoubtedly productive, according to the exacting standards of Lieven *et al.* (1997). For instance, Raivo had a productive formula *more X*, generating such sentences as *More küpsis* ('*More cookie*'). As Vihman points out, such mixed language constructions cannot derive directly from the input, as the adults in this child's environment did not mix languages. It is easy to see, however, that in all cases the combinations represent predicate-argument pairs, although the arguments are drawn from a different lexicon than the predicate words. In some cases, Raivo even learned pairs of predicate words that were translational equivalents in the two languages, generating mixed-language combinations with both, as for example, with the words *ka* and *too*. My daughter Shira, who grew up bilingual between the ages of 1 and 2 years, also produced mirroring mixed language word combinations of this kind, saying in the same week both *give-me halav* and *tni-li milk*, both sentences meaning '*give me milk*'. Such mixed-language combinations are evidence that a child learned some predicate words with their semantic valency, and expresses them in a way derived from the predicates' valency and not through imitation of positional patterns identified in the input.

Vihman also points out that, for some of the frames, reversals in word ordering were quite common, strongly implying that the frame cannot be positionally based. This finding, replicating the 'groping patterns' reported by Braine (1976) and Tomasello (1992), suggests that children might well learn separately the basic semantic valency of a predicate and the syntactic valency of the same word, the latter regulating the linear positioning of the predicate and its expressed valency complement.

1.3.4 Young children prefer immediately adjacent Merge/Dependency pairs

The last piece of evidence for children using the Merge/Dependency syntactic operation for generating sentences comes from consideration of slightly longer sentences, of three words and more, produced by young children. Such sentences involve two or more Merge/Dependency relations among the words of the sentence. Merge/Dependency is a binary operation connecting pairs of words. If the two words involved are not immediately next to each other in the sentence, the production of the word-couple on-line involves memory storage and retrieval processes.

In terms of natural language processing, a Merge/Dependency relation is a computational command to the effect that the information carried by the two separate words comprising the Dependency couple is to be combined, unified, or synthesized. The generation of grammatical sentences requires that each word is to be provided by a Merge/Dependency partner within the sentence. If the two words involved are immediately consecutive, this procedure can be carried out without recourse to storage in, and retrieval from, short-term memory. If the two members of a Dependency couple are to be separated by some intervening material in the sentence, the generation of the sentence involves an interruption in the processing of one Dependency relation by the processing of another, thus creating an *open Dependency* for the duration. Until the second member of the couple is generated, the speaker has to keep in short-term memory the fact that such a closure is pending. For example, the generation of '*Give him apples*' requires that the speaker store the demand for the second dependent of '*give*' (namely, for '*apples*') until after the first dependent ('*him*') is produced.

It is known that in adults these processes place a considerable load on short-term operating memory, making it difficult to deal with sentences where two, three, or more syntactic connected Merge/Dependency operations are simultaneously open and pending. An example with three simultaneously open dependencies is the sentence *Who did the dog which the farmer who the cat licked owned chase?*, which is almost impossible to produce or comprehend (Hudson, 1993).

As expected under the hypothesis that young children produce their sentences using the Merge/Dependency operation, the factor of memory load plays a decisive role in the ordering of acquisition. In Ninio (1994) the first 102 different sentence types of more than two words produced by Travis, an English-speaking child recorded by Tomasello (1992) were analysed. The overwhelming majority (90.2%) of Travis' earliest sentences consisting of three and four words had all Merge/Dependency couples immediately adjacent to each other. For instance, Travis generated very many sentences of the type *Get the pencil* in which *get* is the Head of the determiner *the* and *the* is the Head of the noun *pencil*. She generated very few sentences of the type *Two rugs down* in which there is a gap between *down*, which is the Head word, and the determiner *two*, which is its immediate dependent. The Dependency structure of the two sentences are presented in (5). The arrows connect each Head-Dependent couple, leading from Head to Dependent as usual:

(5)

a.　　　　Get　　　　the　　　　pencil

b.　　　　Two　　　　rugs　　　　down

The long arrow in (5b) symbolizes the increased working load placed on the speaker by the separated, syntactically connected, word-pair *two* and *down*. Apparently, in the first month of producing three- and four-word sentences, Travis very seldom took on separated Merge/Dependency couples.

In following month, Travis gradually increased the production of sentence-types in which Merge/Dependency pairs were not immediately adjacent in the sentence. Of her next 272 'longer' sentence types, only 74.3% were the all-adjacent kind, a difference significant by Chi-square test ($\chi^2 = 11.50$, 1d.f., $P < 0.001$).[18]

The avoidance of open-and-pending Merge/Dependency pairs probably accounts for the old finding that in many children acquiring English, various expansions of the subject noun-phrase to determiner-and-noun, e.g., in the sentence *This glass broke* or *My foot hurts*, do not appear until later than the formally equivalent expansion of the object noun-phrase as in *Take this apple* or *Take my hand* (Bloom, 1970; Brown, 1973; Bloom *et al.*, 1975). The much discussed subject–object asymmetry in production is but a reflection of the processing aspect of children using Merge/Dependency to generate their multiword utterances.

1.4 Conclusions: children learn to merge two words according to their valency

We have shown that classical as well as up-to-date descriptions of the early period of word combinations can be fruitfully 'deconstructed' as approximations to a portrayal of children's two-word utterances as Merge/Dependency couplets. Based on previous descriptions, the earliest word combinations appear to express predicate-argument relations among pairs of words that are inherently asymmetrical as syntactic constituents, the predicate words projecting their valency into utterances while the argument words provide their complements.

Previous descriptions of early word combinations latched on to different aspects of their basic nature. The characterization of early child sentences as 'telegraphic' emphasized the combinations satisfying valency requirements of the sentence's predicate despite the omission of various grammatical functor words that did not contribute to the content. Their characterization as expressions of semantic relations mostly pointed to the semantic predicate-argument relation between the words forming the couplet. Pivot grammar was an early attempt to honour the asymmetrical nature of word combinations, on the most part correctly picking out the predicates as the pivots of the word combinations. Contemporary frame-and-slot descriptions are similar, inheriting the strength and weaknesses of pivot grammar. On the whole, then, empirical generalizations regarding the nature of early word combinations— whatever their theoretical meta-language—appear to describe word-couples that are generated by the syntactic operation of Merge/Dependency.

We may conclude that children apparently begin entry into syntax by mastering the basic building-block of syntactic structure proposed by formal linguistics, namely, the projection of lexical valency into a multiword combination by the operation Merge/Dependency.

Our analysis shows that it is both unnecessary and unwarranted to approach children's syntactic development by positing basic learning processes that are alien in spirit to the conceptualization of syntactic structure by theoretical linguistics (see note 16). This includes all those approaches in which children are said to engage in statistical learning or distributional learning, registering positional frames or co-occurrence patterns, computing transitional probabilities among adjacent words and so forth.[19] Statistical or distributional learning mechanisms incorrectly identify syntactic structure with regularities and patterns of linear positioning (for a similar critique, see Lee, 2004). The main motivation driving the relevant developmental theories is a search for easily noticeable patterns in the linguistic input which children are thought to be able to recognize and store as approximations or substitutes for the supposedly more complex true linguistic units and relations. The main message of the present analysis is that it is possible to attribute to young children a process of syntactic development that respects the fundamental nature of language, using the true units of syntactic structure.

1.4.1 A blueprint for syntactic development

The major outcome of our analysis is a blueprint for the learning process involved in syntactic development, at least at its basic level. It provides a definition of what children need to learn, and apparently learn immediately they begin to produce two-word utterances. It seems that children learn two things: they learn how to use the Merge/Dependency operation to combine two words; and they learn a vocabulary of predicate words, including their semantic and syntactic valency.

According to the empirical evidence reviewed above, children get to understand the Merge/Dependency principle very early, as they appear to master its application as soon as their own first spontaneous word combination is produced.

The Merge/Dependency operation is at its core an operation of semantic specification, carried out by one word on the content of another. The Head word evokes some general concept and the Dependent word provides further specification for it. As Hudson (1990) pointed out, this relation is extremely similar to modification, as in *black shoe*, even when it involves verbs and their subjects or objects. For example, the word *get* evokes the notion of obtaining in general; the addition of the word *bottle* provides information on what is to be obtained in this specific instance. The meaning of the combination *get bottle* is still a kind of obtaining, but a more specific one than the one evoked by the bare *get*.

What was shown in this chapter is that children can be attributed with a control of the Merge/Dependency relation as early as their earliest spontaneous word combination. The suggestion is that children's production of word combinations such as *get bottle* is conditional on, and reflects, an intuitive understanding of the logic of Merge/Dependency. Although this sounds like a very complex idea for children to grasp, that is because we lack a simple vocabulary to talk about intuitions. All it means is that children are able to produce a combination like *get bottle* because they understand that this is a more specific version of the single-word request *get*, not only expressing the request to get but also pointing out what is it that they want the adult to get for them. Two-word combinations thus reflect not only the ability to express two different elements of a scene or event, nor just the ability to order words in linearized strings, nor merely the mastery of multiword prosody, although these skills are important components of what it takes to produce multiword utterances. What they reflect is, at the core, the ability to put two words together so that one specifies the other's meaning.

The Merge/Dependency operation is a very general principle. Some nativist researchers (e.g., Roeper, 1996) suggest that it is innately provided as part of a genetically transmitted Universal Grammar. Others (e.g., MacWhinney, 1975, 1982; Robinson, 1986; Van Langendonck, 1987; Ninio, 1994, 1996; Green, 1997) do not embrace the nativist assumption and propose instead that children master the Merge/Dependency principle on the basis of experience with the linguistic input. This topic will not be pursued in the present book. I will only point out that the main argument for assuming that some piece of knowledge is innate, namely, that it seems unlearnable, does not stand in this case. As Merge/Dependency is neither deep nor invisible, it seems quite easy to learn as a basic operating strategy for producing word combinations, using general human cognitive abilities. Young children figure out many other combinatory principles quite easily and at an even earlier age, such as how to put together two Lego pieces. I will assume that children deduce the principle of the Merge/Dependency operation from sentences adults say to them, leaving the details of this learning process to some other study.[20]

In addition to the Merge/Dependency operation, children need to learn a vocabulary of predicate items, as these items are responsible for the creation of syntactic structure. There are indications that children understand the meaning of predicate words before generating word combinations with them. Very young children who do not themselves produce multiword utterances have been shown to be able to interpret them, judging, for instance, by the findings of the preferential looking paradigm (Hirsh-Pasek and Golinkoff, 1991, 1996). However, the level of skill required for production is higher than for comprehension and it takes children a further 6–10 months of learning until they can actually produce syntactically constructed sentences.

In a syntax projected from the lexicon, the combination resides in an a priori way with the element having the valency for it. As we saw in Section 1.1.2, each word needs to have its syntactic and semantic valencies incorporated into its lexical entry. We might assume that semantic valency is stored in the form of a predicate function such as Sleep(X), with X representing the person or animal asleep, while syntactic valency is stored in the form of a slot-and-frame formula such as 'X *sleep*', X some referential term naming the semantic subject.

Both pieces of information are to be acquired in the process of learning the verb *sleep*. This implies that syntactic development as a process is not clearly distinguishable from the acquisition of a vocabulary of predicate words. It has been proposed before that the emergence of syntax in children is intimately tied to the acquisition of semantically complex vocabulary items (e.g., Bloom, 1970; Bloom and Lahey, 1978; Gleitman, 1990; Ingram, 1979b; McCune-Nicolich, 1981; Ninio, 1988; Naigles, 1990; McCune and Vihman, 1999). For example, Ingram (1979b) showed that children typically postpone learning words with relational meaning to the second half of the single-word period, anticipating the start of word combinations. Ninio (1988) summarizes the connection in the following:

> In producing their earliest word combinations, children demonstrate that they grasp the logical structure of words which encode inherent semantic relations and which therefore take logical-semantic arguments. Thus, the very ability of children to impose formal structure on their utterances follows from their ability to learn the meaning of lexical items that have a variable semantic component.
>
> Ninio (1988, p. 111)

In our review of the developmental literature, we have concluded that children indeed begin acquisition by learning individual predicate terms and their valency, and that, at the start of acquisition, they generate syntactic combinations between specific predicates and their valency arguments. The question we should be asking now is, if each different predicate-argument frame—like *get X*—is learned separately, does it not leave the child with an inventory of isolated mini-grammars, nothing like the interconnected syntactic system of adults? This is the topic to which we turn now.

Notes

1   In mathematical terms, the syntactic structure of a sentence has the characteristics of a directed tree. A directed tree is a completely connected, two-dimensional, directed acyclic graph with a single root. For trees in graph theory, see Tutte (1984).

2   The tree generated by the Dependency relation is also a directed tree. Each node of the tree represents a word and directional arcs between the nodes represent the Dependency relation, leading from Head to dependent. The tree is headed by the highest word in the sentence, the root, which is the word that does not possess a Head of its own.

3   The Merge-type representation is called in computer theorizing a *parse tree*, while *syntax trees* represent the Dependency-type structural description. In a *syntax tree*, operators are the Heads of their operands, rather

than their sister as in *parse trees.* The trees actually used in compiler programs are the syntax trees (Aho *et al.,* 1986, p. 49).

4   Some Dependency Grammars such as Word Grammar (Hudson 1984, 1990) allow multiple Heads, but most do not. Multiple Heads create cyclic graphs, which are not trees; the resultant mathematical structures for sentences are untractable and probably unnecessary for the efficacy of Dependency analysis.

5   Apart from the syntactic tree-structure, Dependency theory also acknowledges another structural representation of a sentence—that of the sentence as a phonetic or orthographic string. The sentence-string consists of the words of the sentence ordered in sequence, when adjacent pairs of words stand in a relation of being a neighbour of each other. The resultant structure is linear or one-dimensional.

According to Dependency theory, the transferral from the two-dimensional tree-structure of a sentence to its one-dimensional phonetic chain structure is regulated by a single rule of the grammar, that of adjacency or projectivity (Robinson, 1970; Mel'cuk, 1988). The rule of projectivity is that a dependent must appear in a sentence immediately adjacent to its Head except that the two may be separated by dependent(s) of either words. This rule is applied recursively so that if the inserted dependent has a dependent of its own, the latter may in turn be inserted between its own Head and the Head's Head. The result is that the deeper the Dependency relation between a pair of words on the tree (the further away from the root), the closer are the words in the linear sentence. In other words, the degree of proximity of two grammatically related words in the sentence chain encodes the relative subordinate-ness of the relevant Dependency relation, in comparison with other relations either word participates in. The technique is similar to that employed in drawing in perspective: the further away a figure from the viewer in the three-dimensional space represented by the picture, the smaller it is drawn in the picture-plane.

6   Phrase Structure Grammars and Dependency Grammars have been shown to be mathematically equivalent (e.g., Bar-Hillel, 1953; Hayes, 1964; Gaifman, 1965; but see Fraser, 1994), despite the differences in the choice of part-whole versus Head-dependent relations as the building blocks of syntactic structure. Evolution of the Phrase Structure Grammar, namely, the development of the Minimalist Program and the adoption of Merge as the basic syntactic operation, makes the previous comparisons somehow dated.

7   Valency was first introduced to linguistics by Peirce (1992[1898]), and see Askedal (1991) and Burch (1992) for a discussion of his work.

8   This is a very oversimplified presentation of valency and the lexicon. In particular, some words—not the English *in*—have several homonyms or polysemous versions with different logical properties. For example, *roll* is a transitive verb with a subject and an object, but it also has an intransitive 'middle' version with a single subject complement, not to mention the nouns sharing the same sound pattern. A theory of the mental lexicon needs to make it clear how these alternatives are stored and related. Another type of complication is posed by languages such as Japanese that allow free dropping of any and all syntactic complement phrases. It is thus questionable whether it is at all possible to talk of syntactic valency in such languages. An opposite problem arises in morphologically rich languages in which verbs are always inflected for subjects and objects—it is a good question whether there is in fact an 'incomplete' verbal lexeme in such languages, or are all verbs in fact already 'saturated'? Can they be seen as having incomplete meaning just because they can get optional noun complements? For some treatment of these issues, see Allerton (1982), Jelinek (1984), and Matsumoto (1996).

9   In addition, there have been various proposals for using 'Typed Lambda Calculus' (Curry and Feys, 1958) and other types of combinatory logic (Church, 1932/1933) as the foundation of syntactic theory, e.g., Moortgat (1988), Steedman (1988), Ninio (1995), and Cormack (1999).

10   Following current practice, both in the Dependency tradition (Hudson, 1990) and in Phrase Structure Grammar (i.e., the DP-Hypothesis; see Abney, 1987; Speas, 1990), determiners are considered Heads of the common noun complementing them. Intuitively, determiners are similar to prepositions: just as prepositions are a type of adverb needing complementation, so are determiners a type of pronoun needing complementation. It should be noted that there are some who disagree with the proposed direction of Dependency (e.g., Van Langendonck, 1994). In addition, some languages do not have determiners, in which case the question of which word is the Head of which is irrelevant.

11   In English as in many other languages, every sentence must have a finite verb as its root; the verb with its direct dependents is considered to be the core of the sentence. The preference for finite verbs as roots of sentences is universal. Some languages allow non-verbal roots (i.e., in so-called nominal sentences), which then behave like verbs, even, sometimes, to the extent of receiving verbal inflections for person and tense/aspect. Even in these languages, if the sentence contains a finite verb, it will be the root, and not a nominal or an adjective.

12 It is often said that the two kinds of theories differ in Phrase Structure Grammars embracing transformations or movements, while monostratal Dependency Grammars such as Word Grammar do not. However, it is possible that transformations can be viewed as special cases of the basic Merge/Dependency operation. In Word Grammar, Hudson (1990) has a special syntactic role of Visitor for, e.g., fronted topics or wh-question words in English. Within Phrase Structure Grammar, Cormack and Smith (2001) suggest that Merge can cover also Move, the second syntactic operation of the Minimalist Program.

13 There are of course other approaches that represent a non-lexicalist view of syntactic structure. The chief among them are Construction Grammars (e.g., Fillmore, 1968; Goldberg, 1995; Croft, 2001) and Usage-based grammars (Bybee, 2001). The former propose sentence-size abstract formats as the building blocks of syntactic structure, which, when filled with actual lexical items and further elaborated with optional adjuncts, generate semantically coherent sentences. The latter are radical theories leaning to the other extreme, proposing that linguists do away with rules and abstractions in toto; instead of rules, they think, speakers store concrete exemplars of actual sentences they heard or said, which then form the basis for the generation of novel sentences by analogy to the stored ones.

14 They also omit inflectional morphology such as the third person singular -s of *makes*, but this will be ignored for the sake of simplifying the present discussion.

15 The expression 'pivot look' was coined by Brown (1973). Among others, Francis (1969), Bloom (1970), Wells (1974), Bloom *et al.* (1975), Mac-Whinney (1975), Smoczynska (1976), Ingram (1979a, 1989), Horgan (1980), Nelson (1981), Peters (1983, 1995), Radford (1990), Tomasello (1992), Pine and Lieven (1993), and Lieven *et al.* (1997) have proposed that at least some children's early word combinations are similar to pivot-open frames.

16 As it is well known, Chomsky explicitly insists that all rules of language are structure-dependent, and see 1971, p. 30, also Piattelli-Palmarini (1980, p. 40).

17 Other bilingual children have been observed to be producing a high level of mixed-language usage in their first word combinations, e.g., Deuchar (1999) reports her daughter mixing Spanish and English in close to half of her two-word combinations in the first 2 months. A similar

phenomenon in two French–German bilingual children is reported by Köppe and Meisel (1995).

18 Similar findings were obtained for Hebrew-speaking children, see Ninio (1998).

19 For example, Finch and Chater (1992, 1994), Altmann *et al.* (1995), Morgan *et al.* (1996), Cartwright and Brent (1997), Lieven *et al.* (1997), Redington *et al.* (1998), Gomez and Gerken (1999), Marcus *et al.* (1999), Newport and Aslin (2000), Saffran (2001, 2002), Mintz *et al.* (2002), Christiansen and Kirby (2003), and Tomasello (2003).

20 In all probability children do not at first master the principle of recursion, which is irrelevant as long as they do not attempt the construction of longer utterances consisting of three words or more. Possibly, the development of longer utterances is conditional on an understanding of the logic of recursion as it is conceptualized in the Merge/Dependency framework (for details see Ninio, 1988). In particular, children are to realize that word combinations inherit the logical combinatorial properties of one of their terms, and with it their formal (i.e., syntactic) combinatorial privileges.

2

The learning curve

2.1 The learning curve in cognitive psychology

2.1.1 The acquisition of syntax as skill learning

In Chapter 1 we concluded that young children learn to produce valency-appropriate syntactic constructions for different verbs and other predicate words, on an individual basis. Among others, they learn to produce a verb–object combination for the transitive verb *get* (as in *get bottle* or *get book*), and for the verb *open* (as in *open this, open box*) and for the verb *want* (as in *want banana, want it*) and so forth. Each different predicate-argument frame—like *get X*—poses a separate learning task.

The emphasis on the individual learning of predicate words and their syntactic frames paints the picture of a learning process that is both very simple and also very similar to any other kind of learning needed to deal with objects in the world. Learning the relational meaning of the word *get* and how to say *get bottle* is not very different from learning that a door has handles and what to do to open it when it is closed.

In more formal terms, we have defined the learning of verb-specific valency combinations (or valency frames) as a type of cognitive skill learning. This conceptualization can be tested. If syntactic development is like skill learning, it should be influenced by well-known factors such as amount of experience with the task. In other words, similar syntactic frames formed by different predicates should sit on their own learning curve, and the rate of their acquisition should adhere to the universal 'Power Law of Practice'. This law states: 'The speed of performance of a task increases as a power-law function of the number of times the task is performed'. We shall discuss the learning curve and the Power Law of Practice in detail, below.

2.1.2 Transfer and analogy

Another way to say experience influences performance is to evoke the term transfer. Theoreticians of learning claim that all new learning involves transfer based on previous learning (Fitts and Posner, 1967; Singley and Anderson, 1989;

Bransford *et al.*, 1999). Transfer is the ability to extend what has been learned in one context to new contexts, by analogy (Byrnes, 1996). Its effect is measured by facilitation of learning if positive, and interference with learning if negative, evidenced by changes in the speed and accuracy of learning. In transfer, learners make use of the common features of the source and the target of the analogy while ignoring irrelevant features, which might be different in the two problems (Thorndike, 1906; Singley and Anderson, 1989; Gentner *et al.*, 2003). The target and all potential sources of analogy are isomorphs: they may differ in terms of superficial features but share structural elements at some deeper level, elements that are directly relevant to the problem-solving operations.

It is important to stress that the ability to notice similarities and to use them in the transfer of learning is a general cognitive bias of the learning system itself and not a higher stage of learning in particular tasks. In fact, similarity matching and transfer operate immediately as soon as the learning of a new task begins. For example, in the analogical reasoning literature it has been claimed that providing learners with as few as two similar concrete exemplars is sufficient to enable them to deal with similar and novel cases (Gick and Holyoak, 1983; Bjork and Richardson-Klavhen, 1989). The best transfer results are achieved if, at learning, only a few exemplars are presented, each with very high frequency (McAndrews and Moskowitch, 1985; Perruchet and Pacteau, 1990).

Analogy making is apparently a very basic cognitive ability in humans, and even young children are able to transfer solutions to isomorphic problems based on analogy between them (e.g., Brown and Kane, 1988; Goswami, 1991, 1996; Blades and Cooke, 1994; Klahr, 2000).

Analogy has been demonstrated in well-controlled experiments in children as young as 3 and younger. For example, Loewenstein and Gentner (2001) tested 3-year-old children on their ability to find a hidden toy in a doll-house room after being shown its location in a perceptually different room. They found that asking the children to point out similarities in two different doll-houses had a significant positive effect on their performance on a spatial mapping task to a third doll-house. Apparently, drawing comparisons focused attention to similarities and commonalities in spatial relations between the doll-houses and this information could then be transferred to the spatial mapping task.

Although quite young children have been demonstrated to use analogy in solving novel problems, detailed examination of their analogical abilities revealed that, mostly, younger children can employ a within-domain 'near transfer' but not a between-domains 'remote transfer' (Chen and Klahr, 1999). Near transfer was defined by Chen and Klahr as the use of a previously employed solution to solve novel problems that use a set of different materials but that are still in the same general domain as the original problem. Remote transfer was defined as the application of an old solution to solve problems within different domains or contexts than the ones of the original training task. It seems that within-domain transfer is within the capacities of children even below the age of 3, as evidenced by studies such as Blades and Cooke's (1994). Despite these early demonstrated abilities, it is clear that older children get progressively better at transfer and analogy, in particular when the transfer is from one domain to another or when it involves ignoring much surface dissimilarity between the problems (Gentner and Toupin, 1986; Chen and Daehler, 1992; Chen and Klahr, 1999).

The most intriguing finding in the problem-solving literature, as far as skill learning is concerned, is that increased experience with, or expertise in a given domain improves the ability to employ analogy and transfer in order to solve problems in that domain. Particularly important for us is the finding that children get better at relations-based analogy with increasing expertise, as shown by studies in which knowledge of domain correlated positively with analogical abilities within the domain (Goswami and Brown, 1989; Goswami, 1992; Rattermann and Gentner, 1998).[1] This finding promises that children would not only transfer skills from one task to another but that their gains from transfer would increase as learning of a particular kind of task progresses.

2.1.3 The learning curve

The quantitative manifestation of within-domain transfer in skill learning is the learning curve, mapping performance on a series of similar tasks. The practice effect is positive transfer or facilitation from previous learning. Similar tasks, involving like stimuli and responses, allow transfer, earlier learning influencing the speed and success rates of later learned items throughout the learning process.[2] It is well known that transfer effects operate at all phases of skill learning. When the learner is a novice, transfer is from previously learned tasks that possess component skills that can help the performance of the novel task. In later stages, transfer is of more task-specific skills or skill components.[3] Even when a skill has been so well learned that it has undergone automatization, it is still vulnerable to be disrupted by negative transfer, demonstrating that previous learning influences performance at all times (Fitts and Posner, 1967, pp. 19–20).

The Power Law of Practice is one of the great success stories of cognitive psychology. It claims that for virtually all learning tasks, the shape of the learning curve plotting performance against amount of experience with the task is an accelerating non-linear curve, best described by the mathematical power-law function. Such a curve has been found for very different types of tasks, perceptual, motor, and higher cognitive. We predict that learning to produce word combinations will also adhere to a power-law function. Namely, the more different predicates the child learns to produce with a particular syntactic construction, the easier it should become to learn a new predicate with the same construction. The practice effects should result in a typical learning curve, with an accelerating power-law shape.

Let us elaborate.

2.1.4 Learning curves and the Power Law of Practice

Learning curves plot some measure of task performance—based on the time it takes to complete a task, the rate of success or both—as a function of amount of experience with the task. Most skilled tasks get better with practice, namely, they take less time to complete and the error rate drops. Unskilled performers at the start of learning perform slowly, namely, it takes them a long time to perform the task to criterion. They may also fail at the task some of the time, be inaccurate, or be able to take on only the less complex tasks. With practice, task performance accelerates and its quality improves. Hence, as the amount of practice increases, so does the proficiency of the individual at the task. There are many ways to measure task performance, and the specific measure to be employed obviously depends on the task we are considering. But on any measure or score, practice brings about an improvement.

The effect of practice is not the same over the course of learning. It has been noted ever since Thorndike (1913) that the benefits from practice follow a non-linear function. Improvement is rapid at first but its rate decreases as the learner becomes more skilled. At some point, the learner reaches an almost-asymptote and the rate of improvements in performance slows down considerably.

In their influential book, *Human Performance*, Fitts and Posner (1967) review half a decade of studies of skill learning and conclude that the relationship of performance to amount of practice can be best described by a power-law function. A power is an exponent to which a given number is raised; the expression x^a therefore means 'x raised to the ath power.' A function, $f(x)$, is a power-law function if the dependent variable, x, is raised to some power, for instance, $y = x^2$. The exponent can be positive or negative: if $y = x^2$ is an example of a positive function, $y = x^{-2}$ is an example of a negative function. The power-law function is a non-linear, accelerating or decelerating, three-parameter mathematical function. If plotted, the resulting graph is a monotonically increasing one for a positive exponent and a monotonically decreasing one for a negative exponent.

The effect of practice on performance is expressed by a power-law function of the form $Y = a + bX^c$, with Y representing some (positive) score of task

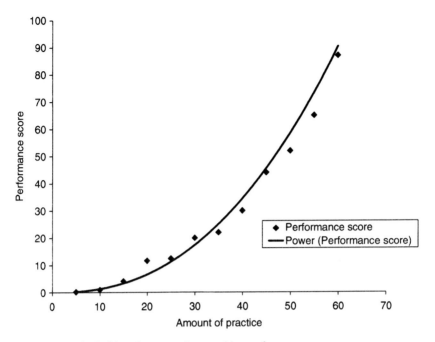

Fig. 2.1 Hypothetical learning curve for a positive performance score.

performance and X, the amount of practice. The parameter *a* is measure of the asymptote the task will arrive at (i.e., as a function of task complexity), *b* is a constant, and *c* is the slope of the function, representing the rate of learning. If the measure of task performance is a score that is expected to decrease with practice, such as reaction-time or error rate, the slope *c* is negative and the power-function decelerates rather than accelerates. Figure 2.1 presents a hypothetical accelerating learning curve.

The power function is characterized by the fact that if we take the logarithm of both variables, X and Y, we find that the logarithm of performance is linearly related to the logarithm of the amount of practice. For this reason, learning curves are often plotted with logarithmic scales on both axes. For example, Fitts and Posner (1967, p. 16) present a graph depicting the gradual improvement of mirror-drawing over 60 days of practice in a study by Snoddy (1926). The performance scores were positive, so that the faster the perform-ance and the higher the accuracy, the higher the score. Snoddy plotted the scores on a log–log scale, with the points sitting quite close to the positively sloping straight line, demonstrating that improvement continues throughout the period, but the rate of improvement slows down. Figure 2.2 presents a log–log version of Figure 2.1.

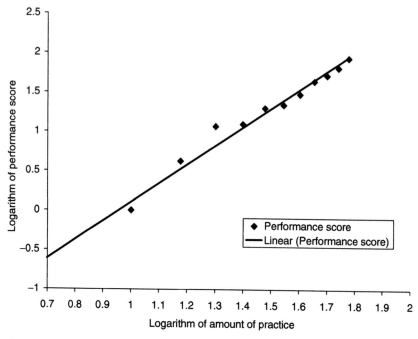

Fig. 2.2 Hypothetical learning curve on a logarithmic scale for a positive performance score.

The performance scores used are sometimes the cumulative number of tasks completed as a function of the cumulative time at performance (e.g., Ohlsson, 1992). This measure, too, is distributed with a power-law function with a positive exponent (e.g., Duane, 1964).

Often, however, the function considered in the skill learning literature is not performance scores *per se* but improvement in performance. For example, if the learning curve is of task time as a function of trial number, the improvement with practice will manifest itself in a negatively accelerating, decreasing curve. Figure 2.3 presents a hypothetical learning curve using task time as the measure.

This kind of negatively accelerating curve emphasizes the fact that at the start of learning there is rapid improvement, followed by ever lesser improvements with further practice. Practice always improves performance, but the most dramatic improvements happen at the start of learning. Subsequently, practice has diminishing returns.

One of the success stories of cognitive psychology is the demonstration that regardless of the task considered and the measure used, the rate of improvement with practice is surprisingly similar: learning curves are well-described by a non-linear, accelerating or decelerating mathematical function.

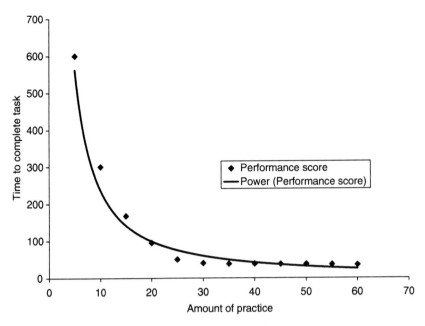

Fig. 2.3 Hypothetical learning curve for a negative performance score.

Apart from power-law functions, other mathematical functions such as the exponential or the sigmoid can also provide this shape. Most researchers concur with Fitts and Posner (1967) that the best fit to learning curves is a power-law function (Newell and Rosenbloom, 1981).[4] In a weaker form, all agree that a power-law function is a good approximation for the effect of practice on learning, at least for the first part of the learning curve. Hence, learning is usually said to follow the 'Power Law of Practice'.

Recently, several authorities have claimed that power-law functions are the best fit only for averaged scores, whether across individuals or sub-tasks, but that more specific and individual results are better fitted with an exponential function (e.g., Heathcote et al., 2000),[5] or with other non-linear mathematical functions such as the logical-sigmoid.[6] The difference between the approximations is not crucial for our argument and we shall stay with originally proposed power-law distribution.

In addition, some authorities use the term 'growth curve' to describe the progress of cognitive learning (e.g., Ruhland et al., 1995). Growth curves are similar to learning curves,[7] except that they are used in biology for phenomena in which temporal changes are not attributed to learning but to other types of effects. For instance, growth curves are used to describe changes in organisms' size (i.e. height and weight), and in the size of populations (Brewer, 1994). It is preferable to keep the term 'growth curve' for such biological phenomena and to use 'learning curve' for learned skills.

Supporters of the Power Law of Practice point out that the shape of the improvement with practice is generally constant across different tasks, whether they are perceptual, motor, or cognitive, small or large, individual or team effort, simple or complex. They claim that the Power Law of Practice is ubiquitous, and deserves the status of a universal law of human performance and cognition. Among the tasks mentioned in the literature as following the Power Law of Practice are mirror drawing, reading inverted text, sending and receiving Morse code, performing mental arithmetic, generating proofs for geometrical problems, rolling cigars, manufacturing machine tools, building ships, and writing books.[8]

Some theorists (Logan, 1988, 1992; Cohen *et al.*, 1990; Palmeri, 1997) consider the power-function speed-up a benchmark test of a viable learning theory. It is often used as a test prediction by which the success of models of skilled performance (e.g., Soar; Newell, 1990) is judged.[9] We shall employ this benchmark test or 'gold standard' of learning theories in order to test if the acquisition of syntactic constructions indeed behaves as a kind of skill learning.

2.2 Implication for acquisition: syntax should transfer right away

Cognitive psychology presented us with a universal law of human skill learning: the Power Law of Practice. This law applies to successive performances of a task on a learning curve. The Power Law of Practice says this series should have the form of a power-law function, performance starting slow and improving with practice.

In cognitive psychology, the shape of the learning curve is a 'gold standard' against which learning theories are tested. We shall employ this benchmark test in order to test the hypothesis raised in Section 2.1 that the acquisition of syntactic constructions is a kind of cognitive skill learning. If learning the valency frames of individual predicates is a learning task just like any other kind of perceptual, motor, and cognitive skill learning, we expect items with a similar type of syntax to show a learning curve with a power-law function.

This hypothesis is not self-evident as there is an alternative: the Verb Island hypothesis (Tomasello, 1992, 2000a). According to this theory, early verbs constitute isolated 'islands' that develop their own mini-syntax independent of each other and unrelated to each other. There is no basis for transfer or facilitation of learning from one verb to another: children do not yet perceive different verbal frames as possessing syntax-relevant commonality. Defining connectedness between individual syntactic frames in terms of belonging to a shared more general category, the Verb Island hypothesis suggests that young children's grammar is devoid of transfer and generalization at the early stages because their grammar lacks as yet the verb-general thematic roles 'actor', 'patient', and so forth that would apply equally to different verbs and make transfer and generalization of syntactic marking for participant roles possible. The theory proposes that children at this stage can learn verb-specific rules like how to express the 'thing hit' argument of the verb *hit*, but not, at this time, relate it to the 'thing seen' argument of the verb *see*. The explanation offered is that young children apparently cannot generalize across pragmatic scenes in which each verbal construction was learned. As Tomasello and Brooks say: 'This limited generality is presumably due to the difficulty of categorizing or schematizing entire scenes, including both the events and the participant roles involved, into a more abstract construction.' (1999, p. 170).

According to the Verb Island hypothesis, integration of the isolated patches of syntax is a later process, occurring at some future date well beyond the period that a child learns to generate multiword positional combinations with her first 20 or 30 verbs. Until that date, children's learning curves are not expected to accelerate, as the individually acquired verbal constructions do not in fact form a temporal series. Thus, according to the Verb Island hypothesis, syntactic acquisition in its early phase is not a typical cognitive learning task but has unique features that preclude transfer and practice effects.

Against these arguments, the Skill-learning hypothesis is based on the assumption that children do not need abstracting or categorizing participant roles, nor do they need to generate abstract constructions in order to relate one verbal frame to another. It is sufficient that the frames are similar in their syntax, and this formal similarity can support transfer and generalization by analogy. The major reason is that abstract participant roles such as 'actor' and 'patient' do not serve any function in adult syntax and it is unlikely that children would go to the trouble of actually forming them. Nor are abstract syntactic schemas such as a generalized Verb-Phrase construction rules operative in adult syntax; in fact, it is quite likely that argument-structure constructions never go beyond lexically-specific valency formats. We have already seen that lexically-specific valency formats are a given in Chomskian linguistics; these subjects will be further dealt with in the following parts of this monograph.

Thus, we have two competing hypotheses regarding the learning curves of children's earliest valency frames: the Skill-learning hypothesis according to which syntactic development is like any other cognitive skill learning, with practice effects and accelerating learning curves under the Power Law of

Practice; and the Verb Island hypothesis, according to which early syntax is not like skill learning, and children's early learning curves should not accelerate under a power-law, exponential or any other non-linear function.

2.3 Developmental evidence: learning curves and generalizations in early syntax

2.3.1 Learning curves in child syntax

The temporal course of development of individual syntactic constructions has not been a preferred focus of investigation in studies of syntactic development. Nevertheless, already in the classical longitudinal studies carried out by such researchers as Braine (1976) and Bowerman (1978), the authors commented on the speeding up of the learning of new word combinations after an initial period of slow advance, at least in the speech of some children.

Later studies, concentrating on verbal valency constructions, calculated the learning curve of development for specific verbal frames. The measure of performance used was in most cases the cumulative type frequency, plotted as a function of age at first production. Namely, the measure was the cumulative number of different verbs in a given syntactic pattern such as the subject-verb construction, plotted according to the age at which the child was first observed to have produced each type of word combination. This produces a monotonically increasing graph, expected to speed up with a positive power-law function under the Law of Practice.

To summarize the existing developmental evidence, it appears a safe generalization that young children's syntactic development advances in typical learning curves, with power-law speed-up. There have been several studies of children's mastery of basic syntactic constructions in three languages—English, German, and Hebrew—and in the vast majority of cases, the learning curves show a slow start, followed by a non-linear acceleration.

Learning curves for transitive constructions

Ninio (1999a)[10] documented the cumulative type frequency of the first 20 verbs in the transitive subject–verb–direct object (SVO) pattern in Travis, a child acquiring English as her first language. Travis is the child whose development is reported in Tomasello (1992). Tomasello's was a diary study concentrating on emergent patterns; all utterances that were not identical verbatim to already recorded ones were included. Travis's speech was daily recorded by her parents, and in addition they made 60-minute long audiotaped and videotaped recordings of her once a month. The start of the systematic recording was at 1;0, and continued till 1;8.8; in this period every sentence was recorded, thereafter only if its structure was more complex than of those produced previously. The source for the following analysis was the appendix of Tomasello (1992), listing all utterances produced by Travis as well as date of production and contextual notes for each sentence. With the exception of perfect repetitions of the same expression in the same context, the data base is close to a complete record of all Travis's multiword sentences involving some predicate word.

For this analysis, Travis's corpus was searched for sentences in which a verb was expressed with a subject and direct object in an SVO construction, optionally with additional elements included in the same clause. Before the systematic observations ended, Travis produced SVO sentences for 19 different verbs. Table 2.1 presents all the SVO sentences produced by Travis since she started to produce such utterances and until 1;8.8.

Figure 2.4 presents the learning curve of Travis' SVO, plotting the accumulation of SVO constructions as a function of the age at which each new verb started to be used in an SVO pattern.

We fitted a power-law function to the graph, which resulted in an excellent fit, with $R^2 = 0.97$. The R^2 statistics measures the per cent of variance in the plotted time-series accounted for by some mathematical function fitted to it; namely, the power-law function accounted for 97% of the variance in the time series. The best linear function fitted to the same learning curve had a lesser fit, $R^2 = 0.84$. Figure 2.5 presents the same learning curve with the two trendlines generated by the power-law and linear mathematical functions.

The difference of 13% between the per cent of variance accounted by the power-law and the linear functions indicates that the learning curve is indeed an accelerating graph, covered by the Power Law of Practice. Inspection of Figure 2.5 makes it clear that the linear function misses both the slow start of learning and the speed-up of the later period.

It should be noted that we are taking the time that has passed since the child last produced a new verb in the SVO pattern as the measure of how much time and effort it has taken her to learn the present, new verb in the pattern. It is customary to use such measures in the skill learning literature as estimate of the time it takes to complete a task to criterion, even if the tasks are self-imposed and the researcher cannot know for sure when the task was in fact taken on (e.g., Ohlsson, 1992). Take note that the period between two points on the graph could have been devoted to either practising the already learned verb(s) in the SVO construction, to learning the new verb in SVO, or to any combination of the two. Of course, the child also devotes attention at this time to dealing with other elements of her grammar, with possible complicating effects on her acquisition of the SVO construction. At the

Table 2.1 Travis's first sentence with each of her first 20 different verbs participating in a Subject–Verb–Direct Object (SVO) construction, with the age of emergence

Age	First SVO utterance with verb
1;06.29	Maria made this duck
1;07.08	Big Bird ride horsie
1;07.11	Weezer did it
1;07.22	Cinnamon lick-it hands
1;07.23	Girl have that umbrella
1;07.23	Pete hurt the fingers in there
1;07.26	Maria hit me
1;07.26	Maria told me have one too
1;07.27	Dana called me Lauren
1;07.28	Danny got me
1;07.28	Daddy take the bottle
1;07.28	Weezer drinking the eggs
1;07.29	Mommy get sauce
1;07.30	Daddy buy this
1;08.03	Cookie Monster love cookies
1;08.04	… Weezer climbing a tree
1;08.04	Bunny Rabbit playing music
1;08.06	Daddy singing chicken
1;08.07	Daddy put-a … new pajamas on

Reproduced from appendix D2 of Ninio, A. (1999a). Pathbreaking verbs in syntactic development. *Journal of Child Language*, with permission from Cambridge University Press.

moment we shall assume that other things being equal, all these complications do not bias the significance of the learning curves as demonstrations of the Power Law of Practice in syntactic acquisition.

To summarize the learning curve for Travis's acquisition of the SVO construction, it looks as if the more verbs she already knows how to combine with a subject and an object, the faster she can learn a new verb in the same pattern.

One troubling question remains. How can we be sure that the accelerating learning curve truly represents transfer of learning between subsequent verbs and thus reflects a practice effect? Unless we find a way to discount other explanations, it remains a possibility that the acceleration of the learning curve

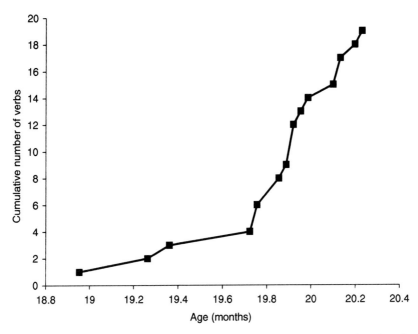

Fig. 2.4 Cumulative number of different verbs in the SVO construction as a function of age at first production—Travis; redrawn from figure 2 of Ninio (1999a). Pathbreaking verbs in syntactic development. *Journal of Child Language*, with permission from Cambridge University Press.

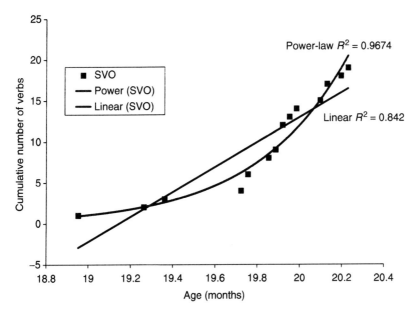

Fig. 2.5 Cumulative number of different verbs in SVO construction as a function of age at first production, with power-law and linear trendlines fitted—Travis; redrawn from figure 2 of Ninio (1999a). Pathbreaking verbs in syntactic development. *Journal of Child Language*, with permission from Cambridge University Press.

for SVO is due to some general advance the child has undergone in the relevant developmental period and not, specifically, to the increasing number of previously learned verbs in the same construction.

In principle, accelerated acquisition could be due to some general developmental advance to which many aspects of language acquisition are sensitive. For instance, many plottings of the mean length of utterance in longitudinally collected samples have the gradual speed-up shape (e.g. Bloom *et al.*, 1975), so it could have been the case that children get faster at combining verbs with subjects and objects between the ages of 1;06.29 and 1;08.07 as a function of getting better at combining morphemes in general. Another possibility is that the accelerating graph reflects children's improved retrieval of items from the lexicon, improving prosodic capacity and so forth.

The way to test this possibility is to look at another learning curve for Travis, one that covers a different age and hence a different developmental period. The logic of this control is that if the learning curve of SVO accelerates because of something that happens in the age period between 1;06.29 and 1;08.07, it is highly unlikely that the same developmental advance would repeat at a different time period.

The syntactic construction we compared with Travis's SVO is her acquisition of VO. The two constructions are quite closely related in that both involve transitive verbs getting a postverbal direct object; the difference is that in the SVO pattern the verbs have in addition to receive an expressed subject. Because VO involves only the control of one single Merge/Dependency couple, it is expected to be easier and earlier than sentences with SVO. Table 2.2 presents Travis's first 30 VO sentences.

We have added the learning curve for Travis's VO to her SVO learning curve, both fitted with a power-law trendline. Figure 2.6 presents the result.

Travis started to produce VO sentences at 1;05.01; her first was *Get-it hat.* By the time she produced her first SVO sentence at 1;06.29 she had already produced VO sentences with over 20 different verbs. Figure 2.6 presents the first 30 verbs in this pattern, thus providing for some overlap between the periods in which the two constructions are beginning to be produced.

Our results show that the learning curve for VO also accelerates: the R^2 for the power-law function is 0.94, while the matching linear function only gets a $R^2 = 0.84$.[11]. In fact the two power-law curves (for VO and SVO) are quite similar in their slope and other formal aspects.

The crucial point is that the learning curve for SVO begins at a very slow rate at a point when the learning curve for VO is already highly speedy. In plain language, by the time Travis started to slowly produce SVO sentences, a new

Table 2.2 Travis's first sentence with each of her first 30 different verbs getting a post-verbal Direct Object, with the age of emergence

Age	Utterance	Age	Utterance
1;05.01	Get-it hat	1;06.25	Fix this
1;05.26	Find-it funny [picture]	1;06.25	Blow balloon
1;05.27	Open door	1;06.25	Hit ball
1;05.27	Yaya [draw] mans	1;06.25	See this
1;05.28	Catch rocks	1;06.25	Read this
1;06.01	Ride horsie	1;06.29	Maria made this duck
1;06.02	Hammer table	1;06.29	Stop-it bike
1;06.06	Hold Weezer	1;06.29	Close this
1;06.06	Get-out kisses	1;06.03	Drop-it ice
1;06.07	Bite finger	1;06.03	Brush-it hair
1;06.11	Throw da ball	1;06.03	Watch TV
1;06.13	Got-it Weezer	1;07.00	Clean this;
1;06.16	Touch light	1;07.00	Driving car
1;06.22	Step-in water	1;07.03	Break this
1;06.24	Lock that Lulu	1;07.03	Bring chair

Reproduced from appendix D1 of Ninio, A. (1999a). Pathbreaking verbs in syntactic development. *Journal of Child Language*, with permission from Cambridge University Press.

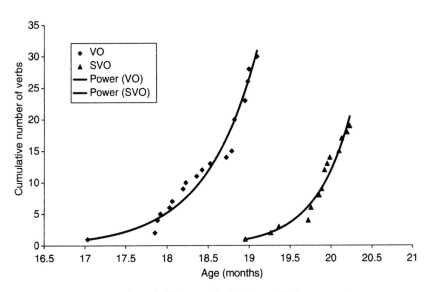

Fig. 2.6 Cumulative number of different verbs in VO and SVO constructions as a function of age at first production, with power trendlines fitted—Travis; redrawn from figure 2 of Ninio (1999a). Pathbreaking verbs in syntactic development. *Journal of Child Language*, with permission from Cambridge University Press.

verb every few weeks, she was already using VO sentences with a new verb or two every single day. If we look at her SVO graph, she seems to be a slow learner, held back by some developmental difficulty suggested above, such as slow retrieval from the lexicon, or general clumsiness with combining morphemes. If, however, we look at her VO curve, we see a fast learner of syntax, who apparently overcame whatever developmental difficulties slowed down her learning of VO 2 months before.

Obviously, this is an unacceptable paradox. The child cannot be at the same time both enjoying the benefits of some 'non-specific general developmental factor' and, with another task, suffering from the negative effects of the same 'non-specific general developmental factor'. In other words, these results refute the hypothesis that learning curves accelerate because of some non-specific developmental advance that is unrelated to the Practice Effect of previously learned verbs in the same construction. A non-specific developmental advance would not generate two temporally separate gradually-increasing graphs, each beginning with a very slow learning rate. If there were no specific effects of the particular combinatory pattern on the speed of learning, the second—SVO—graph would start with the slope already achieved by the first learning task, and learning would not slow down afresh.

To check the generality of these results, we have repeated the two-graph analysis for another child, a girl acquiring Hebrew. Ruti was audiotaped by her parents twice a week between 1;6 and 2;4, for 20 minutes at a time. In addition, her parents also kept an extensive diary on utterances they heard in between observations. Ruti's first 20 sentences in the VO pattern and the SVO pattern are given in Tables 2.3 and 2.4. The source is Ninio (1999a).

Figure 2.7 presents Ruti's learning curves for her first VO and SVO sentences.

We fitted a power-law function and a linear function to each of the graphs. The power-law function had an excellent fit, with $R^2 = 0.98$ for VO and $R^2 = 0.99$ for SVO. The linear function had a less good fit, $R^2 = 0.85$ for VO and $R^2 = 0.83$ for SVO. The difference between the two functions is 13% variance accounted for in the case of VO and 16% in the case of SVO, demonstrating that as with Travis, both learning curves accelerate, and they are well-described by a power-law function.[12]

As with Travis, the same acceleration recurred in the case of the two different combinatorial rules explored, demonstrating that the speed-up is specifically tied to the number of previously produced verbs in the same kind of combination. As before, the separate acceleration of the two learning curves makes it difficult to attribute the gradual speed-up of the learning curves to non-specific factors. It is much more likely that the acceleration is directly

Table 2.3 Ruti's first sentence with each of her first 20 different verbs getting a post-verbal Direct Object, with age of emergence

Age	Utterance	Gloss
1;07.29	Roca ze	want this
1;09.00	Yavi daysa	will-bring porridge
1;09.14	Ose raash	makes noise
1;09.14	Oci etze	I'll-take-out this
1;10.11	Lasim mayim	to-put water
1;10.11	Al taase ze	don't do this
1;10.11	Ima takri ze	mommy will-read this
1;11.09	Ima kax ze	mommy take this
1;11.09	Lisgor ze ima	to-close this mommy
1;11.09	Lehorid et-ze	to-take-down ACC-this
1;11.13	Ima kanta et-ze	mommy bought ACC-this
1;11.13	Talbish et-ze	wear ACC-this
1;11.23	Lekapel et-ze	to-fold ACC-this
1;11.23	Liftoach et-ze	to-open ACC-this
1;11.27	Aba ciyer ze	daddy drew this
1;11.27	Lehaziz et-ze	to-move ACC this
1;11.27	Aba letaken et-ze	daddy to-fix ACC-this
1;11.27	Aba tadbik et-ze	daddy, glue ACC-this
2;00.00	Ima tikshor et ha-seret	mommy will-tie ACC the-ribbon
2;00.03	Ima tenaki et-ze	mommy, clean ACC-this

Reproduced from appendix C1 of Ninio, A. (1999a). Pathbreaking verbs in syntactic development. *Journal of Child Language*, with permission from Cambridge University Press.

attributable to a practice effect, connecting the gradually increasing speed of learning to facilitation, generalization, or transfer from existing verbs that the children already know how to combine in the relevant pattern.

The results reported above were replicated in further longitudinal corpora. In a study of the development of the VO pattern in Hebrew-speaking children (Ninio, 2005a), the earliest six different verbs in VO sentences of 20 children (12 girls and eight boys) were fitted with power-law and linear trendlines.[13] The first six verbs in the VO pattern were learned within 3.41 months on the average (SD 1.79, range 0.90–6.93 months). In all 20 children there was a very good fit of the power-law function to the cumulative distribution, explaining 90% or more of the variance. The linear trendlines fit the distribution less well.

Table 2.4 Ruti's first sentence with each of her first 20 different verbs participating in a Subject–Verb–Direct Object (SVO) combination, with the age of emergence

Age	Utterance	Gloss
1;09.00	Shay roce kadur	Shay wants (a) ball
1;09.28	Ish ose raas	man makes noise
1;10.11	Ima takri ze	mommy will-read (FEM) this
1;11.20	Ima kanta et-ze	mommy bought (FEM) ACC-this
1;11.20	Sheima talbish et-ze	that-mommy will-CAUS-wear ACC-this
1;11.23	Ani ekra et-ze	I I-shall-read ACC-this
1;11.23	..ani sama ze	I put (FEM) this
1;11.27	Aba ciyer ze	daddy drew this
1;11.27	..aba asa cafcefa	daddy made (noise of) horn
2;00.00	Ima tikshor et ha-seret	mommy will-tie ACC the-ribbon
2;00.11	Ruti lo shomaat shir	Ruti not hear (FEM) (a) song
2;00.14	At axalt hakartiv hahu	you ate-2sgf the-popsicle the-that
2;00.14	..ani mocet et aba	I find (FEM) ACC daddy
2;00.18	Ata roe ze ratuv	you see this (is) wet
2;00.21	Tali carix laasot hakol	Tali needs to-do everything
2;00.24	Aba tiken et ze	daddy fixed ACC this
2;00.24	Aba hidbik et ze	daddy glued ACC this
2;00.24	Aba lakax et hamocec sheli	daddy took ACC pacifier my
2;00.28	Ani mesaderet ze..	I put-in-order (FEM) this
2;00.28	Ani axzik et ze	I I-shall-hold ACC this

Reproduced from appendix C2 of Ninio, A. (1999a). Pathbreaking verbs in syntactic development. *Journal of Child Language*, with permission from Cambridge University Press.

The mean fit of an accelerating power-function was $R^2 = 0.95$ of the variance (SD 0.03, range 0.88–1.00). The mean fit of a linear function was $R^2 = 0.86$ of the variance (SD 0.10, range 0.68–1.00). Namely, on the average the power function explained 9% more of the variance than the linear function. The comparison of the fit of the power function with the fit of the linear function by paired t-test revealed that the difference is highly significant ($t(19) = 5.00$, $P < 0.001$). Of the 20 children, 19 or 95% had a better fit to their learning curves with a power-law function than with a linear function. Against a null hypothesis that graphs will be non-accelerating, this result is significantly higher than chance by binomial sign test ($P < 0.001$).

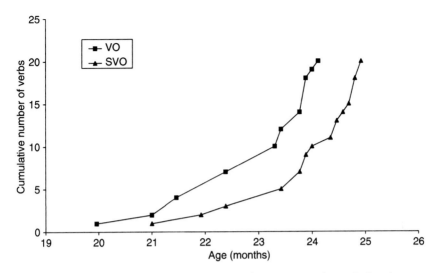

Fig. 2.7 Cumulative number of verbs in the VO and SVO constructions—Ruti; redrawn from figure 1 of Ninio (1999a). Pathbreaking verbs in syntactic development. *Journal of Child Language*, with permission from Cambridge University Press.

It can be summarized that children's acquisition of transitive verbal frames is apparently well-described by a power-law function. This learning pattern appears to be quite general, judging from the replication in a large sample.

Learning curves for ditransitive constructions

Children's acquisition of ditransitive verbal constructions and their components also appears to be well-covered by the Power Law of Practice. This includes the basic verb-dative pattern, as well as the full double-object or prepositional ditransitive, in three languages: Hebrew, English, and German.

The Hebrew dative object—as of the recipient of *give*—is always a prepositional object with the preposition *le-* '*to*'. Ninio (2005b) studied the acquisition of the verb–indirect object combination in Hebrew, in 14 children.[14] In all 14 children the cumulative frequency of the first 10 verbs in the verb–indirect object construction as a function of age at first production showed an accelerating learning curve. The mean fit of a power-law function was $R^2 = 0.93$ (SD $= 0.06$). The mean fit of a linear function was $R^2 = 0.79$(SD $= 0.13$). On average the power function explained 14.3% more of the variance than the linear function (SD $= 0.08$). The comparison of the fit of the power-law function with the fit of the linear function by paired two-tailed t-test revealed that the difference is highly significant ($t(12) = 7.00$, $P < 0.001$). In all 14 children the power-law function had a better fit to the accumulative graph relative to a linear function.

Against a null hypothesis that graphs will be non-accelerating, this result is significantly higher than chance by binomial sign test ($P < 0.001$).

The acquisition of the full ditransitive SVO–indirect object pattern in three Hebrew-speaking children was investigated by Keren-Portnoy (in press). In all three children, the power-law function had a higher fit to their learning curve than a linear function.[15]

The complete trivalent ditransitive construction was also investigated by Kiekhoefer (2002) in two children, one acquiring English, the other, German. The children were observed in an unusually dense observational schedule: their speech was recorded 5 days a week, for 1 hour each time during the relevant period. The German-speaking child used 39 different verbs in complete ditransitive constructions between 1;11.14 and 3;0.0 (Mean Length of Utterance in words or MLUw 1.12–3.86), generating a total of 329 utterances in this construction. The English-speaking child used 29 different verbs in complete ditransitive constructions between 2;0.12 and 3;2.11 (MLUw 1.53–2.66), generating a total of 196 utterances in this construction. Kiekhoefer reported that the learning curves of both children were non-linear, accelerating curves. Table 2.5 presents the first 10 verbs that the German-speaking child, Leo, produced in the ditransitive construction, together with the age the first ditransitive utterance was produced.

Figure 2.8 presents Leo's learning curve for his ditransitive sentences.

A power-law function ($R^2 = 0.83$) and a linear function ($R^2 = 0.64$) were fitted to Leo's graph. The power-law function had much better fit; 19% more of the variance was accounted for by it.

Table 2.5 The first 10 verbs produced by Leo in the ditransitive construction, with age of emergence

Age	Verb	Gloss
2;1.3	geben	Give
2;1.11	(ein)kaufen	Buy
2;5.16	machen	Make
2;5.27	nehmen	Take
2;5.28	erzaehlen	Tell
2;6.13	bringen	Bring, get
2;6.20	nennen	Call
2;6.20	schenken	Give x to y
2;6.24	ziehen	Pull
2;6.24	holen	Get, fetch

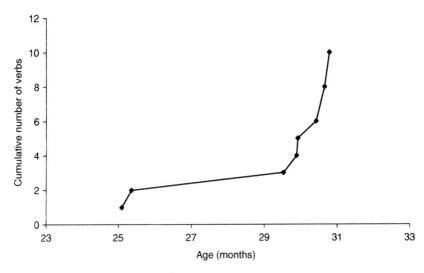

Fig. 2.8 Cumulative number of different verbs in the ditransitive construction - Leo; redrawn from Kiekhoefer (2002), Figure 1.

Kiekhoefer (2002) also provided information about the last 11 verbs Leo produced in the ditransitive pattern before observations ended, between 2;9.18 and 2;11.23. The learning curve for these 11 verbs—fitted separately—did not accelerate; it was well-fitted with a linear trendline while a power-law trendline did not result in as good a fit. As the most pronounced non-linear segment is at the very beginning of the power-law curve, it is expected that later segments of the same curve appear to be linear. For this reason, it is imperative to sample a child's speech from the start of the acquisition of some construction—otherwise the acceleration will not be observable.[16]

It may be summarized that the three types of basic verbal valency patterns of accusative-nominative languages, namely, the combination of a verb with a subject, an object, and a dative complement (or any combination of these) show consistent acceleration, with learning curves demonstrating the Power Law of Practice. The Power Law of Practice is the quantitative manifestation of transfer from previous learning. Apparently, children's lexically specific, item-based learning of individual word combinations for some verbs facilitate the lexically specific, item-based learning of the same construction for other verbs.

The effect of inter-construction transfer

An interesting complication to the Power Law of Practice was observed in a study on the acquisition of two kinds of German passive, carried out by Abbot-Smith and Behrens (2002). Using the same dense observational base as

Kiekhoefer (2002), they mapped the development of two German passive constructions in the speech of Leo, the *werden*-passive and the *sein*-passive. The *werden*-passive uses the auxiliary verb *werden 'become'* in sentences like (1):

(1) der   Ball   wird   angemalt
     the   ball   become-3rdPRES   paint-PARTICIPLE
     'the ball is being/will be painted'

referring to an event or process, i.e., the ball is going through, or will go through the process of being painted.

The *sein*-passive uses *sein 'be',* as in (2):

(2) der   Ball   ist   angemalt
     the   ball   be-3rdPRES   paint-PARTICIPLE
     'the ball is painted'

referring to a state, i.e., the ball is in the state of 'paintedness'.

I fitted power-law and linear functions to the cumulative learning curves of the first 20 verbs produced in each passive, as a function of age in months.[17] While the learning curve of the *werden*-passive accelerated as usual under a power-law function ($R^2 = 0.98$, linear function $R^2 = 0.84$), the learning curve of the *sein*-passive was close to a straight line. The linear trendline had a much better fit to the *sein*-passive's cumulative type frequency time series than the power-line function (linear $R^2 = 0.93$, power-law $R^2 = 0.84$).

Abbot-Smith and Behrens tie the linear developmental trend of the *sein*-passive to its apparently having received a great deal of transfer from previously learned and formally similar constructions using either the relevant auxiliary, the participle or both. In fact, they found that in a set of related constructions that they had examined (including the two passives), all the constructions acquired late had a linear trendline, while all the constructions acquired early had an accelerating learning curve.

Such results are expected on the theory of skill learning that ties transfer from one learning task to another to similarity in the tasks. In particular, the identical-element theory of transfer (mentioned in Note 8) attributes the degree of transfer between the source and the target tasks to the quantity of shared task components, namely, to the amount of elements, features, or principles shared by the two (e.g., Thorndike, 1913; Singley and Anderson, 1985). In the domain of syntactic development, the acquisition of two different items with the very same syntactic construction (e.g., two verbs with preverbal subjects) relies on the maximum degree of task similarity, while the acquisition of two items with related but not formally identical constructions will have transfer and facilitation relative to how much the constructions share. It should be kept in mind that the cross-construction transfer and facilitation seen in the Abbot-Smith and Behrens study was achieved on the basis of formal, rather than semantic, similarity between the components of different learning tasks. This topic will be further discussed in later parts of this monograph.

In summary, naturalistic studies investigating learning curves in syntactic development find that particular syntactic constructions, over different participating verb types, show typical power-law acceleration: The more verbs children are already able to combine in a certain syntactic pattern (such as the subject–verb–object or the ditransitive construction) the faster they learn new ones in the same pattern. These results—including the apparent exception of the passives study—support the hypothesis that the acquisition of valency frames of individual verbs is a type of skill learning, similar to cognitive tasks in general.

No verb is an island

In Section 2.2 we presented a counter-claim to the hypothesis that the acquisition of syntactic valency frames is a kind of skill learning. This is the Verb Island hypothesis, offered by Tomasello and colleagues as a characterization of children's early syntactic development (Tomasello and Brooks, 1999; Tomasello, 2000a). The Verb Island hypothesis proposes that the combinatory patterns of individual verbs are not only learned in a piecemeal fashion, but also form isolated 'verb islands', unrelated to each other, so that children's emerging syntactic knowledge does not organize into a system (e.g., Tomasello, 2000a). Each word is said to acquire its individual valency frames in isolation from any other word's; this type of lexical-specific learning does not rely on transfer.

The results presented above make it unlikely that the Verb Island hypothesis is a correct description of even children's earliest syntactic knowledge.[18] The recent findings suggest, instead, that the syntactic characteristics of words, their lexical valency, is learned in ways similar to the words' semantic and phonetic content. In all cases, the lexical content is learned on the active background of previous learning, and once learned, each piece of new information joins an interconnected network of related items, facilitating further learning.

2.3.2 Experimental evidence for transfer of syntactic knowledge

Learning curves based on naturalistic spontaneous production are not sufficient by themselves to demonstrate all that children know or the way they have learned it. In particular, the acceleration observed does not necessarily reflect transfer of learning from previous items learned with the same kind of syntactic valency format. Learning curves can accelerate for many reasons and not only because of transfer from previous items. Naturalistic observations of spontaneous speech, the kind of studies we have been reviewing so far, do not fully rule out other explanations. In order to demonstrate that transfer indeed takes place in syntactic acquisition, the analysis of learning curves needs to be complemented by other research paradigms, in particular, experimental manipulation of the learning situation.

To date, there have been several such experiments conducted, for instance, Tomasello and Brooks (1998), Brooks and Tomasello (1999), Childers and Tomasello (2001), Abbot-Smith *et al.* (2004), and Ono and Budwig (2005). In the experimental paradigm transfer has been measured by the effect of priming on the probability of children using a novel item in a particular syntactic construction without previous modelling. In such experiments children are presented with some transitive sentences (the priming sentences) and with a nonce verb that they do not hear used as a transitive verb but only as an intransitive one. They are then prompted to use the target verb in a transitive sentence, changing the valency this verb was presented with. Generalization of novel verbs beyond the input is then taken as the positive effect of transfer from the priming sentences.

The simplest and most elegant study using this paradigm was carried out by Tomasello and Brooks (1998). The children were taught just two new nonce verbs, *meek* and *tam*, one as a transitive verb and one as an intransitive verb. The same verb was taught to some children as a transitive verb and to others, as an intransitive. The verbs meanings were such that lent themselves to this type of lability in English, similar to such true verbs as *swing, roll, float* and the like. *Tam* referred to an object swinging from a pendulum, or else being swung by some other agent. *Meek* referred to pulling an object up a ramp, or else the object ascending the ramp on its own (see pp. 383–384 for a description). The relevant events were enacted with puppets. The participants were 16 children with the mean age of 2;0, and 16 others with the mean age of 2;6. Half of each subsample heard *tam* as a transitive and *meek* as an intransitive, half *tam* as an intransitive and *meek* as a transitive. Each verb served as a prime for the other verb to be used in the unmodelled construction: the transitively introduced verb for the intransitively introduced one and vice versa.

The children heard the experimenter use each new verb in 88 utterances modelling it either as a transitive or intransitive verb. In addition, the children were asked throughout the experiment, for each verb, 25–30 eliciting questions encouraging its use in the format of the introducing construction, 25–30 questions eliciting its use in the 'opposite' construction, and 25–30 questions neutral as to format. For instance, the experimenter prompted transitive answers with questions of the kind 'What is AGENT doing?'. There was a final elicit-ation task in which the children were shown the same actions with two new objects, and encouraged to use the nonce verbs with regard to these objects.

The results of the study showed that 2-year-old children were not very good with producing undemonstrated constructions with nonce verbs, regardless of the priming provided by the other verb. However, the 2;6-old children were astonishingly good: nine of the 16, namely 56.25% used the intransitive verb in a transitive format, either VO or SVO, and 10 of the 16, that is 62.5%, used the transitively introduced verb in an intransitive SV format.

Other studies supporting the positive priming effect at 2;6 were carried out by Childers and Tomasello (2001) and by Abbot-Smith et al. (2004). The methodology of these studies was roughly similar to the Tomasello and Brooks (1998) study reviewed above, with one difference: the children were presented with a much higher number of priming sentences. In the Childers and Tomasello (2001) study 40 children at the age of 2;6 heard 575 transitive sentences with real verbs as primes for an intransitively introduced nonce verb. The majority of the children, 26 of the 40, namely, 65% produced a transitive sentence with a direct object undergoer in the postverbal position, whether or not there was an actor subject. A control group of 10 children of the same age did not receive training with priming sentences; only two children of this group (20%) used the same nonce verbs in an unmodelled transitive frame. In the study by Abbot-Smith et al. (2004) the children received only 128 training sentences (in all of which the subjects and objects were filled with nouns only); of the 24 children at 2;6, 11% or 46% produced an unmodelled transitive construction with the nonce verb, consisting at least of the verb and a postverb object. It is clear that children at 2;6 can generate unmodelled constructions with newly learned verbs, if this construction is primed with other verbs. The priming effect does not require the 'flooding' of the child with extremely many priming sentences; in fact the modest model-ling of Tomasello and Brooks (1998) and Ono and Budwig (2005) achieved as high a priming effect as the Childers and Tomasello study that used a much bigger number of primer utterances.[19]

Some of the priming experiments reviewed above included samples of older children, for example 4½ year olds. Older children are clearly better at producing unmodelled constructions with novel verbs as a result of priming and elicitation questions. It is not clear at present if the increased productivity after priming is a result of older children's better learning of the source-constructions or of an enhanced ability to employ transfer and analogy to produce unmodelled sentences on their basis.

We might summarize that children before the age of 3 years, apparently at the start of acquiring their earliest basic syntactic formats, demonstrate transfer of syntactic behaviour from primer sentences to novel verbs, if such transfer is prompted by eliciting questions. Apparently, children at the earliest stages of producing combinatory speech are quite capable of transferring knowledge gained through the enhanced modelling of a syntactic construction for some items, to novel items. Without priming, young children tend to be more conservative and to avoid using a new verb with unmodelled and contrastive valency patterns; priming serves as a source for transfer and analogy.

2.3.3 Further evidence of transfer

Yet another research paradigm was employed by McClure and Pine (2002) in their demonstration that the insularity claim of the Verb Island hypothesis was incorrect. If at the start of syntactic development verbal formats were learned independently of any other construction already in the child's repertoire, there is no reason why new verbs should not enter the child's grammar at the same average level of complexity. However, McClure and Pine offered evidence that verbs entering slightly later into children's grammar start at a more complex entry level than verbs learned earlier. They measured level of complexity by Mean Length of Utterance (MLU) and number of arguments expressed in utterances using the relevant verbs. They found that for 10 children acquiring English, verbs first appearing at Brown's Stage II, namely at MLU 2.0–2.49, are immediately used in utterances with significantly more complex structure than verbs that first appeared at Stage I (MLU = 1.0–1.99). This study demonstrates that the existing level of syntactic knowledge at the time a new verb is learned, influences the learning event. The more a child knows of other words' combinatory properties, the more she is able to learn of a novel word's syntax. Individual predicates' valency frames do not constitute 'islands' of mini-syntax; instead, from the very first stages of word combinations they form an interconnected system with mutual transfer and facilitation.[20]

2.4 Conclusions: lexical-specific syntactic frames facilitate others

We have learned that the Power Law of Practice applies to children's acquisition of syntactic valency formats, as expected under the hypothesis that lexical-specific learning of syntactic frames is a kind of cognitive skill learning.

This result should come as no surprise. Although the derivation of learning curves for individual syntactic constructions is a very recent methodological strategy, previous research often targeted the temporal course of development of other kinds of language skills. The present results come on the background of ubiquitous transfer of learning found in children's language; accelerating acquisition has been demonstrated in most of the major domains of language development. In a study we have already mentioned above (Bloom *et al.*, 1975), it was found that the MLU, a composite score of morphological and syntactic development counting the number of different morphemes per utterance gradually speeds up as a function of age. This shows that the task of learning new morphemes in general, and learning to combine them in utterances, has its own learning curve. Studies in which specific morphemes are targeted also find the same kind of learning curves, e.g., in the development of German noun plurals (Szagun, 2001).

In particular, lexical development is well-known for its learning curves. Graphs of overall vocabulary size measured by cumulative type frequency typically show acceleration as a function of age in the initial stages of vocabulary learning, for example in Nelson (1973).[21] The curves depicting the onset of acquisition are well-fitted with a power-law or exponential function; however, at later stages of development the learning of new items typically slows down and the learning curve decelerates, resulting in an overall S-shaped or logistic curve (e.g., Ruhland *et al.*, 1995; Ganger and Brent, 2004).

There is, as we can see, much connectedness and systemic linking in children's accumulating vocabulary. It is beyond dispute that each vocabulary item—each word—has to be learned individually. Word learning usually refers to words' semantic and phonetic content; the accelerating learning curves reviewed above show that this task gets gradual facilitation from previously learned items. It is undisputed that item-specific learning—which is the heart of the acquisition of the lexicon—does not preclude connectedness between the items and that the vocabulary in fact forms an interconnected system. It is only regarding the grammatical content of children's lexical items—the valency of words—that the hypothesis of disconnection between individual lexemes has ever been advanced.

It may be concluded that the Power Law of Practice applies to children's acquisition of syntactic valency formats, as it does to lexical learning in general. Children learn lexical-specific syntactic formats and generate word combinations on their basis, but these individual formulae are interconnected, with inter-item and inter-construction transfer and analogy facilitating the learning process. In all probability, the same kind of systemic connectivity and analogy-making also underlies the priming effects that enable very young children to use novel verbs in unmodelled valency frames. Children's developing grammar is not a collection of insular formulae. It is probably much more like a web, with all items connecting to each other by various dimensions of similarity. And, if language is like a network, learning it can be considered as the growth of the network. More on this subject in Chapter 5.

According to studies of problem-solving in young children reviewed in Section 2.1.2 above, children's skills at analogy-making continue to develop and improve throughout the years (Klahr, 2000; Loewenstein and Gentner, 2001). As processes similar to analogy in problem-solving presumably underlie transfer in children's dealing with syntactic constructions, it is to be expected that children would get much better at generalization as they get older. Indeed, older children find it much easier to employ a novel verb in a syntactic frame unmodelled in the input (e.g., Abbot-Smith *et al.*, 2004). Nevertheless, the ability to transfer is already there in very young children who are just starting to learn syntactic word combinations.

Indeed, one of the interesting properties of learning curves following a power-law function is that the greatest changes in performance occur early in practice (e.g., Logan, 1988). Namely, the improvement in learning apparently due to transfer is substantial in particular at the start of learning. This implies that the first few valency formulae, undoubtedly learned on an item-specific basis, are already powerful sources of transfer for other, related, pieces of syntax.

It seems that there is no need for a critical mass of items to accumulate in order for transfer to happen. Nor is it very likely that the practice effect is achieved by abstraction and schematization. These processes are generally taken to occur at a relatively late stage in the development of a particular syntactic structure, as they are thought to require that the child already possesses at least three or more item-specific formulae over which processes of abstraction can operate. Instead, the learning curves show the typical maximal improvement right at the start of learning. Syntactic transfer is, apparently, a process that uses one item as a source of analogy for another, and it does not involve the generation of abstract constructions in order to relate one verbal frame to another. This result is well-compatible with proposals regarding similarity matching rather than rule-formation as the basis for analogy, made by researchers in cognitive psychology (e.g., Nosofsky, 1988; Barsalou, 1990; Hahn and Chater, 1998).

Nor is it likely that the early-observed transfer is a reflection of innate abstract knowledge. Whatever our general view of innate categories, we are concerned at present with the acquisition of lexical-specific and language-specific valency frames (see Chapter 1), and there is a wide consensus embraced by nativists and empiricists alike that these are indeed learned on an item-specific basis (e.g., Maratsos, 1983; Ninio, 1988; Clahsen *et al.*, 1996; Trueswell and Gleitman, 2004). For example, Radford (2000) succinctly defines the component of lexical learning associated with the latest nativist theories:

The revised model of Minimalism presented in Chomsky (1998, 1999) raises interesting questions about the nature of language acquisition. If the Language Faculty specifies a universal set of features (Chomsky 1999, p. 7), a child acquiring language L has to learn which subset of these features are assembled into lexical items in L, and how. If innate architectural principles determine how lexical items project into syntactic structures, the major task facing the child in acquiring the syntax of a language is assembling features into lexical items.

Radford (2000, p. 57)

Lexical-specific syntactic learning is not only necessary but probably also sufficient; modern-day linguistic theory makes it unlikely that more abstract phrasal schemas are in fact needed in order to characterize adult competence. We shall turn to this subject in the next chapter.

Notes

1 The claim that gains in domain knowledge drive analogical development was offered by Gentner and Rattermann (1991), who proposed that with increased exposure to a domain, children as well as adults switch from object-based analogy to one based on similarities in relational structure. For an extensive review of the evidence, see Loewenstein and Gentner (2001).

2 Authorities sometimes formally distinguish between two kinds of practice effects: those involving the repetition of identical items, and those reflecting facilitation in the learning of so-called unique stimuli. In both cases, the learning curve shows a power-law function, demonstrating that the two effects are in fact the same type of facilitation (Logan, 1990; Kirsner and Speelman, 1996; Gupta and Cohen, 2002).

3 The identical-element theory of transfer attributes the degree of transfer between the source and the target tasks to the amount of identical elements, features, or principles shared by the original and new learning situations (Thorndike, 1913; Singley and Anderson, 1985; Bransford et al., 1999; Caplan and Schooler, 1999).

4 Some researchers who found that a power-law function has the best fit for learning curves are Bryan and Harter (1897), Roberts (1972), Mazur and Hastie (1978), Newell and Rosenbloom (1981), Anderson (1982, 1993), Logan (1988, 1992), McKay (1988), Shrager et al. (1988),Cohen et al. (1990), Kramer et al. (1990), Anderson and Schooler (1991), Ohlsson (1992), Delaney et al. (1998), and Williamon and Valentine (2000).

5 Heathcote et al. (2000) argue that the power-law practice function is an artefact of averaging over subjects, and that individual practice curves are better described by an exponential function. A different argument is made by Newell et al. (2001) who suggest that measures of learning

distributed with a power-law function combine several different micro-processes, each of which is better fitted by an exponential function.

6   S-shaped learning curves were reported for by Hull (1943) by Atkinson *et al.* (1965). An S-shaped or sigmoid pattern has a three-phased curve: initially, it shows slow growth, which then speeds up, before slowing down to approach an asymptotic limit. This pattern can be modelled using several mathematical functions, e.g., the generalized logistic and Gompertz curves.

7   Biological growth phenomena are also covered by the same accelerating or sigmoid curves as learning. In fact, biological growth curves most often have a pronounced three-phase logistic shape, with growth checked by limited resources sometimes called the environmental carrying potential (Krohne, 2001). It is interesting to speculate what are the limiting 'environmental resources' contributing to the slowing down of learning curves such as the ones mapping cumulative vocabulary size.

8   For examples of tasks following the Power Law of Practice, see Fitts and Posner (1967), Newell and Rosenbloom (1981), Anderson (1982), Logan (1992), Ohlsson (1992), Delaney *et al.* (1998), Nerb *et al.* (1999), and Williamon and Valentine (2000).

9   Other models of skilled performance tested for power-function are ACT (Anderson, 1982; Anderson and Schooler, 1991; Anderson and Lebiere, 1998), the Chunking model (Newell and Rosenbloom, 1981; Rosenbloom and Newell, 1987a,b), the Component Power Laws model (Rickard, 1997), instance theories (Logan, 1988, 1992; Nosofsky and Palmeri, 1997), and network models (MacKay, 1982; Cohen *et al.*, 1990).

10 The present graph is based on Ninio (2003), incorporating some marginal corrections.

11 Repeating the same analysis with exactly 19 verbs for comparison with the 19 of SVO makes very little difference to the results.

12 In accordance with our methodological guidelines, we have included among Ruti's VO sentences every sentence with a novel verb that had an expressed VO combination, regardless of other elements in the clause. This resulted in our including among her first 20 sentence-types three that were already SVO combinations (the 7th, 11th, and 15th). In order to control for the overlap, Ruti's VO graph was re-drawn so that the three SVO sentences were excluded from it. This made no significant difference to the graph; it still shows a gradual speed-up of learning with a power-law function, only the slope of the curve at the later period reduces somewhat.

13 Ruti, reported above, was part of this sample. Her data are left in the sample because it is not necessarily true that her first six verbs would form an accelerating curve just because her first 20 or 30 did. The other children were observed weekly at home for 30 minutes at a time, in naturalistic interaction with their mother. Observations started when the children were still in the single-word stage and continued for 8–11 months. The children were between 1;06.00 and 2;06.00. In addition to the weekly observations, parents also kept a diary on emergent constructions of the children.

14 The children belong to the same pool of longitudinal corpora as those described in Note 12, namely, they were observed longitudinally in weekly observations augmented by parental reports. None of the children produced verb–indirect object combinations when observations started. We included in the analysis all children who produced at least 10 different types of verb–indirect object combinations until observations ended.

15 Keren-Portnoy (in press) also investigated the acquisition of another basic syntactic format of accusative-nominative languages, the subject–verb construction. She mapped the subject–verb utterances of six Hebrew-speaking children, three boys and three girls, longitudinally observed. In all six children the learning curves were better described as accelerating than as linear.

16 An example is a study by Campbell and Tomasello (2001) on the acquisition of the full-ditransitive construction in seven children acquiring English, taken from the CHILDES archive. Although Campbell and Tomasello did not attempt to fit power-law functions to their data, they do present the data in the form of line graphs and conclude that these do not support an acceleration hypothesis. However, the data are most probably inappropriate for testing the hypothesis of the Power Law of Practice. Three of the children already produced several different ditransitive sentences on their very first observation, suggesting that the start of the learning curve is missing. In addition, the full ditransitive was quite rarely observed in these corpora, resulting in very short curves with as few as four points in two children. Compare with Kiekhoefer (2002), who did find accelerating full-ditransitive curves for an English-speaking child, relying on a much denser observational schedule.

17 The results are very similar to Abbot-Smith and Behrens's, although they fitted a function only to the set of sentences with a third person singular subject, whereas I fitted functions to all sentences. In addition, they fitted an exponential and not a power-law curve. When the power-law function

reported in the text above is compared with an exponential function computed from the same data, the two explain an almost identical percentage of the variance.

18　See also Ninio's (2003) re-examination of Tomasello's (1992) data according to which many of Travis's SVO sentences and other longer utterances were not based on simpler constructions with the same verbs, thus questioning the basic motivation for the Verb Island hypothesis.

19　It should be noted that the Tomasello and Brooks (1998) study is sometimes reported by mistake as if the children at 2;6 were avoiding using verbs in unmodelled constructions, in particular in a transitive construction (e.g., Tomasello, 2003, p. 151). The source of the mistake is relying on the percentage of children generating the full SVO sentence as an indication of productive use of the transitive construction, rather than, as in other studies such as Childers and Tomasello (2001), the percentage of children producing *any* transitive sentence, whether SVO or VO. Although it is true that only three of the 16 children of the sample of Tomasello and Brooks (1998) generated unmodelled SVO sentences, a much higher number, nine of the 16 children or 56.25%, produced Verb–Object sentences with verbs they had previously heard only in an intransitive frame. This percentage falls into the same range as the percentage of children producing unmodelled transitive sentences of any kind, SVO or VO, reported for the Abbot-Smith *et al.* (2004) and the Childers and Tomasello (2001) studies, namely 46% and 65%.

20　Transfer has also been found in a connectionist simulation of the acquisition of grammatical constructions. Morris *et al.* (2000) simulated the learning of grammatical relations with a connectionist simple recurrent network, which was trained to assign semantic categories ('agent' or 'experiencer') to words in a series of different constructions involving action verbs (e.g., *kiss*) and experience verbs (e.g., *see*). They found that the system becomes productive with a grammatical construction more quickly the larger the amount of experience which it had with that particular construction, as well as the amount of experience with previously learned, simpler related constructions.

21　Accelerating learning curves for vocabulary were also found by Dromi (1986), Elman *et al.* (1996), and Kauschke and Hofmeister (2002), among others. See Ingram (1989) for a review.

3

Lexicalism

In the previous two chapters I proposed that children begin the production of multiword combinations by combining specific predicate words and their arguments, using the cognitive equivalent of the linguistic Merge/Dependency operation. These combinations were said to be based on the words' lexically stored syntactic and semantic valency. I have also shown that despite their lexical-specific nature, valency-based syntactic frames do not form isolated patches of grammatical knowledge but, rather, connect to each other, facilitating new learning from models in the input as well as priming creative syntactic uses for words in the absence of specific models. In this chapter, I want to argue that such lexical valency-based syntax is all that children need to learn to get to the adult syntactic system. In particular, children do not need to form abstractions because the adult system itself is fully lexicalist, devoid of abstract rules. As I shall show presently, language development theory has been lagging behind linguistics in its treatment of abstract concepts of language.

Throughout the chapter, it is important to remember that lexicalism does not imply the absence of the ability to go beyond the item-specific combinatory formula. As we saw in Chapter 2, transfer, generalization, and all types of mutual influence among lexically-specific formulae can take place through item-to-item analogy. The linguistically based objection developed in the present chapter is aimed at hypothetical processes of abstraction and abstract schema construction said to be taking place in child language, and not at all against phenomena of generalization. Generalization does not have to rely on abstraction, and the connection often made between the two in the literature is a mistake we should not hold on to.

As usual, the discussion in this chapter will concern the production but not the comprehension of multiword utterances. As we pointed out in Section 1.4.1, our interest is the characterization of cognitive skill used for producing syntactic word combinations. It is thus possible that any generalizations we make here, apply only to young children's construction of multiword utterances but not to their interpretation of utterances. At the moment, we shall make do with examination of the arguments for a lexicalist productive syntax.

3.1 **The linguistic basis to lexicalism**

In the earliest versions of the Chomskian grammar (Chomsky, 1957, 1965, 1975), his strategy of theory construction was closely guided by a desire for economy, elegance, and parsimony of description. In order to achieve the utmost efficiency in a theory of grammar, these early phrase-structure grammars defined maximally general grammatical rules, applying to the largest group of individual elements possible. In particular, in the syntactic component of the grammar use was made of a set of category symbols standing for sets of words in the lexicon, such as Noun, Verb, Adjective, and so forth, namely, form-classes or lexical categories. The motivation for lexical categories is provided by a central organizational phenomenon of language: whereas the lexicon contains a very large number of items, the grammatical rule system governing combinations of lexemes consists of a few sets of intercorrelated rules, each applying to a subgroup of words.

The one-to-many mapping of rules to words makes it possible to minimize the number of rules in a grammar. Instead of item-specific combinatorial rules, general or abstract rules can specify which group of words they are written on, and it is possible to specify for each word which group of rules applies to it. Such specification is carried out by means of (sub)category symbols such as N(oun) or V(erb). Category symbols like these appear in terminal strings of 'phrase-markers', which are abstract structural descriptions of composed units, shortly to be described. They are place-keepers for the actual lexical items that will turn the abstract 'phrase-marker' structure into a concrete sentence in a further operation of 'lexical substitution'. These symbols appear also in every entry in the mental lexicon, marking the category the word belongs to, namely, specifying the kind of syntactic contexts the relevant item may be inserted into. Thus, the subcategory symbols provide a bridge between the base component of the grammar and its lexical component, and drastically reduce the number of rules in the grammar.

The maximally general structure-building operations of the early Chomskian grammars were the so-called phrase structure rules. These are rewrite rules that generate phrase structure from top to bottom. Phrase structure rules are usually of the form A→B C D, where A is the name of the phrase and B C D defines its structure in terms of ordered subconstituents B, C and D. First, the sentence is broken into its constituents (1):

(1) S→NP VP

(S is the familiar abbreviation for Sentence, NP is Noun Phrase and VP, Verb Phrase). Each of the latter is then broken down into its own allowable constituents, for example (2), in English:

(2)

a. NP→(D) N

b. VP→V (NP) (NP) (PP) (COMP)

c. PP→P NP

d. AP→A (P)

and so forth.

In this notation, round brackets indicate that a phrase is optional. The rewriting continues until every constituent unit reaches its lower limit in the form of word-level, non-phrasal, or terminal categories such as Noun, Verb, Adjective, Determiner, and so forth. For each sentence it is possible to derive a 'phrase marker' based on the actual phrase structure rules that are steps of its derivation. The phrase marker represents the structure of the sentence in abstract terms; as mentioned above, a further step of 'lexical insertion' substitutes concrete words for the terminal symbols of the phrase marker to generate an actual sentence. I am skipping over the fact that the a priori ordering provided by the phrase structure rules often did not represent the actual linear order of the same elements in the sentence; phrase structure rules generated the invisible and underlying Deep Structure of a sentence, which was then further changed by transformations into its ultimate Surface Structure.

3.1.1 The elimination of phrase-structure rules

The critically important development of Chomskian linguistics, from the point of view of a theory of language acquisition, happened much before the adoption of the Minimalist Program. This was the elimination from the theory of phrase-structure rules with the formulation of the Principles and Parameters approach.

Returning to the English phrase structure rules presented above in (1)–(2), it is clear that there are several different alternative ways that a given phrase can be rewritten as a set of lawful constituents. This is in particular true when it comes to verb phrases. The following (3) is just a few of the alternative VP rewriting rules, exemplified by a sentence:

(3)

a. VP→V   Sara awoke.

b. VP→V NP   She drank some coffee.

c. VP→V NP NP   The postman brought her a package.

d. VP→V NP PP   He gave it to her.

There are, according to Hornby (1945) and Allerton (1982), about 25–30 different syntactic patterns for English verbs, each characterized by a different combination of complements. It has long been obvious (Bresnan, 1978) that the information how many complements a verb takes and what kind, needs to be entered in the lexical entry of each verb. In order to ensure that each verb selects the correct VP rewrite rules out of the alternatives, even the earliest versions of phrase-structure grammars acknowledged the need to mark the lexical entry of the verb for the verbal subclass it belonged to, namely, to subcategorize it. The lexical markers specify the information about the syntactic contexts into which the verb can be inserted, which makes them equivalent to a listing of all the phrase-structure rules applying to the relevant verb. Indeed, the common shape of the lexical markers of subcategorization are simply a repetition of the syntactic frames specified by the phrase structure rules. For example, one of the 'subcategorization frames' of the verb *give* would be [__ NP PP], the empty slot representing the positioning of the verb relative to its VP complements.

The doubling of information subcategorization frames introduced into the Chomskian Standard Theory did not long go unnoticed. As early as the 1970s, Heny (1979) showed that the general phrase-structure rules were completely redundant, as they duplicated information available in lexical entries. It was impossible to eliminate the redundancy by retaining only the abstract phrase structure rules; the individual subcategorization frames had to be specified in the lexicon in any case. The lexical specification made the phrase structure rules otiose; they served no function in the grammar (see Baltin, 1989, pp. 1–3 for a discussion).

In order to eradicate the redundancy from the grammar, and as a response to other problems,[1] in the next version of the theory called the Principles and Parameters framework (Chomsky, 1981, 1986; Stowell, 1981), phrase structure rules have been completely eliminated from the model, that is, except for the expansion of S (sentence). In their stead, the theory turned to a different type of characterization of the structure-derivational process: first to the X-bar schema,[2] then to the operation Merge. This move did away with abstract syntactic rules with units above the level of the lexeme.

In current Chomskian theorizing, phrase structure is built 'bottom-up', rather than, as in the earlier versions, 'top-down'. This is a severely lexicalist account of structure-building: Syntax is now seen as projected by the lexicon (Chomsky, 1995). The earlier account saw syntactic structure as originating from a separate grammar component that generated abstract phrase-markers for sentences. The lexicon came into action only at the last stage of derivation in which the abstract string was turned into a concrete sentence by 'lexical insertion'. The present theory starts with the lexicon and with the valency information stored there for individual predicates; it does not make use of abstract schemas, which then have to be applied to particular lexemes.[3]

In other words, present Chomskian theorizing has no role in the grammar for abstract syntactic schemas such as the transitive frame [V NP] or [NP V NP] if we add the subject. To generate the sentence in (3b above), namely, *She drank some coffee*, there is no need to store a general rule for generating transitive verb phrases such as the now outdated phrase-structure rule VP→V NP. Instead, the system needs to register on a lexically-specific manner that the verb *drink* can be inserted into a transitive syntactic context. All that is necessary and sufficient for structure-building is the lexically-specific valency information.[4]

Giving up on general rules defined on category symbols has an obvious domino effect on other categories and abstractions that used to play functional roles in previous versions of Chomskian syntactic theory. Two in particular stand out. First, the current theory has no formal use for general linking rules connecting verbal arguments' 'thematic roles' to syntactic configurations, and in fact there is no 'theta-theory'. Instead, the specification of the argument-taking requirements (namely, valency) of words takes place in the lexicon, for each word separately. Second, the syntactic component of the grammar refrains from employing lexical category symbols such as N, V, or A, preferring in all cases actual words even as labels for the nodes of syntactic trees. As the consistent lexicalism of the Minimalist Program is so different from the image of the Chomskian framework entrenched in developmental psycholinguistics, it is worthwhile to dwell on the reasons why such an influential theory of syntax turns its back on abstract categories and the regularities of language they seem to embody.

3.1.2 The problem with linking rules

One of the major reasons why it is necessary to register each verb's syntactic valency in the lexicon is that there is no simple way to derive this information from the verbs' semantics. In Chapter 1 we said logical-semantic valency and syntactic valency are partially disparate concepts. Nor, despite some undoubted regularities, can they be mapped isomorphically on to each other (e.g., Helbig, 1992). The result is that attempts to define 'linking rules' or 'mapping rules'[5] that would systematically map verb semantics to the syntactic construction that the verb forms with its dependents are doomed to be failures.

There is an unquestionable degree of correlation between verbal arguments' semantic properties and their syntactic embodiment. For instance, in nominative-accusative languages such as English, there is a strong tendency for agents of a depicted action to be expressed as the subject of the clause, and for the patient or undergoer of actions to be expressed as a direct object if the verb is transitive, but as a subject if the verb is intransitive (Anderson 1977; Pinker, 1989; Dowty, 1991). The problem with such linking rules is that although it is true that the tendency exists, unfortunately this is not the whole truth. There is many an agent that does not get expressed as a subject, and many a subject that does not express anything like the agent of an action. The regularity in the system is tantalizing; but up till now, no linking theory has been successful in embossing it in a deterministic set of mapping rules.

To remind us, the earliest proposition had been that syntactic structures are directly mapped from a small set of semantic or 'thematic' categories for verbal complements, such as Agent, Patient, Theme, Goal, Source, Recipient, Experiencer, Path, and Location, as proposed, for instance, by Fillmore (1968). However, in the linguistic literature it has been long and persuasively argued that such simple category systems are undefensible, as is the effort in general to define direct links between syntax and semantics. For instance, Dowty (1991), in a seminal treatment of the subject, summarizes the disagreements and arbitrariness plaguing the attempts to define an acceptable list of thematic roles. He also cites an early study by Blake (1930), which, as Dowty says, provides the most comprehensive and organized list compiled to date, consisting of 113 temporal, locative, and other roles. It is obvious that such a large class of thematic roles does not provide linguistic theory with the desired short list of semantic universals, but it is not at all clear that any of it is superfluous or ill-motivated. The feeling is that a truly systematic mapping of types of thematic relations in all languages could in fact end up with an even larger, and basically infinite, set, achieving no generality beyond the semantics of individual predicates.

Instead of direct mapping, it is argued, the mapping of semantics to syntax is better conceptualized as complex and indirect (e.g. Jackendoff, 1990 or Levin and Rappaport Hovav, 1995). However, even when the analysis is detailed and complicated, it still does not quite shape up, and see recent criticisms by Koenig and Davis (2001) and Goldberg (2005).

In fact, both within a single language and across languages, the repeated finding is that semantics maps to syntax by many-to-many mapping. On the one hand, verbs depicting identical or very similar semantics possess different syntax. Examples abound, such as the English change-of-location verbs of the *load, fill,* and *pour* class that not only differ in their syntactic expression but also possess a potential for alternative realizations without an obvious difference in their meaning. It is clear that the syntactic frame cannot be picked out with certainty from verb semantics, as a given type of semantic argument can be mapped to more than one complement type (see also Hudson *et al.*, 1996). Moreover, one type of syntactic format can map to a varied and unpredictable range of semantics, and see the non-agentive subjects of stative transitive verbs such as *want* or *forget*. Neither type of one-to-many mapping is a marginal phenomenon involving idiosyncratic fringes of the verb lexicon, but, rather, a critical feature of such major verbal constructions as the transitive verb–direct object combination.

To give a feel for the magnitude of the linking problem, I shall bring some yet-unconsidered data from English and Hebrew. Hebrew is a nominative-accusative language with an subject–verb–object canonical word order. Its repertoire of verbal constructions is quite similar to that of English, the core complements consisting, except for the direct object, of an indirect object using one of a set of obligatory prepositions *le-* ('to'), *mi-* ('from'), *be-* ('in'), and so on. There is no a priori typological reason why the syntax-semantics mapping should be different in the two languages.

Nevertheless, there is a considerable and unexplainable difference in the treatment of the two languages of translationally equivalent verbs. A non-systematic search unearthed 22 rather active verbs (see Table 3.1) that get a direct object in English but whose translation equivalents in Hebrew get indirect objects for the same 'undergoer' argument. The verbs in the table are a chance collection, and they can be added to easily.

These examples represent a no-win situation for linking rules of all persuasion, whether the 'direct linking' theory of Fillmore (1968) using thematic roles, the decompositional theories of Foley and Van Valin (1984), Pinker (1989), Jackendoff (1990), or Levin (1993), or the cluster-concept approach of Dowty (1991) and so forth. Whatever deterministic or probabilistic rules account for the mapping of the English verbs to the direct-object syntax, fails in the case of the Hebrew equivalents, despite the pronounced likeness between the basic diathesis system of the two languages.[6]

Note that among the verbs exhibiting the unexpected indirect syntax in Hebrew are some of the most prototypical transitive verbs, according to the criteria proposed by Hopper and Thompson (1980, 1984) for the cross-linguistic expressions of transitivity, expressing a high degree of impact of the act on the patient-entity, such as *harm*, *influence*, and *injure*. The very verb meaning *cause* in Hebrew (*garam*) has an oblique object with a *le-* preposition. Thus, the linking problem demonstrated by these examples affects the very core of the

Table 3.1 Examples of verbs taking a direct object in English, but their Hebrew translation equivalents getting an indirect object

English verb	Hebrew verb
abuse	hita'lel be-
cause	garam le-
command	paqad al
contact	hitqasher im
defend	hegen al
fight	nilxam be-/neged
forbid	asar al
harm	hiziq le-
hit	hirbic le-
influence	hishpia' al
injure	paga' be-
kick	ba'at be-
oppress	rada be-
order	civa al
press	laxac al
pull	masak be-
pursue	radaf axarey
repeat	xazar al
resist	neevaq neged
seize	axaz be-
stop	acar bead
use	hishtamesh be-

transitive verb class, not leaving much room even for a weakened claim about the category being a graded 'prototype category' where at least the core items invariably follow the canonical syntactic mapping even if more marginal items with a less prototypical semantics might not do so (*pace* Levin, 1999).[7]

These findings should not surprise us. The virtual impossibility of matching typical or prototypical semantics to the transitive construction has been extensively discussed in the linguistic literature of both languages, for example, by Goldberg (1999, p. 207) and Lyons (1968, p. 439) for English and by Glinert (1989) for Hebrew. Glinert says it quite simply: 'There are no recognized semantic criteria as to which verbs take direct objects.' (p. 159). The transitive construction is highly heterogeneous semantically and, as we saw in Table 3.1, the same kind of verbal arguments that appear as direct objects can easily appear as indirect objects as well. In fact, in both languages it is easy to find almost synonymous verbs with different complements, such as two Hebrew verbs for hitting, *hika* and *hirbitz*, the first getting a direct object, the second, an indirect one with the preposition *le-* ('to'). In English, the same phenomenon is seen in such arbitrary contrasts as the direct object form of the Theme argument of *trust* but the indirect objects taken by the Theme of the quite similar verbs *believe in* and *rely on.*

We might summarize that mapping from semantics to syntax and *vice versa* is messy, often arbitrary, at the most semi-regular, and under no circumstances deterministic.[8] Formally, words' semantic valency cannot fully predict their syntactic valency, hence the need to register both pieces of information in the lexicon. But once we do that, it is but a short step to the elimination of now-useless phrase-structure rules from the grammar.

3.2 Implication for acquisition: no abstract schema formation

The elimination of phrase-structure rules from Chomsky's theory of syntactic structure has revolutionary implications for the study of child language. Over the years it has been the unquestioned dogma of the field that developmental psycholinguistics needs to account for children's acquisition of abstract syntactic schemas. For instance, a considerable proportion of Ingram's (1989) influential review of the field was devoted to competing theories regarding the formation of abstract rules and categories, as was the edited collection by Levy *et al.* (1988). Nativists offered processes by which such abstraction can be triggered from dormant genetic storage (e.g., Pinker, 1984).[9] Empiricists offered elaborate explanations how the same abstractions can be induced from the linguistic input that consists of concrete sentences (e.g., Maratsos, 1979 or MacWhinney, 1982).[10]

Undoubtedly, much of this can be directly attributed to Chomsky's influence. Not only is Chomsky the single most influential linguist of his generation, but he has also repeatedly proposed that his theoretical-linguistic models of language be taken as characterizations of 'psychologically real' definitions of human internalized knowledge of language. When he argued that the target grammar of natural language acquisition must incorporate phrase-structure rules (Chomsky, 1957, pp. 21–33), this sent a strong message to the field that made it mandatory to account for the acquisition of phrase-structure rules, for nativists and empiricists alike.

The Minimalist Program's lexicalist conceptualization of syntactic structure signifies a major change in the character of the target grammar of natural language acquisition from the point of view of the Chomskian tradition. The message for the field of developmental psycholinguistics is that lexical-specific combinatory rules, item-specific syntactic schemas should be quite sufficient for the generation of grammatical sentences in children of any developmental stage, as they are the theorized forms of syntactic knowledge in adults as well, underlying the whole of the generative process. It should be unnecessary for developmental theory to deal with the consolidation of abstract syntactic rules by children, rendering such proposals without theoretical support.

I want to emphasize that the choice of a lexicalist syntax in developmental psychology is not one of preference, leaving it open for researchers so inclined to continue to use abstract and general rules applying to groups of predicates such as verbs. If linguistics cannot justify as theoretically sound a description of syntactic generativity by abstract and general 'Phrase-Structure Rules' but requires, instead, lexical-specific combinatory formulae registered in each word's lexical entry, the same should be true for speakers, whether adults or young children. The arguments for an internalized lexicalist syntax are identical to the arguments for a theoretical lexicalist syntax: There is too much unpredictable diversity in the mapping of semantics to syntax, and it is impossible to guess on the basis of a word's meaning its syntactic combinatory possibilities. And, once the combinatory potential of each word is registered in the lexicon, there is no need nor use for an extra abstract rule that cannot but list each word to which the relevant syntax applies.

The switch to a lexicalist syntax is a potential paradigm change—we can assume the continuity of the earliest syntactic competence with adult knowledge, and all of it is lexical-specific. Apparently, developmental psycholinguistics has been out of date and operating with a phrase-structure type grammar developed in the days of the Standard Theory (Chomsky, 1957, 1965), which has long been abandoned by linguists as a model because it cannot be sustained on linguistic basis. Current Chomskian syntax is lexicalist, and in order to follow in its footsteps, we should conclude that apparently children do not form anything more general than lexical-specific combinatory formulae.

3.3 Developmental evidence: no change in the form of syntactic schemas

3.3.1 Earliest word combinations are lexically specific

It is almost superfluous to bring empirical evidence to back up the claim that children indeed learn lexical-specific syntactic formulae. There is a wide, wall-to-wall consensus in the field that children's earliest syntax consists of item-specific rules regulating the combinatory behaviour of individual predicates rather than abstract rules applying to whole classes of words. Namely, most researchers agree that children start off with a lexicalist syntax, at least as far as the production of utterances is concerned.[11]

The grounds for this near-certainty is a set of robust findings regarding the conspicuously slow spread of novel morpho-syntactic patterns over different predicates and in particular, different verbs in the first period of their acquisition. Typically, it takes children several months to extend each new grammatical frame to 10 or 20 different verbs, and see the studies reviewed in Section 2.3.1 (e.g. Ninio, 1999a, 2005a; Abbot-Smith and Behrens, 2002; Kiekhoefer, 2002). The syntactic constructions for which such piecemeal learning has been documented include wh-question constructions (Klima and Bellugi-Klima, 1966; Forner, 1979; Kuczaj and Brannick, 1979; Johnson, 1980, 2000; Bloom *et al.*, 1982; Dabrowska and Lieven, 2005); auxiliaries, e.g., in yes/no questions (Kuczaj and Maratsos, 1983; Pine *et al.*, 1998); complement-taking matrix verbs getting *to* infinitives and other connectives (Bloom *et al.*, 1983, 1989); verbal argument frames and other syntactic multiword constructions (Braine, 1963; Bowerman, 1976; Clark, 1978; Slobin, 1985; Gropen *et al.*, 1989; Tomasello, 1992; Clancy, 1995; Lieven *et al.*, 1997).[12]

In some cases, there is an inordinately long period of time in which children produce a certain type of syntactic combination with a few select lexemes before they even begin to acquire the other instances of the same lexical category to which the novel construction could be applied. For example, most children begin the production of complex sentences with a very few complement-taking verbs like *want* or *can't*; other verbs of this type are not acquired at all until months later (see Pinker, 1984, pp. 215–219 for a review of this phenomenon).

The lexical-specificity of early combinatory rules appears especially clear when some of the candidate lexical items for the same syntactic frame are already within the child's productive vocabulary, but she does not generate the relevant word combination with these items for a discernible time period. For instance, Bowerman's daughter Eva started to produce verb–object combinations with the verb *want* at 1;5, combining the verb with various object nouns and verbs referring to activities. At this point she already had a sizeable verb vocabulary, which, however, she only used in the form of single-word utterances. Verb–object combinations with other verbs such as *open, close, break* and *fix* only appeared a month later. A similar phenomenon occurred with the verb *do*, which was the only verb combining in a subject–verb–object pattern in the first month when such combinations first emerged, although Eva already produced quite a few transitive verbs in combination at the time (Bowerman, 1976, p. 157, 1978, pp. 378–379).

As long as children use a particular syntactic format with only a few select verbs, it seems indisputable that they have learned to construct these word combinations in a lexeme-specific manner. As far as the early days of word combinations go, the data certainly support the lexicalist hypothesis we are testing.

3.3.2 **Nothing changes**

Several months after the very first sentence is produced in some particular syntactic format, children typically come to use the construction with many different verbs. At this point, it is less immediately obvious that their word combinations continue to be generated on a verb-specific basis and not derived from an abstract syntactic schema. Indeed, the great majority of the researchers in the field assume that by this stage children will have developed a generalized combinatory rule for the relevant construction, underlying the production of any further word combinations of that kind.

However, close examination of the evidence for abstract rules in children's internalized grammars fails to convince that such a process of abstraction indeed takes place in children's syntactic development. On the contrary; the empirical facts clearly support the lexicalist hypothesis of formal linguistics.

According to the relevant authorities, two things should change as children develop abstract rules. First, abstract rules should bring in enhanced productivity, and more precisely, a sudden across-the-board change in the use of the group of relevant lexical items (MacWhinney, 1982, p. 106; Tomasello, 2000b, p. 68). Second, abstract rules should bring in an enhanced ability to generalize the pattern to novel items the child has not heard modelled in the relevant frame in the linguistic input, this type of creativity sharply increasing relative to the initial period of word combinations (e.g., MacWhinney, 1982, pp. 106–108; Tomasello, 2000a, pp. 221–223).

When we closely examine the evidence for the hypothesized sudden changes against the alternative hypothesis that development is smooth and gradual, it appears that the empirical data supports the conclusion that syntactic combinations continue to be produced as they were from the beginning, namely, by a piecemeal learning of lexical-specific syntactic formulae.

First, the productivity (or range of application) of a given syntactic pattern such as the transitive verb–object format is expected to increase with development whether the child constructs an abstract verb-general transitive schema or continues to accumulate lexically-specific verb–object formats.

The crucial evidence that can distinguish between the two alternatives is whether or not there is a sudden discontinuous jump in productivity at some point in development. Examination of the learning curves for syntactic development computed on the basis of the empirical data in Ninio (1999a, 2005a,b), Abbot-Smith and Behrens (2002), Kiekhoefer (2002), and Keren-Portnoy (in press) revealed no evidence of such a discontinuity in development. A discontinuous jump in productivity should have caused a so-called inflection in the graphs. No such inflection is discernible in the learning curves we presented and mentioned in Chapter 2. Instead, there is a gradual smooth acceleration covered by a single mathematical function. In all cases, the power-law function we fitted to the graphs had a very high degree of fit, with the percentage of variance accounted for (the R^2) at or above 96%. Had there been a significant discontinuity or inflection in the graphs, the degree of fit of the single power-law curve would have been much lower. For example, let us look again at Figure 2.7, repeated here as Figure 3.1, presenting Ruti's learning curves for her first verb–object and subject–verb–object sentences.

I have added the power-law trendlines and the values for degree of fit to the two graphs presented in Figure 3.1. For both graphs, the degree of fit of the power-law trendline is 99%, namely, an almost perfect fit. In other words, the single power-law function fitted to a graph give such a good description of the data series that it precludes the possibility of there being two discontinuous functions instead.

Such results do not support the hypothesis that there is a discontinuous jump in productivity in the children's various syntactic combinations during the period it takes them to accumulate 20 or more verbs in a given pattern. We should accept it that development can be rapid and still be gradual. Travis was a fast learner, and her cumulative graphs show a steep acceleration; for example, the learning curve of her verb–object pattern, presented in Figure 2.6, climbed from the first verb that stayed the only one in this pattern for one whole month to five different new verbs per a single day at the end of this 2-month period. Nevertheless, her learning was gradual and there is no sudden jump in it; it is all accounted for by the practice effect embodied by the learning curve.

Interestingly, the very same issue of continuity versus 'burst' of productivity has already been discussed and decided on similar grounds in the domain of vocabulary growth. Bates *et al.* (1995) objected to the characterization of the rapid development of vocabulary size seen in most children in terms of a 'vocabulary spurt', pointing out that this notion is a mistake stemming from a mathematically naive look at an accelerating graph.[13] Similarly to

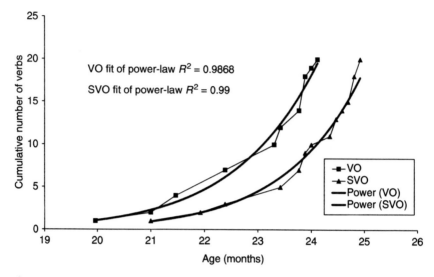

Fig. 3.1 Cumulative number of verbs in the VO and SVO constructions—Ruti; redrawn from figure 1 of Ninio (1999a). Pathbreaking verbs in syntactic development. *Journal of Child Language*, with permission from Cambridge University Press.

their analysis, it is apparent that in the case of syntactic development, the dynamic features of the complete graph (power-law or exponential) is characterized by just one single parameter, the slope, and the slow change at the lower values and the swift change at the high values are part and parcel of the same single mathematical function characterizing a continuous learning curve.

To summarize, the changing pace of syntactic learning does not mean that it is possible to cut the process into separate phases or stages; it is one and the same single learning process. We get similarly accelerating learning curve with an unchanging single motor task (for example rolling cigars; Crossman, 1959) where there is no possible way of talking about generalization, abstraction and so forth, and the acceleration represents nothing else than a practice effect. Learning the syntactic behaviour of verbs is a more complicated task but still, the mere fact that at some stage many new items are produced within a short time does not indicate a qualitative change in the process that produces the items. Instead, the findings demonstrate that all of syntactic acquisition is a single indivisible learning process in which children learn the semantic and syntactic valency of individual predicate words on a word-by-word basis, and in which item-specific knowledge facilitates the learning of other item-specific pieces of knowledge of the same type in children of all ages and at all stages of development.[14]

The second type of evidence for children switching at some point from item-specific formulae to abstract syntactic rules would be a sudden, sharply enhanced ability to use the syntactic pattern with novel items, without hearing them so used in the linguistic input, for example as a result of priming with many similar constructions presented to the child in a short time. The alternative hypothesis is that generalization to novel items derives from item-to-item transfer built on similarity and analogy, and, as such, the relevant effects (priming, facilitation of learning, overgeneralization errors and the like) should show a gradual, rather than sudden, development. Another crucial difference is that item-to-item analogy and transfer are expected to be available immediately to the child as soon as she learns a novel syntactic pattern for the first item, whereas the inducing of an abstraction from item-specific formulae is thought to require a critical mass of already-learned word combinations and thus it is not expected to be happening before the age of 3–3.5 years (Tomasello, 2000a, pp. 216–222).

The evidence on this issue has already been reviewed in Chapter 2, in Section 2.3. It appears that transfer of learning, priming effects, and experimentally induced novel-item generalization are all very early, both in terms of children's age and in terms of the stage of the learning process at which they happen. Improvement due to facilitation of learning is in fact maximal at the very start of learning a novel syntactic construction, as this is a basic feature of the Power Law of Practice (Logan, 1988). Indeed, accelerated learning curves were generated by as few as the first six items in some syntactic patterns (Ninio, 2005a). As to transfer to unmodelled novel items, the majority of children as young as 2;6 are perfectly able and willing to be affected by priming and other experimental manipulations encouraging going beyond the input (e.g., Tomasello and Brooks, 1998; Abbot-Smith et al., 2004). The ability to generalize to novel items does get better with learning, but the improvement is gradual rather than sudden. There is nothing in these findings[15] that makes it necessary to assume that syntactic acquisition ever departs from being concrete and lexically-specific, or that at any point in development children induce or otherwise form abstract syntactic rules of the phrase-marker-plus-lexical-insertion type now outdated in linguistic theorizing.

3.4 Conclusions: children learn a lexicalist syntax

3.4.1 Children do not form abstract rules or schemas

It can be summarized that there is not one shred of developmental evidence for a discontinuity in children's internalized syntactic rules from a set of lexical-specific combinatory formulae we have been calling individual predicates' syntactic valency, to a system consisting of abstract rules applying to whole groups and classes of predicates. This is not surprising as Chomskian linguistics and in particular the Minimalist Program have eliminated such entities as abstract phrase-structure rules from the grammar many years ago. It seems that the field of developmental psycholinguistics would do well to give up on the idea of 'teaching' children abstractions when it is so much easier to account merely for the acquisition of lexical-specific formulae.

3.4.2 What children do learn

If we follow the Minimalist Program, syntactic development should be conceptualized in terms of three kinds of learning.

1. Children need to learn the lexicon of their language, complete with logico-semantic valency and syntactic valency information for each word. This is no mean feat as words have multiple arity and they can appear in multiple syntactic environments. For instance, Bloomfield (1935, p. 265) mentions that the word *one* in English belongs to no less than five different form-classes. Similarly, Dixon (1991, p. 339) points out that English verbs can have an extremely varied semantic and syntactic range, as evidenced by the number of different senses they are listed with in the Oxford English dictionary; for instance, the verb *have* is listed with 27 senses, *give* with 64, and *take* with 94. Each semantic variant has a potentially different syntactic behaviour. Children need ultimately to learn and master all the richness of the lexicon.

2. Children need to learn to operate with the combinatory operation Merge/ Dependency. This means both to be able to generate the relevant word combination with its formal features but no less to be able to combine the content of the Head-word and the Dependent-word into a unified concept, giving each its correct role in the combination. In some respect, children need to learn to perform what is called in the Computational Linguistics literature the act of 'unification' (cf. Shieber, 1986), namely, to combine partially overlapping feature structures belonging to two different words.[16] We showed in Chapter 1 that in all probability children start to use Merge/Dependency already with their very first word combinations; understanding the principle of unification is apparently a precondition to multiword speech.

3. Children need to learn to apply the Merge/Dependency operation recursively; recursion is the crucial feature of syntax (Hauser *et al.*, 2002). It is needed in order to build infinitely long sentences and not just Merge/ Dependency couplets consisting of two words. This skill is beginning to be

acquired relatively late, starting with the build-up of three-word combinations. Some evidence on how children come to master recursion can be found in Ewing (1982), Hill (1984), Elbers (1990), and Ninio (1994).

One thing children do not need to learn is how to create abstract representations on the basis of groups of word-based concrete syntactic rules. The system we are proposing allows for transfer of learning and for generalization to novel items through the process of similarity-based analogy and not through a rule-based process using abstract representations. To remind us, transfer is the ability to extend what has been learned in one context to new contexts (Byrnes, 1996). Analogy is transfer based on structural similarity; for example, in the problem-solving or 'analogical reasoning' literature, analogical transfer is a process of problem-solving by drawing on analogous solutions (Reeves and Weisberg, 1993; Paas and Van Merrienboer, 1994).

Here we should face the often asked question, don't we smuggle in abstraction under the cover of similarity? Why is similarity less abstract than abstract rules?

This subject has been extensively discussed in the cognitive psychology literature. The clearest exposition was made by Hahn and Chater (1998) in a lucid analysis of the different processes through which people perform acts of categorization. The situation is one in which there is a set of rules, each with its own antecedent entities to which the rule applies, and the present decision is which rule is to be applied to the current item. Hahn and Chater distinguish (especially on p. 202 ff) between similarity-based and rule-based systems by two major factors: first, what is the status of the representations to which the to-be-categorized item is compared with, namely, are these more abstract representations of the antecedents of a rule or else equally-abstract ones? And, second, is the criterion for categorization a full match or a partial match to the antecedent? They show that rule application is a matter of strict matching to knowledge that is more abstract than the new item to be matched, while similarity-based processes involve partial matching to a representation that is not more abstract than the to-be-matched item. The process of matching itself, with its possibility of partiality, does not by itself involve abstraction; it is a process available due to the fact that representations (abstract or concrete) possess a complex internal feature structure. They assume that, on the basis of the complex feature system, which is the representation, people are able to make judgements of similarity (also of analogy, which they define as structural similarity) and not only judgements of identity.

An abstract representation is one in which the representation 'abstracts away' from the details of the particular instance, focusing on a few key properties. Hahn and Chater point out that all abstraction involves loss of information relative to the corresponding specific representation and, basically, entails underspecification. Unless we are ready to believe that people store actual exemplars of sentences they have heard or said as the basis for their syntactic rule system (as it is proposed by Bybee, 2001, for the phonological rule system), it is impossible to avoid some underspecification in syntax. The lexical-specific valency information we are talking about probably uses something that has the status of variables instead of actual words to represent the arguments of predicates; however, this can be no more abstract than the description 'the thing to be eaten' as the patient argument of the verb *eat*. However, this is no feat of abstraction, but, rather, the very core process of acquiring words. When children learn the meaning of a predicate word, they already deal with its possessing logical-semantic arguments. For example, the word *sit* is meaningless unless it is understood to entail that there is someone to do the sitting (Ninio, 1988, p. 111). Learning *sit* as a meaningful vocabulary item also means learning that *sit* takes a 'sitter' argument; this is a fact about the semantics of this word and not a separate piece of abstracted-out information.

To summarize, similarity based analogy does not imply that people (children) use an abstract representation instead of actual lexical items for the process of generalization or transfer of learning. It only means that people are ready to accept a partial match between the present item and its closest antecedent when making a decision of which syntactic rule to apply to the former. This process is probably available to children from birth, as it is impossible to function in the perceptual world without accepting partial matches between stimuli and stored representations. Our analysis of the processes of syntactic development merely adds another context for the operation of the same general cognitive process, but does not import the concept of abstraction through the back door.[17]

The lexicalist conclusions of this chapter herald in a paradigm change in the treatment of syntactic development. There is a continuity in children's syntactic competence with adult knowledge, not because (as in some nativist theories) young children operate with innate abstract categories like adults are supposed to but because adults operate with the same lexical-specific combinatory schemas as children do.

A radical possibility that emerged in this chapter was that semantic similarity is not a good basis for transfer of learning and generalization in syntactic development. In the following chapter I shall examine this possibility in more detail.

Notes

1 In addition to redundancy, phrase structure rules turned out to be inadequate because also they failed to account for the endocentricity of phrases (Lyons, 1968). In the phrase structure rule conceptualization, all 'sisters' are equal, and there is no formal means to acknowledge the special role of the Head-sister that gives the resultant phrase its own features, e.g., the verb to the verb phrase.

2 The X-bar schema conceptualizes structure building as a bottom-top process; phrase structure is projected from the lexicon and every phrase is required to have a lexical Head. Not as in the symmetrical phrase-structure rules, the X-bar schema explicitly acknowledges the asymmetry between Heads and Dependents in the 'sister' relationship, namely, the fundamental endocentricity of phrases (Chomsky, 1970, Jackendoff, 1977). The notion of Head is used in this theory very much like in Dependency Grammars (see Hudson, 1990, p. 111), and in fact Covington (1994, p. 3) showed that X-bar theory can be interpreted as equivalent to a kind of Dependency grammar. See also Bennett (1995, p. 15). For our purposes, it is important to note that X-bar principles are extremely abstract and fundamental in all structure-building. Like Merge and Dependency relations, they do not characterize particular phrases on a more abstract level so much as constitute the means by which all phrases are constructed.

3 Except for the Minimalist Program, there are many other completely or partly lexicalized theories of grammar in which the main responsibility for projecting syntactic structure is borne by the lexicon, for instance Montague-Grammar (Montague, 1974; Dowty, 1982); Categorial Grammar (Venneman, 1977; Moortgat, 1988; Oehrle, 1994); Combinatory Categorial Grammar (Ades and Steedman, 1982; Steedman, 2000); Relational Grammar (Perlmutter and Postal, 1984); Lexicalized Tree Adjoining Grammar (Schabes, 1990; Rambow and Joshi, 1994); Link Grammar (Sleator and Temperley, 1991); and Slot Grammar (McCord et al., 1992). Some of these rely heavily on valency information being stored in the lexicon but maintain the use of unlexicalized rules, including Lexical Functional Grammar (Bresnan, 1978, 2001; Bresnan and Kaplan, 1982); Head Driven Phrase Structure Grammar (Pollard and Sag, 1987, 1994); and some versions of Dependency Grammar (Mel'cuk, 1979; Hudson, 1984; Starosta, 1988).

4 In some other linguistic theories the lexicon incorporates in addition to words also higher-level units such as abstract constructions, for instance, in Radical Construction Grammar (Croft, 2001) and in Cognitive Grammar (Langacker, 1987).

5 Different proposals for a ruleful mapping between lexical semantics and syntax, involving, variously, sets or hierarchies of thematic roles and macroroles, argument alignment, semantic primitives, and the like have been made by, among others, Fillmore (1968), Jackendoff (1972, 1990), Anderson (1977), Foley and Van Valin (1984), Lebeaux (1986), Baker (1988, 1997), Dowty (1989, 1991), Pinker (1989), Speas (1990), Bouchard (1991), Gleitman (1990), Hale and Keyser (1993), Levin (1993), Van Valin (1993), Levin and Rappaport Hovav (1995, 1996), Wechsler (1995), and Davis and Koenig (2000).

6 Other accusative-nominative languages in which English transitive verbs have translation equivalents that take dative, instrumental or other oblique complements are, for example, Russian (Dezso, 1982) and Hungarian (Blume, 1998). In addition, linking generalization based on English are sometimes not replicated in other languages (see for instance Filip, 1996, on Czech). For a recent review of the weaknesses of cross-linguistic linking generalizations see Goldberg (2005).

7 See for instance Ross (1972, 1973), Lakoff (1987, pp. 462 ff), and Taylor (1989, pp. 192 ff).

8 It should come as no surprise that mapping of grammatical rules to lexical form-classes suffers from the same type of problems (e.g., Crystal, 1967); however, this topic is beyond the scope of the present monograph.

9 See also Hyams (1986), Pinker (1989), Bloom (1990), Clahsen (1990), Gleitman (1990), Naigles (1990), Radford (1990, 1996), Fisher et al. (1991), Poeppel and Wexler (1993), Clahsen et al. (1996), Lust (1999), and Trueswell and Gleitman (2004).

10 See also the developmental processes proposed by de Villiers (1980), Ingram (1981), Maratsos (1982), Peters (1983), Berman (1986, 1988), Ninio (1988), Bowerman (1990), Pine et al. (1998), Tomasello (2000a), and MacWhinney (2004)

11 Among the very many authorities who suggested that children's initial combinatory rules are lexically-specific are Francis (1969), Macnamara (1972), Brown (1973), Schlesinger (1974), Bowerman (1976), Braine (1976), de Villiers and de Villiers (1978), Baker (1979), Berman (1982a), Chiat (1982), MacWhinney (1982), Maratsos (1983), Peters (1983), Roberts (1983), Pinker (1984), Brown and Leonard (1986), Robinson (1986), Van Langendonck (1987), Ninio (1988), Gropen et al. (1989), Gleitman (1990), Tomasello (1992), Braine and Brooks (1995), Clark (1996), Ingram and Thompson (1996), Berman and Armon-Lotem (1997), Lieven et al. (1997), Uziel-Karl (2002), and Trueswell and Gleitman (2004).

12 Item-specificity has been found also for verb-morphology such as inflection for tense, aspect, and person (Bloom *et al.*, 1980; Berman and Dromi, 1984; Clark, 1996; Wilson, 2003).

13 It is worthwhile to cite their arguments verbatim:

> A second problem comes from the discontinuity implied by the word 'burst', and by most of the theories that seek to explain accelerations in word learning. Van Geert (1991) and Bates and Carnevale (1993) have noted that individual growth curves described in longitudinal studies of vocabulary development during the second year (see especially Dromi, 1987) are best fit by a smoothly accelerating exponential function, or by related non-linear functions such as the quadratic or the logistic. By appropriate variation in their parameters, such non-linear models could lead to growth curves marked by apparently intense bursts, weaker bursts, or no significant acceleration at all. The key insight here is that there is no inflection point in the exponential portion of the so-called vocabulary burst, i.e., no single 'take-off point' of the kind assumed by most of the theories cited above.
>
> Bates *et al.* (1995, p. 100)

14 The analysis of the process of learning in terms of the gradual acceleration of learning curves puts into a questionable light the practice of using the criterion of co-emergence as an indicator of the productivity of some grammatical pattern in young children. This method has been routinely employed by researchers wishing to make a distinction between productive categorial rules (syntactic or semantic) and item-specific formulae (e.g., Bowerman, 1973a, 1976; Bloom *et al.*, 1975; Braine, 1976; Lieven *et al.*, 1997; Pinker, 1984, 1989; Pine *et al.*, 1998; Abbot-Smith and Behrens, in press). If, however, development is a continuously accelerating process of accumulating item-specific syntactic formulae, it is expected that at some point in development many different lexical-specific constructions emerge at approximately the same time, some of them semantically and syntactically similar. Co-emergence may simply reflect the fast pace of item-specific learning rather than a categorial process.

15 The hypothesis of lexicalism in syntactic acquisition is also supported by the finding that measures of grammatical development are strongly correlated with vocabulary size (e.g., Fenson *et al.*, 1994; Bates and Goodman, 1999; McGregor *et al.*, 2005).

16 For some Unification-based grammars and automatic parsers see Hellwig (1986), Pollard and Sag (1987), Covington (1990), Sleator and Temperley (1991), McCord *et al.* (1992), and Fraser (1993).

17 We cannot explore this subject in sufficient depth; for treatments see Medin and Schaffer (1978), Nosofsky (1984, 1992), and in particular the contributions in the special issue of *Cognition* devoted to this topic (1998, Vol. 65), for instance, Gentner and Medina (1998).

4

Similarity

In Chapter 3 we concluded that, in most probability, the process of syntactic acquisition does not involve the formation of abstract rules on the basis of groups of word-based, concrete, combinatory formulae. Namely, the item-specific valency formulae with which children begin acquisition remain the only form in which syntactic potential is represented in their language system. Whenever there is a need to relate two or more item-specific formulae, as in transfer of learning and in generalization to novel items, this is likely to be accomplished through similarity-based analogy and not through a rule-based process using abstract representations.

This conclusion is radical enough to warrant further and more detailed examination. In particular, there is an alternative hypothesis with a very long history in the field of developmental psycholinguistics claiming that during syntactic development children form—at least temporarily—combinatory schemas applying to semantic categories of wide or narrow scope. However, as the major use that model builders envisioned for such categorial schemas is to 'bootstrap' the child's system into abstract syntax, the present lexicalist approach is left without a major motivation for them in the developmental process. It seems more likely that children do not, in fact, carry out anything like semantic categorization as part of their learning of item-specific syntactic formulae.

In more formal terms, we have defined syntactic development as the acquisition of an autonomous lexicalist syntax. In this model, development is the accumulation of lexical-specific combinatory schemas, each mapping a specific predicate's semantic valency to its individually specified syntactic valency. As semantics is an unreliable guide to the form in which a particular syntactic dependent is to be expressed, the relationship among individual combinatory schemas making up a child's syntactic system can only take into account a similarity of form, not the degree of similarity of meaning. If the child cannot rely on semantic similarity in order to predict syntactic form, we expect transfer of learning and generalization not to make use of similarity of verb semantics or similarity of the semantics of verbal arguments between the source and the target of the transfer process.

This hypothesis will be tested in this chapter against the alternative that children do form semantically based general combinatory schemas and make use of them in the learning process. We shall discuss the alternatives in detail, below. We shall start with the construct of similarity and its application to syntactic development.

4.1 Similarity for transfer and generalization

We said children need to learn and adults to use in sentence generation lexical-specific syntactic formulae and not abstract phrase structure rules. This appears to remove abstraction and category formation as learning tasks, leaving for syntactic acquisition the task of accumulating a repertoire of lexical items furnished with syntactic and semantic valency. But, the question of abstract categories in the learning process is not yet settled. Even if there is no linguistic need to form general rules applying to groups of items, it could be that people still form them for the sake of transfer and generalization.

The need for generalization arises because even if syntactic combinatory regulations are fundamentally lexical-specific, there are several processes in which there is a requirement to go beyond the individual item-specific formulae. One is transfer and facilitation of learning. It is unlikely that human beings learn to carry out a task without bringing old learning to bear on the new one. Transfer of learning entails the existence of some relationship among the various lexical-specific syntactic formulae.

Second, children at some point in development generalize syntactic frames beyond the lexemes for which they had learned the said formulae from the linguistic input. Some of these are mistakes (or overgeneralizations), some represent intentional and creative innovations, which in adults go by the name of *coercion* (Pustejovsky, 1991), and some others are the result of elicitation pressures by experimenters. Applying a familiar formula to a novel item is evidence of the child's actively establishing a relationship between the previously learned lexical-specific formats and the innovated one.

In Chapter 3 we suggested that processes going beyond individual item-specific syntactic formulae make use of item-to-item similarity-based analogy rather than abstract rules and categories. This proposal immediately raises the question whether similarity is able to ground cognitive processing. In particular, we have to see if we can save it from criticism that the notion of similarity is too flexible and not sufficiently well-determined to be used in cognitive theorizing.

4.1.1 **Similarity in cognitive psychology**

Similarity is a central theoretical construct in cognitive psychology, and, as we mentioned in Chapter 2, it is thought to be essential in transfer of learning and in making generalizations.[1] What appears to be important for people's judgements of similarity is not only the overlap of individual features or attributes but also the higher-level relational or structural analogy between the concepts compared (e.g., Gentner, 1983, 1989; Gentner and Markman, 1997; Hummel and Holyoak, 1997).

There is, however, a fundamental problem with similarity and analogy and it needs to be addressed before we can assume these constructs can successfully substitute for abstraction and categorization. The problem is that without further constraint, analogy and similarity are vague and unbound concepts. Any two objects are similar to some extent on some feature, but also unique and dissimilar in other respects. Similarity is universal: any pair of things are potentially infinitely similar to one another (but also infinitely dissimilar). For example, both pencils and houses have mass and they are not alive; but pencils weigh less than a kilogram and houses weigh more, and pencils are used for writing and houses are not. We cannot actually answer the question if pencils and houses are similar or dissimilar; it is a meaningless question. Similarity by itself lacks any explanatory power for cognitive processing; to say that X is similar to Y is an ill-defined claim unless we can specify the dimensions on which the relevant similarity resides (Watanabe, 1969; Goodman, 1972).

In our chosen topic of interest, namely, words in the lexicon, similarity is correspondingly unbounded. Two words can be similar on many dimensions, for example how do they sound, what is their onset, what is their rhyme, what is their stress-pattern, how many syllables they have, what is their morphological behaviour, how they get plural or gender, how they get past tense, what kind of meaning they encode, how many complements they need to have, and what is the acceptable syntax for their arguments. In addition, words can be similar in terms of the feelings or associations they evoke (see Osgood *et al.*'s 1957 work on the 'Semantic Differential'). As Medin, Goldstone and Gentner point out, a random choice of some dimension of similarity among words would not provide the cognitive underpinnings necessary for transfer or generalization: 'A model for generating past tense may be successful if it bases its generalization on phonological similarities (e.g., Rumelhart and McClelland, 1986), but it is likely doomed to failure if it formulates generalizations in terms of semantic similarity.' (Medin *et al.*, 1993, p. 256).

If all pairs of items potentially share at least one of an infinite number of commonalities, we need to be able to specify some external principle by which learners can pin-point a priori the relevant dimensions of similarity and ignore all irrelevant ones. According to an influential theory of cognitive psychology, such a principle is provided by the goal of the task for which the construct of similarity is to be used. Apparently, learners are quite capable of choosing the right dimensions for a given cognitive context because they are guided in this decision by the nature of the learning task itself, by the goal of action. The theory claiming this is known by the name of Goal-Driven Learning and it is associated with such cognitive psychologists as Barsalou, Solomon and their colleagues (see for instance the papers in Ram and Leake, 1995), but some of its intellectual roots can be traced to the work of the philosopher Ludwig Wittgenstein. As it is well known, in his book *Philosophical Investigations* (1978[1953]) Wittgenstein defended a use-conditional (as opposed to truth-conditional) theory of meaning. The aspect of his proposal that concerns us touches on the way people classify words into categories of similarity:

> Think of the tools in a tool-box: there is a hammer, pliers, a saw, a screw-driver, a rule, a glue-pot, glue, nails and screws.—The functions of words are as diverse as the functions of these objects. (And in both cases there are similarities.) [...] It will be possible to say: In language (8) we have different *kinds of word*. For the functions of the word 'slab' and the word 'block' are more alike than those of 'slab' and 'd'. But how we group words into kinds depends on the aim of the classification,—and on our own inclination. Think of the different points of view from which one can classify tools or chess-men.

Wittgenstein (1978[1953], #17, pp. 6–8.)

Wittgenstein opened the way for the cognitive psychologists who emphasized the context-dependent, *ad-hoc* nature of similarity and equivalence categories. For example, in a seminal paper Tversky (1977) argued that similarity is context-bound, and cannot ever be extracted out of context. Similar points were made by also by Murphy and Medin (1985).

In the Goal-Driven version of this theory, the context is identified as the ongoing task. According to the tenets of this theory, the learning process is strongly influenced by the learner's goals. Learning is seen as an active process in which the learner identifies the information needed for the successful completion of the task on the basis of his prior knowledge, his skill level, and the environmental context of the learning situation. Thus, it is claimed that during task-performance and in particular in a learning situation, people create *ad hoc* categories of similarity in response to the goals of the learning situation. The dimensions and features of similarity that are then chosen to guide transfer and generalization are those most relevant to the successful completion of the ongoing task (e.g., Barsalou, 1983, 1991; Johnson and

Johnson, 1991; and see the chapters in Ram and Leake, 1995). Moreover, Barsalou (1991) also showed that goal-derived categories are not fixed but flexible and can change during task performance as the learner becomes more skilled. The model has received much empirical support and it is probably a valid characterization of learner's use of similarity in learning.

The theory of Goal-Derived Learning as well as corresponding models by Wittgenstein, Tversky, and others, provides a coherent basis for constraining the overly flexible constructs of similarity and analogy. It appears that in actuality people do not choose randomly among the infinite dimensions of similarity on which two items may be compared; rather, they choose strategic-ally in a way that focuses on the task-relevant features. This approach provides us with a principled way to reduce the excessive flexibility of similarity and enable it to ground cognitive processing.

4.1.2 Similarity of form and meaning of grammatical relations

Syntactic formulae can be similar to each other on an infinite number of dimensions, but only a few of these define them as expressing an identical grammatical relation. The relevant similarity function refers solely to the *form* of the syntactic frame and not at all to its *meaning*. The term 'form' refers to such coding features as word-order and casemarking on the dependent phrase (Keenan, 1976). For example, a subject is a such a noun phrase that is canonically placed pre-verbally and it is in the nominative case. Grammatical relations have other features as well, such as so-called behavioural features, for instance, accessibility to passivization or relativization, which are not part of the directly observable surface structure of the word combination. Each sub-type of grammatical relation is identified by a correlated cluster of features, not all of which is present for each individual exemplar.[2] The semantics of the word combination is not one of the defining features of a grammatical relation, and in fact grammatical relations are purely structural relationships beyond semantics (Andrews, 1985). See for example a definition by the typological linguist Payne (1997): 'Grammatical relations are often thought of as relations between arguments and predicates in a level of linguistic structure that is independent (or 'autonomous') of semantic and pragmatic influences.' (p. 129).

The reason is that one particular grammatical relation can and does express many different semantic relations between the verb and the complement phrase.[3] In the terminology of Chomsky *et al.* (2002, p. 113) some case forms such as the English Accusative and Nominative do not have semantic interpretations. We saw in Chapter 3 that linking semantics to syntax is less than regular, so that items with similar semantics can be mapped to different syntactic frames. The same is true for the other side of the linking equation: different items with the same syntax possess a wide range of semantic roles. Linguists such as Fillmore (1968), Allerton (1978), Foley and Van Valin (1984), Levin (1985), Jackendoff (1987), Mel'cuk (1988), Dowty (1991), Zaenen (1993), and so forth have described in great detail the rich repertoire of different thematic roles possessed by subjects, direct objects and indirect objects. We shall present some of it below in Section 4.3 when we come to discuss children's acquisition of grammatical relations. A thorough discussion of linking theories is beyond our scope. At the moment it is sufficient for our purposes to take note of Dowty's (1989) warning that it might require a very large number of different thematic roles to fully categorize all possible argument roles even in one language.

The mapping of syntax to semantics is many-to-many, turning the linking of meaning to form and form to meaning to a large part unpredictable. One kind of argument semantics (e.g., agent of action) can be mapped to more than one complement type, and one kind of syntactic formula can map to many different type of semantics, often in an idiosyncratic manner. This is the reason that syntax is said to be autonomous (e.g., Hudson *et al.*, 1996). Our best bet is to conclude that grammatical relations are purely syntactic relations, and the dimension of similarity relevant for their definition (and hence, their acquisition) is only that of similarity of form.

The potential complication to the claim of 'autonomous syntax' comes from the existence of local islands of regularity in linking in the otherwise semantics-neutral syntactic system. Although overall a given grammatical relation such as the verb–object one is semantically heterogeneous, there is, nevertheless, some degree of orderliness in the syntax-semantics mapping. We know that the verb lexicon is composed of many small and semantically homogeneous subclasses or semantic fields. Theoreticians such as Bolinger (1975), Dixon (1982), Pinker (1989), and Levin (1993) claim that members of such subgroups are not only semantically similar but they also share much of their overall syntactic behaviour. These suggestions by linguists can be quite elaborate. Levin describes hundreds of verb classes defined by diathesis alternation and it is possible that she underestimates the number of syntactically distinct lexical subgroups.[4] Indeed, Bolinger (1975) raises the possibility that there are literally an infinite number of such classes, if the grouping is done on the basis of semantic similarity among the participating words:

> There are lesser classes too, no one knows how many. Since meanings can cluster in
> infinite ways, it should not be surprising that many smaller groups of words embrace

some common feature that reflects itself in a freedom, or lack of it, to combine with other items or classes. A great deal of current work in syntax has to do with discovering and defining these classes and their syntactic effects, largely in the hopes of finding which ones are widespread and perhaps universal.' (p. 149).

Within the set of constituents standing in a specific grammatical relation with the verb, semantic similarity generates subgroups filling different thematic roles. For example, the thematic role alternatives for syntactic subjects are so that some subjects express an *Effector of action*, some others express an *Initiator*, an *Instrument*, a *Force* and yet others are *Locations*, as in 'The garden swarms with bees' (Salkoff, 1983; and see examples in Note 3). The verbs that appear in each of these constructions (defined by the conjunction of syntactic form and semantic role) probably share much of their lexical semantics, or, at least, groups of them possess some quite specific semantic components. For example, English locative subjects are restricted to a very few classes of verbs only, one of verbs depicting small repetitive movements (as in *crawl, drip, bubble,* and *dance*), another group referring to kinds of light emission (*beam, blaze,* or *brighten*) and yet another depicting smells and tastes (*reek, smell,* or *taste*), and a few others (all the examples from Dowty, 2000).

Take note that the semantic homogeneity is only within each subgroup of a subgroup. That is, verbs referring to smells and tastes might be quite close in their meaning, but *smell* and *taste* do not have a lot in common with small repetitive movements such as *crawl* or *drip*. Namely, even for such an unusual version of thematic roles such as locative subjects, there is no overall commonality among all the verbs taking this kind of structure. Then, the verbs taking locative subjects are not like verbs taking instrument subjects, and as all verbs in English take subjects, we end up with a totally heterogeneous category, whose semantic diversity encompasses the whole of the verb class.

We might summarize that although it is true that the lexicon contains many small groups of items with similar syntax that also have a similar semantics, semantics does not provide a second and parallel organizing principle to the structure of the syntactic lexicon. If there are an infinite number of dimensions along which linguistic items can be said to be similar, some must be ultimately irrelevant for syntax, and, apparently, semantics is one of them.

Instead of an a priori group of general 'syntactically relevant semantic features' that would predict the syntactic behaviour of classes of predicates, it seems that the mapping of syntax to semantics is determined on an individual basis. Each predicate registers in its lexical entry its logical-semantic arguments, as well as the syntactic form their expression takes. Certain verbs get a direct object argument not because they possess some a priori semantic feature or other, but because their lexical entry specifies it.

4.2 Implication for acquisition: no role for semantic linking in learning syntax

The analysis presented above implies that there is no role for semantic linking in learning syntax. In all probability, children use similarity of form for generalization and transfer of learning, disregarding argument semantics and thematic roles.

Grammatical relations are purely formal relations, and there is no one-to-one mapping between complement form and argument semantics. As we saw in Chapter 3, semantics is mapped in a one-to-many manner to syntax; in Hebrew, for example, it is difficult to find semantic criteria as to which verbs take direct objects and which, indirect or oblique ones because any given semantic content can be mapped to either (Glinert 1989, p. 159). The arbitrariness means that children need to learn for each verb separately that it takes a direct or an indirect object, on an item-specific basis. In such circumstances, it might be risky to rely on semantic analogy for predicting that some new verb with a meaning similar to a previously learned one will also take a direct object, as the prediction will often turn out to be incorrect. In this chapter we saw that the mapping of syntax to semantics is not one-to-one either; instead, there are many different thematic roles filled by the very same syntactic dependent. As similarity of meaning cannot be relied on, it is probably the best learning strategy to ignore meaning and rely on only one dimension of similarity between old and new formulae to be learned: that of similarity of form.

It might be thought that despite the overall unreliability of syntax-semantics linking, it might still be worthwhile for children to develop many small abstract schemas in which semantics is homogeneous, at least on a temporary basis. Such schemas could for example apply to all verbs to do with ingestion and their 'ingested' direct object. If a child develops such a general schema on the basis of three to four different ingestion-verbs such as *eat, drink,* and *swallow,* the schema can then be applied to all kinds of other verbs with at least similar semantics such as *chew, lick,* or *taste* without the effort it takes to learn the VO combination from the input.[5] At first glance this sounds like an efficient route of development until we realize that forming such abstractions has its price. Assuming that some syntactic pattern is linked to a particular semantics for the argument might help learn the pattern for similar arguments but for the same reasons it might well cause negative transfer for learning the same pattern for other semantics. For instance, if a child learns to expect the direct object to be associated with ingested substances, she might resist learning the same pattern for things you perceive, as in the case of objects of verbs such as *see, hear,* or *feel.* As a result, if children form abstract schemas in which syntax is linked to some specific semantics, they must soon unlearn them, as the same syntax is also linked to other semantics.

The formation of abstract schemas is not only inefficient and problematic but also a developmental blind alley; the system, as we now know, does not contain abstract phrase-structure rules and especially not ones with a regular linking to semantics. As the making of abstractions is a quite laborious cognitive task, and given the low return in efficiency and the lack of a clear role in the overall system, it is of questionable value for the learning process. As before, I am assuming that the developmental process is guided by the true nature of the to-be-acquired syntactic system, and that children do not waste energy on learning incidental associations that do not fit into it.[6]

It follows that children probably do not at any stage form general and abstract rules applying to semantically homogeneous groups of predicates, as has been claimed to happen by many authorities in the field. Hypothesized processes such as semantic bootstrapping, syntactic bootstrapping, abstraction and generalization, schema formation and so forth, to be discussed below, appear to be based on the assumption that children very much take notice of argument semantics and are in fact engaged in forming generalizations about the way semantics and syntax map to each other. What seems to emerge in our analysis of the linguistic and cognitive conditions to the acquisition of syntax is that in all probability children merely learn item-specific formulae, taking advantage of the similarity of form to generalize the format to novel items or else to facilitate new learning, but ignore argument semantics as irrelevant to either transfer of learning or to generalization of old knowledge to new items. In consequence, their representation of syntactic rules does not change from item-specific formulae to semantically homogeneous abstract schemas but remain lexically specific even when they go beyond individual formulae for the sake of transfer and generalization.

It should not surprise us that this conclusion—based on the linguistic evidence regarding the autonomy of syntax from semantics—is completely congruent with another implication of present-day theoretical linguistics for a model of syntactic development, and that is the absence of Phrase-Structure rules and the full lexical-specificity of combinatory rules in the internalized syntax. We have a already pointed out (in Section 3.1.2) that one of the major reasons for the need to register each predicate's individual syntactic and semantic valency in the lexicon is the failure of linking regularities to make the syntax predictable from verb semantics. The two components of the model of syntactic development emerging from theoretical linguistics—the lexicalism of combinatory formulae (and the absence of abstract rules) and the sole reliance on similarity of form (and not of semantics) in going beyond item-specific formulae—are one and the same principle, stemming from the fundamental autonomy of syntax.

Although creating semantically homogeneous abstract schemas in the course of syntactic development is an inefficient strategy if we take into account the true nature of the end-state syntactic system, we cannot assume that children are only influenced by adult principles. The existing local regularities in syntax-semantics linking could seem for a time like an efficient way to generate semantically supported transfer and generalization, and children could be motivated to generalize across individual instances as far as the data allows. In fact there exists a competing hypothesis to our lexicalist one, assuming precisely these processes in children. The hypothesis is that children will make use of the local patches of semantic homogeneity and form abstract schemas with coherent semantics. Such a hypothesis has been promoted by many developmental psycholinguists,[7] mostly as a temporary route to the formation of the abstract rules and categories that older versions of the Chomskian theory demanded. For example, Morris *et al.* (2000) proposed a process by which children's verb–specific syntactic formulae gradually 'merge' into more and more abstract schemas. The order of these 'mergers' is determined by how close the semantics of the relevant verbs is, so that at the start of the process only very similar verbs will 'merge' into a larger grammar, e.g., *eat* with *drink*, or *hit* with *kick*, while later on more distantly similar groups of verbs will also 'merge' into more abstract schemas. At the end of the process, children are said to arrive at a completely abstract syntactic schema (for example, for the verb–object combination) in which semantic similarity has no longer a functional role. A very similar developmental process is proposed by Tomasello (2000a, pp. 242 ff), who elaborates on the need for such abstract schemas for generalization. In his approach, semantically based schema formation and schema application are seen as necessary and sufficient conditions for productive syntax, ending a hypothesized initial stage in which verb–specific formulae are 'isolated' from each other and therefore cannot serve for transfer and generalization. He proposes that children create more general and abstract linguistic constructions by extracting the common structure of a set of different verb–specific constructions possessing similar semantics. He gives as an example the verbs *give*, *tell, show, send,* and so on, which share both their semantics and syntax: they share a 'transfer' meaning and also appear in an identical syntactic structure, namely, NP + V + NP + NP. The outcome of this process is, according to his hypothesis, an abstract ditransitive construction possessing the prototypical semantics of 'transfer', which then can be used as a template for the generation of ditransitive sentences with novel verbs possessing the same semantics.

Although present-day theoretical linguistics does not encourage us to look for processes of semantically based abstraction during development, and, moreover, we already know (see Chapter 2) that in fact item-to-item transfer and facilitation is a robust process for going beyond individual syntactic formulae, it is not logically impossible that children do create semantically homogeneous local abstractions of the kind described above, even if they are inefficient in the long run. The empirical question is whether they actually do so.

We will test the two hypotheses one against the other: on the one side, the claim that children's syntactic system is completely lexical, and that transfer and generalization ignore semantic similarity and concentrate on similarity of form only; and the alternative, that children do form generalizations or categorial schemas with homogeneous semantics, in order to use them in transfer and in other circumstances where they need to go beyond individual formulae. In particular, the 'semantic schema'-type theories thus make a quite precise prediction that should be possible to check on the basis of developmental data. First, according to such theories, the degree of semantic similarity between verbs needs to be high in order for schema formation and schema application to be possible, at least at the start of this process. Second, semantic similarity can only be of use when a child has already learned, in an item-based manner, the mini-grammars of a number of verbs with similar semantics, such as the 'transfer' set *give, tell, show,* and *send* mentioned above. At the least, two different verbs are required for semantics-based abstraction or 'merger' to apply. In addition, transfer and facilitation based on semantic similarity can only apply to novel items that are very similar in meaning to some already-learned ones, as the abstract schemas themselves are defined for quite specific semantic content such as 'transfer', 'ingestion', or 'physical assault'.

'Semantic schema'-type theories thus make a quite precise prediction regarding the developmental preconditions for schema formation and application in young children, in terms of the composition of their already-learned lexically specific word combinations. Semantically based transfer and facilitation is expected to occur when and only when the children's inventory of item-specific schemas includes two or more earlier-learned items to which the current item is closely related semantically.

4.3 Developmental evidence: no semantic effects in generalization and transfer

There are three kinds of possible evidence for a functional role of semantics in syntactic development. First, demonstration of semantically based generalization of syntactic formulae to novel verbs in the absence of overt modelling. Second, evidence for naturally occurring semantically based overgeneralization of a given syntactic pattern to novel items. Third, demonstration of semantic effects in naturally occurring transfer of learning.[8] We shall review these in order.

4.3.1 Generalization without semantic similarity

In recent years several training and priming studies have been carried out in which young children were tested for generalization of syntactic formats to unmodelled items. Unfortunately, in most, the semantics of the training and the testing verbs was equated, probably to ensure that semantics-based transfer, if it exists, can indeed take place. There has been one study in which the semantic similarity of the training and testing verbs was not identical (Abbot-Smith *et al.*, 2004) and this is our sole source of information on semantic effects on generalization. This study (and the one with which it is contrasted, Childers and Tomasello, 2001) employed a method of priming while attempting to elicit unmodelled transitive sentences from children.

In a priming experiment focusing on the transitive construction, children are trained with a large number of transitive sentences using familiar verbs. It has been found that such a training increases significantly 21/2-year-old children's tendency to use the transitive construction with novel nonce verbs, which have not been introduced to them in this construction but, rather, either in intransitive or in passive sentences. Childers and Tomasello (2001) carried out a typical study of this kind, and in this study the majority of training verbs and all testing verbs expressed caused motion (such as dropping or rolling). After presenting the experimental group with 576 transitive sentences using 16 (real) verbs, they tested them on the novel nonce verbs, and found that the children produced a significantly larger number of transitive sentences with these than a control group who did not undergo training.

Although the results show that training helps to elicit unmodelled syntax from young children, the results do not demonstrate that the effect has to do with the semantic similarity of the training and testing verbs. For such a demonstration, the results need to withstand the test of a control condition not included in the original study, in which the semantics of the training and testing verbs is not closely related. Such a control study has been performed by Abbot-Smith *et al.* (2004). In the new study the testing verbs were from a different semantic class than the training verbs. While the training verbs were verbs of caused-motion (such as dropping or rolling) as were most verbs in the previous study, the testing verbs were nonce verbs signifying light emission and sound emission.

Despite the semantic difference between training and testing verbs (and a much lower number of training sentences), the Abbot-Smith *et al.* study found the same amount of facilitation in the 2½ year olds' production of transitive constructions without prior modelling as did the Childers and Tomasello study; about twice as many children in both studies used the nonce verbs in the unmodelled transitive (S)VO construction after training (with a nouns-only set of sentences) than did children without the training.

The positive results of training without close semantic similarity and the lack of an effect for the degree of similarity in the two studies make it questionable that semantic analogy plays a decisive role in the facilitation effected by the enhanced input. In particular, it is unlikely that the transfer process was schema formation, a procedure that requires, according to Morris *et al.* (2000) and Tomasello (2000a), that the semantics of the training and testing verbs be closely related (see Section 4.2 above). Instead, the results suggest that, just like transfer of learning in natural conditions, the priming effect of these experiments was triggered by similarity of form and not of semantics.[9]

4.3.2 Overgeneralization on semantic basis: a late phenomenon

A second type of evidence sometimes said to exist for semantic effects in syntactic development are overgeneralizations, whether the unmodelled frames are employed creatively or due to mistakes in the learned argument structure of lexical items.

After systematic examination of this phenomenon in the context of a longitudinal study of her two daughters' speech, Bowerman (1982) concluded that syntactic overgeneralization errors are a late phenomenon, occurring in her two girls as late as a year to a year and a half after they had attained a level of adult competence in the expression of argument structure constructions. Before mastery of the basic syntactic patterns, and in particular during the initial period of learning we are interested in, she did not find evidence of analogy or generalization from one pattern to another. Bowerman proposed that patterns such as VO are learned on a word-by-word, piecemeal basis for each verb, up to the attainment of adult competence by about 2;6. Only a year later do children start to generalize from one pattern to another on a semantic basis, this development bringing in its course overgeneralization errors. The implications are that semantics-based generalization (and overgeneralization) belongs to a different developmental stage than the early phases of syntactic development and such processes do not serve children in the acquisition of the basic syntax of their language. It is beyond the scope of the present work to speculate about the processes bringing about late overgeneralization and it is sufficient for us to note that they appear to be irrelevant for our concerns.

4.3.3 Transfer of learning without semantic similarity

The last piece of evidence regarding semantic effects in acquisition asks whether such effects can be found in transfer and facilitation of learning. The answer appears to be negative. Two recent studies (Ninio, 2005a,b) demonstrated that semantic similarity has no role in naturally occurring transfer of learning. The studies concentrated on two core grammatical relations in nominative-accusative languages, namely, the verb–direct object and the verb–indirect object (VI) relations.[10]

Transfer of learning without semantic similarity in the acquisition of the verb–direct object combination

Ninio (2005a) tested the hypothesis of semantic similarity underlying transfer of learning on the first verbs in the VO pattern in the spontaneous speech of a group of Hebrew-speaking children. Twenty children were observed longitudinally, the observations starting before the children began to produce any VO combinations. The parents also kept diaries, to supplement the observational data. Each child's first sentences with the first six different verbs in the VO pattern were tested for transfer and facilitation of learning by computing the relevant learning curve, as well as categorized for the thematic role of the direct object (direct object). Under the hypothesis that syntactic facilitation is based on semantic similarity, a positive correlation was predicted between the presence of semantic similarity among the direct objects and facilitation of learning. The alternative hypothesis was that no such correlation will be found, namely, that syntactic facilitation will be independent of the degree of semantic similarity among the items. Hence, the first six items in a VO constructions could facilitate each other or be insular and unrelated to each other, but their facilitation or lack of it will not be correlated with the degree of semantic similarity to each other.

Sentences with the first six verbs in the VO pattern were produced within 3.41 months on the average (SD 1.79; range 0.90–6.93 months). There was facilitation of learning, as evidenced by accelerating learning curves.

A power-law function gave a better fit to the learning curves than a linear (non-accelerating) function; the comparison of the fit of the two functions by paired t-test revealed a highly significant difference ($t(19) = 5.21$, $P < 0.001$). It is important to note that the power-law function has exactly the same degrees of freedom as the linear one, as the log-log transformation of the former produces a straight line. The comparison of degree of fit is a fair one, and does not give an advantage to the power-law trendline.

Next, the thematic roles of the direct objects were categorized, using an eight-category system derived from Levin (1985).[11] The following categories were used (Hebrew examples in parenthesis): Affected Object = Patient (*shavar* 'break', *mila* 'fill'); Moved Object = Theme (*sam* 'put', *heziz* 'move'); Transferred Object and Object of Desire (*natan* 'give', *laqax* 'take', *raca* 'want', *carik* 'need'); Transferred Information (*amar* 'say', *her'a* 'show'); Object of Result = Effected Object (*asa* 'make/do', *bana* 'build'); Ingested Entity (*akal* 'eat', *shata* 'drink'); Object of Perception and Cognition (*raa* 'see', *shama* 'hear', *yada* 'know', *lamad* 'learn'); Contacted Object and Object of Emotion (*hika* 'hit', *nisheq* 'kiss', *ahav* 'love', *sana* 'hate').

For each child, the number of different semantic roles for the first six direct objects was counted[12]. The mean in the sample was 3.95 (SD 0.76). None of the children had less than three different semantic roles among their first six VO types, and the majority had four or more. The large number of different semantic categories implies that each was represented by only one or two exemplars in a given child's speech. On the average, there were 1.57 different VOs per semantic category (SD 0.31), less than two per category.

Usually, in theories of category formation it is assumed that an abstract schema is based at least on two different exemplars. In order to check if it was possible that later-learned direct objects relied on a schema built on two previously learned similar direct objects, the number of semantically similar antecedents were counted for each candidate direct object (which were the third, fourth, fifth or sixth by a given child). There were 80 later-learned direct objects in the whole corpus; of these, only four (5%) were preceded by two semantically similar antecedents. The other 76 (95%) were not preceded by two or more semantically similar antecedents. Namely, the basic conditions for the formation of abstract schemas based on semantic similarity do not exist in the set of verb–object types comprising children's first six VO constructions. Although we observed facilitation among the first six VO types, this cannot be a consequence of the formation of general schemas or 'mergers' of mini-grammars on a semantic basis. The amount of semantic similarity among the first six types of VO constructions is too low to support

Table 4.1 Udi's sentences with his first six verbs with a DO, with classification of the direct objects' semantic role

Sentence	Gloss	Semantic role of direct object
Roce et-ze	'want this'	Transferred/desired object
Lo roce lishon	'don't want to-sleep'	
Lo roce bakbuk	'don't want bottle'	
Roce laredet	'want to-get-down'	
Roce hakadur	'want the-ball'	
Roce lishtot	'want to-drink'	
Lehoci ecem	'to-take-out bone'	Moved object
Lehoci kof	'to-take-out monkey'	
Lehoci et-ze	'to-take-out this'	
Ima, lehoci madaf	'Mommy, to-take-out shelf'	
Lehoci et-ze madaf	'to-take-out this shelf'	
Liftoax et-ze	'to-open this'	Affected object
Liftoax et shulxan	'to-open table'	
Liftoax, Ima, ze	'to-open, Mommy, this'	
David, tiftax kadur	'David, open ball'	
Tetate et-ze	'sweep this'	Affected Object
Lo torid Udi	'don't take-down Udi'	Moved Object
Udi lishtot mic	'Udi to-drink juice'	Ingested Object

Reproduced from Table 4 of Ninio, A. (2005a). Testing the role of semantic similarity in syntactic development. *Journal of Child Language*, with permission from Cambridge University Press.

a facilitatory process based on semantic commonality among the different VO types.

As an example of the analysis, Table 4.1 presents one child's first six verbs with a direct object. The sentences were produced by child no. 8, hereafter referred to by the pseudonym Udi. For each verb the table presents all the different VO sentences recorded with that verb (excluding exact repetitions) before Udi went on to produce a VO combination with a novel verb. This child generated his first six types of direct objects with four different general semantic roles.

Udi's sentences demonstrate that thematic roles of the kind we coded for, incorporate a very liberal criterion of semantic similarity. In fact, the degree of semantic similarity coded for in this study is considerably more distant than the close semantic similarity deemed necessary by Morris *et al.* (2000) and others for the semantics-based abstraction process at its initial stages. Had we adopted a more detailed semantic coding system only acknowledging close semantic similarity, none of Udi's first six types of direct objects would have fallen into a common category. There is no close semantic similarity between sweeping the floor and opening up a table-top, although in our coding system both are coded as operations on a Patient or Affected Object. There is no close semantic similarity between extracting a bone from a piece of chicken and being taken down from a chair to the floor, although in our coding system both are seen as operations on a Theme or Moved Object. In other words, coding for thematic roles rather than semantic fields maximized the chances that children's early-produced direct objects be seen as semantically homogeneous, and made it more likely that the hypothesis of semantic schema-formation be accepted. Despite the liberal coding, the hypothesis was rejected.

Another and somewhat weaker method of examining a possible semantic factor is to see if the number of different semantic categories in a child's first six verb–object combinations predicted the amount of facilitation of production in that child's development. However, the correlation between number of semantic categories and the exponent (i.e., slope) of the power-law function was not significant ($r = -0.24$, d.f. $= 18$, $P > 0.05$, NS). Namely, it was not the case that children who produced more direct objects, which were semantically related among their first six VO types, accelerate their acquisition faster than children who learned a set of unrelated semantic roles for the first six direct objects.

Thus, the prediction that facilitation would rely on semantic similarity is not supported by the data. There is facilitation among the first six verbs in VO, but it cannot rely on similarity in the general semantics of the first six direct objects, at least not in the way semantic roles of direct objects are usually conceptualized, such as Patient vs. Theme, or Affected Object vs. Object of Result and so forth. It is even less likely that the observed facilitation can be attributed to the similarity in the specific lexical meaning of the verbs, as informal examination of the participant verbs revealed that the first verbs the children learned in the VO pattern were quite unrelated semantically, as we saw above for child no. 8, and see Note 7.

Transfer of learning without semantic similarity in the acquisition of the verb–indirect object combination

The second study mentioned above, namely, Ninio (2005b), strongly replicated these finding for another grammatical relation. The study examined the first 10 different verbs in the VI combination, produced by 14 children acquiring Hebrew as their first language. In all 14 children the learning curves accelerated. The mean fit of an accelerating power-function was $R^2 = 0.93$ of the variance (SD $= 0.06$) while the mean fit of a linear function was $R^2 = 0.79$ of the variance (SD $= 0.13$). On average the power function explained 14.3%

more of the variance than the linear function (SD $= 0.08$); the difference highly significant by paired two-tailed t-test ($t(12) = 7.00$, $P < 0.001$).

The children's VI were coded for thematic relations using a 10-category coding system, plus nine idiosyncratic items, based on the semantic categories listed for indirect-dative objects (IOs) in Berman (1982b), Borer and Grodzinsky (1986), and Glinert (1989, pp. 148–163). All the children expressed at least four different semantic roles by their first 10 IO types, and most expressed six or more (mean 5.79, SD $= 1.25$). On the average, there were 1.72 different IOs per semantic category, less than two per category. Of nine second- to tenth-learned IOs in the VI construction, only a mean of 4.21 (46.8%) had one or more antecedents in the form of an IO belonging to the same thematic category, while 4.79 (53.2%) of these later-learned IOs were not preceded by any semantically similar antecedent. Namely, the majority of later-learned IOs were without a single semantic antecedent among previously learned ones. In addition, a correlation coefficient was computed between number of different semantic roles of the first 10 indirect objects and the estimate of acceleration in the graphs, namely, the slope or exponent of the power-law function. As in the VO study, this correlation was not significant ($r(12) = 0.28$, $p > 0.05$).

It is clear that semantic similarity cannot, by itself, account for the accelerated learning seen in the learning curves. However, it is still possible it plays at least some part in the transfer and facilitation observed in the acquisition process. As we saw above, about 47% of all later-learned IOs in each child's series of 10 did have some semantically similar antecedents in previously produced combinations. The question was, could these items account for the acceleration of the learning curves? In order to test for this possibility, all IOs with semantic antecedents were removed from the series and the remaining items once again tested for acceleration. The argument was that if the similarity in the formal pattern of verb–IO constructions, regardless of their semantics, is a sufficient basis for transfer of learning, the remainder-graph will also show acceleration. If, however, similarity in the formal pattern among the VI items is not enough to feed facilitation of learning, the remainder-graph will not accelerate, demonstrating that the acceleration in the original learning curve should be attributed to the semantically similar items it contained.

The results of this analysis showed that the deletion of items possessing semantic antecedents had a negligible effect on the learning curves. Among the items without semantic antecedents, the mean fit of an accelerating power-function was $R^2 = 0.92$ of the variance (SD $= 0.04$), while the mean fit of a linear function was $R^2 = 0.85$ of the variance (SD $= 0.12$); the difference was highly significant ($t(12) = 3.15$, $P < 0.01$). Namely, when items with semantic antecedents are removed from the series, the learning curves remain accelerating, indicating that the acceleration in the original learning curve did not originate in the semantically similar items it contained. Instead, it is similarity in the formal pattern among VI sentences that in all probability underlies the observed transfer and facilitation of learning.

Transfer of learning without semantic grouping in the acquisition of the subject–verb–direct object combination

A common method of hypothesis testing in computational disciplines is to compare functions, curves and other mathematical objects obtained under differing assumptions on the basis of the same set of empirical data. This method was applied to the issue of semantic grouping in the acquisition process. We examined the acquisition of the SVO (subject–verb–direct object) pattern by Ruti, a child whose learning curve was presented in Chapter 2 (in Figure 2.7), and whose SVO sentences were presented in Table 2.4 of that chapter.

First, we categorized Ruti's first SVO sentence types according to the thematic role of the direct object of the combination, using the category system mentioned above in 'Transfer of learning without semantic similarity in the acquisition of the verb–direct object combination'. This categorization summarizes most of the semantic typing of the SVO sentence as there is a very strong and obvious correlation between the thematic role of the object and the lexical semantics of the verb as well as the semantic category of the subject argument. Table 4.2 presents the sentences with the categorization, sorted by thematic roles and age.

Figure 4.1 presents the learning curve of Ruti's SVO, with each point coded for the semantic category of the relevant direct object. The learning curve was fitted with a power-law function which had a very good fit ($R^2 = 0.99$). The exponent of the power-law curve was 17.131. The figure shows clearly that items belonging to the various semantic categories sit in a smooth line along the power-law accelerating curve. We saw in Chapter 2 that when the two girls Travis and Ruti started to generate SVO sentences, their learning slowed down considerably, relative to the pace of producing new VO sentences. For example, at the beginning Travis produced one new verb in the SVO pattern every few weeks, although by then she was already using one or two new verbs in the VO pattern every single day. The difficulty she is showing demonstrates that semantic similarity to already-produced word combinations is insufficient to retain the speed of learning if the syntax is significantly more complicated. Examination of her VO sentences shows that before she started on SVO sentences, she already used direct objects in the thematic roles of Affected object (*Open door*); Moved Object (*Throw da ball*); Transferred Object/Object of Desire (*Bring chair*); Effected Object (*Yaya (draw) mans*); Object of

Table 4.2 Ruti's first 20 different SVO combinations by the thematic role of the DO

Age	Utterance	Gloss
Affected Object = Patient		
1;11.20	Sheima talbish et-ze	that-mommy will-CAUS-wear ACC-this
2;00.00	Ima tikshor et ha-seret	mommy will-tie ACC the-ribbon
2;00.24	Aba tiken et ze	daddy fixed ACC this
2;00.24	Aba hidbik et ze	daddy glued ACC this
2;00.28	Ani mesaderet ze..	I put-in-order (FEM) this
Contacted Object		
2;00.28	Ani axzik et ze	I I-shall-hold ACC this
Effected Object = Object of Result		
1;09.28	Ish ose raas	man makes noise
1;11.27	Aba ciyer ze	daddy drew this
1;11.27	..aba asa cafcefa	daddy made (noise of) horn
2;00.21	Tali carix laasot hakol	Tali needs to-do everything
Ingested Object		
2;00.14	At axalt hakartiv hahu	you ate-2sgf the-popsicle the-that
Moved Object = Theme		
1;11.23	..ani sama ze	I put (FEM) this
Perceived Object		
1;10.11	Ima takri ze	mommy will-read (FEM) this
1;11.23	Ani ekra et-ze	I I-shall-read ACC-this
2;00.11	Ruti lo shomaat shir	Ruti not hear (FEM) (a) song
2;00.18	Ata roe ze ratuv	you see this (is) wet
Transferred or Desired Object		
1;09.00	Shay roce kadur	Shay wants (a) ball
1;11.20	Ima kanta et-ze	mommy bought (FEM) ACC-this
2;00.14	..ani mocet et aba	I find (FEM) ACC daddy
2;00.24	Aba lakax et hamocec sheli	daddy took ACC pacifier my

Perception (*Watch TV*); and Contacted Object (*Touch light*); these are the same thematic roles that she later used in her SVO sentences. The semantic similarity between the VO and the SVO sentences as well as the partial overlap in the syntactic formulae does not suffice to retain the speed of learning of VO for this novel and more complicated three-word composition.

The question we are asking now is whether the SVO pattern is perceived as a separate learning task for groups of sentences that have a different semantics. If it is, we expect the child to start afresh with slow learning each time she faces an SVO sentence with a new type of semantics. Already the smooth graph of Figure 4.1 makes this highly unlikely. We do not see any special discontinuity in the curve when a new semantic symbol appears on the graph; instead, sentences with a new type of semantics fit into the temporal pattern already achieved at that point. Remember that the curve fits the 20 points of this sequence so that it explains 99% of the variance, namely, there is an almost-perfect fit. We wanted, however, to test this hypothesis in a formal manner. To do so, we took apart the 20 SVO sentences into sets with homogeneous semantics. Some sets included only a single sentence (e.g., Ingested Objects); these were ignored in this analysis. The residue consisted of four groups. There were four sentences each with Transferred Objects, Effected Objects and with Perceived Objects, and five with Affected Objects. The examples can be found in Table 4.2 above. Next, we treated the mastery of SVO with each type of thematic role for the direct object as a separate learning task and fitted individual learning curves to the acquisition data. The idea was that if the child starts the acquisition of each syntax-semantics bundle as a separate task, for example in order to generate from it an abstract construction or schema, the slopes or exponents of all the separate learning curve should be very similar, and at the most, the slopes should

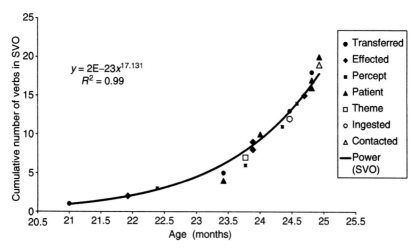

Fig. 4.1 Ruti's learning curve for the first 20 different verbs in the SVO pattern, with semantic categories and a power-law graph fitted. Redrawn from figure 1 of Ninio (1999a). Pathbreaking verbs in syntactic development. *Journal of Child Language*, with permission from Cambridge University Press.

get somehow steeper to account for a minimal amount of inter-schema transfer. Under the hypothesis of separate learning for these semantically homogeneous sets, we expect a very low positive correlation between the age at which the first of the set is acquired and the exponent of the learning curve for the set. All slopes or exponents should be quite similar, resembling the overall slope of the combined curve, which was 17.131.

The alternative hypothesis predicts a very strong correlation between the age of first production of SVO sentences of a particular semantic type and the steepness of the learning curve for that bunch of items. This because the semantic subgroups are considered to form a single SVO set, and the only difference between the subgroups, which is thought to be relevant to the speed of learning is the age at which the first item of the set joins the overall learning curve. The later the emergence of a particular semantics, the more steep the curve should be, as the power-law curve is a sharply accelerating graph and what we are doing is cutting it into segments at differing points of its acceleration.

The results of this analysis are presented in Figure 4.2. All four semantic subsets of the SVO pattern formed accelerating learning curves of their own, but the slopes were very dissimilar. The first-emerging semantic pattern, which was first produced at the age of 21 months (expressing an action on transferred objects), resulted in an exponent of 7.8386 for its four items. The second-emerging pattern (involving effected objects), which began to be produced at about 22 months, resulted in a power-law exponent of 11.886 for its four items. The third pattern (involving objects of perception), starting to be produced at 22.385 months, showed an exponent of 14.125 for its four

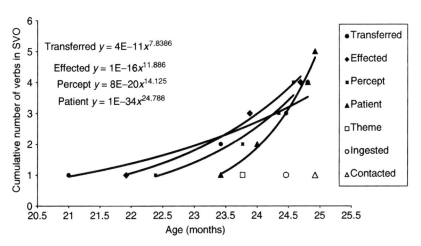

Fig. 4.2 Ruti's first 20 SVO types with individual power-law learning curves fitted to each semantic category.

items. Finally, the pattern involving affected objects (namely, patients) that started at 23.423 months, had a truly high exponent of 24.788 for its five items. The correlation coefficient between age at first production and the exponent of the power-law function was $r = 0.97$. The later-emerging a pattern, the steeper the slope of the learning curve for that group of sentences.

The most obvious explanation for this correlation is statistical. Each subgroup covers a successively higher-placed segment of a single power-law learning curve, thus the slope becomes steeper. When we represent the four segments as separate curves, their power-law exponent reflects the increasing steepness of the overall SVO learning curve from the point of the first-produced item in each group and till the end of the measured development, namely, when the child completed producing 20 different sentences in the SVO pattern. The particular content of the items should be quite irrelevant for the statistical pattern to emerge.

We wanted to be sure that this explanation is correct, and to test it, we predicted that the exponent of these individual learning curves would become steeper in just the same manner whatever the semantics of the items we linked to the first-produced items, as long as these items followed in time the first-produced ones. To test this hypothesis, we used the 'Table of Random Numbers' (the first lines of table 25 in Arkin and Colton, 1950) in order to allocate items (numbered 1–20 by their order of appearance) to semantic subgroups in a random manner. To each 'starting sentence' we added the requisite number of following sentences, so that we ended with the same four- or five-member groups as before, but this time, the verbs were picked without regard to their true semantics. For example, the first sentence with an Effected Object (*Ish ose raash*, 'man makes noise') was provided with the random class-mates *Ima tiqshor et ha-seret* 'mommy will tie the ribbon', *..ani mocet et aba* 'I find daddy' and *Aba laqax et hamocec sheli* 'daddy took my pacifier' that in reality have Affected and Transferred objects.

Figure 4.3 presents the learning curves of these artificial groups in which the first item is the true one but the following ones are randomly assigned.

As we can see in the figure, we got four accelerating curves quite similar to the real ones. When we compared the mean fit to the power-law function by comparison with the fit to a linear function, we got about the same difference: in the true data set, the mean fit to the power-law function over the four groups was $R^2 = 0.9825$, while the fit to the linear function was $R^2 = 0.8996$, a difference of 0.0829. In the randomly assembled groups, the fit of the power-law had a mean of $R^2 = 0.9083$, the fit of the linear function had a mean of $R^2 = 0.8461$, a difference of 0.0621. Namely, the acceleration of the random learning curves was not noticeably different from that of the true curves.

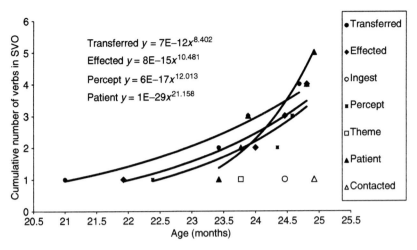

Fig. 4.3 Ruti's first 20 SVO types with randomly assigned semantic categories and individual power-law learning curves fitted to each semantic category.

Lastly, we tabulated the exponents of the four bogus learning curves and found that they, too, got gradually larger in quite the same manner as in the real sets. The first-emerging transferred object group had a slope of 8.402, the second-emerging effected object group had an exponent of 10.481; the third-emerging percept group had an exponent of 12.013 and the last-emerging group with affected objects had one of 21.158 (see also in Figure 4.3). We then computed the correlation coefficient between age of first emergence and the power-law exponent in the random set and found that it was $r = 0.94$. This is almost identical to the true value we got before, which was $r = 0.97$. Namely, we succeeded in reproducing the gradually steepening learning curves for the four subgroups with randomly assembled items, despite their semantic heterogeneity. The conclusions are that in most likelihood the semantic subgroups we isolated from the overall SVO set were not in fact treated as separate learning tasks by the child; rather, they were part of a single continuous learning task in which the learning of SVO formulae got relatively easier with each new verb, hence the accelerating power-law learning curve. The learning task apparently consists of mastering the SVO pattern for 20 different verbs with 20 different individual semantic roles for the direct objects.

We performed the same analysis with Ruti's VO sentences as well as Travis's VO and SVO sentences, with similar results. There is no evidence that, during the learning process, children group items with similar semantics, and that the latter especially facilitate each others' acquisition. Syntactic acquisition appears to be a learning process in which semantic similarity is irrelevant, and all items are treated to the same facilitation. The only thing relevant to how fast a child progressed in mastering the VO or SVO pattern for a new verb is how many verbs she learned already in the same pattern. The facilitation strictly follows a power-law curve, a single one for the first 20 verbs, and the theoretical subgrouping to semantically homogeneous subsets is an exercise that does not lead us to the true learning process.

The results of the studies reviewed above suggest that facilitation of learning of early syntax is not mediated by semantic similarity, and in particular, it is highly unlikely that the facilitation we have observed is the result of children's generating semantically defined abstract or general schemas for combining verbs with their objects. This leaves us with the only other dimension in which the various VO-, VI-, and SVO-type sentences are similar to each other, and that is their syntax. It seems that learning to express some verbs with their subjects or objects facilitates the learning of other verbs in such constructions, regardless of the semantics of the verb–subject or verb–object combination. Children seem to register and make use of similarity of form.

4.4 Conclusions: children utilize similarity of form to organize the process of acquisition

Our review of the developmental evidence found no role for semantic similarity in early syntactic development. The hypothesis that children create abstract combinatory schemas with narrow homogeneous semantics, gradually merging them into schemas with wider semantics and ultimately into an abstract formal rule applying to an abstract form-class was found to be incorrect and not supported by empirical evidence.

We saw that children are efficient learners and do not follow the blind alley of temporary semantic generalizations. It is a sound linguistic generalization that syntax is autonomous of semantics; syntactic development only follows the ecologically given.

This conclusion strengthens the one reached in Chapter 3 according to which children do not form abstractions in general during syntactic development. Instead, they learn an item-specific grammar in which items relate to each other by task-relevant similarity.

The developmental results signal that similarity of form and not of meaning is the organizer of the internalized syntactic system, just as it is of the syntactic module of theoretical linguistics. The internalized syntactic system appears to be a syntactic lexicon. In the following chapter, we shall investigate in greater detail its nature.

Notes

1   Among the central texts on similarity in learning are Thorndike (1931), Osgood (1949), Gick and Holyoak (1983), Ross (1984), Novick (1988), and Singley and Anderson (1989).

2   Subjecthood and objecthood are graded categories, with some exemplars possessing more of the characteristic properties of the concept than others. Keenan (1975, 1976, p. 312) says subject and object are multifactor concepts, while Givón (1997, p. 92) talks about grammatical roles having a 'basket of properties'. Ross (1972, 1973) in particular has emphasized the unclear boundaries between grammatical categories, inventing the term 'the category squish'. These categories are notoriously difficult to define with any rigidity, and discrete classification can only be achieved by ignoring evidence of gradation.

3   For example, Payne (1997, p. 131) provides the following examples of the diversity of English subject semantics:

> 1. (a) George opened the door.
> subject = agent
> (b) This key opened the door.
> subject = instrument
> (c) The wind opened the door.
> subject = force
> (d) The door was opened by the wind.
> subject = patient

4   The number of distinct verb classes identified by Levin (1993) is a result of selective choice among the morphosyntactic features on which the classification is based. Levin's goal is to identify the linguistically relevant meaning components that determine the verb's behaviour. She sets up verb classes with distinctive behaviour with respect to diathesis alternations, and she expects this class will be semantically coherent, and its members will share at least some aspect of meaning, or have meaning components in common. However, Levin points out that a consistent application of this strategy generates, in English, a very large number of lexical categories, in fact, as many as there are verbs:

> In this book, I have chosen a level of classification characterized by interesting clustering of verbs that should further the isolation of meaning components [which trigger the linguistic behaviors]. The classification system does not take into account every property of every verb, since such a system would be liable to consist of classes having only one member, a state of affairs that would not provide much insight into the overall structure of the English verb lexicon.
>
> Levin (1993, p. 18)

5 Considerations of efficiency and potential economy of learning were among the major reasons that authorities such as Brown (1973, p. 122) and Bowerman (1976, p. 158) proposed that children form semantic schemas rather than learn piecemeal the position associated with each semantic role of each verb. However, *pace* Brown, children cannot in fact be spared the need to learn the valency pattern of each verb separately, as the amount of unpredictability in the system is too high, and see, for example, Table 2.6.

6 The same creed directed my objection in Chapter 1 to the model of 'statistical learning' that did not obey the so-called principle of structure-dependency (Chomsky, 1971).

7 Such suggestions have been made, for instance, by Schlesinger (1971), Bowerman (1973b, 1982), Brown (1973), Bloom *et al.* (1975), Braine (1976), MacWhinney (1982), Pinker (1984, 1989), Goldberg (1995, 1999), Tomasello (1998, 2000a), Dabrowska (2000), and Morris *et al.* (2000).

8 One of the major methods believed to reveal semantic schemas underlying children's speech involves looking for utterances expressing the same kind of semantic relations that emerge at about the same time in the child's speech (Brown, 1973, p. 142; Bowerman, 1973a,b, 1976; Schlesinger, 1974; Bloom *et al.*, 1975; Braine, 1976; Greenfield and Smith, 1976). The principle was outlined by Schlesinger (1974): 'If two items in a list of possible relations begin to appear in children's speech simultaneously, and if they use the same syntactic patterns to express these, there is good reason to regard them as belonging to one and the same underlying relational concept' (p. 136).
If, instead, utterances expressing the same semantic relations emerge not at once but sequentially, it is concluded that the putative relational category has no psychological reality for the child (Bowerman, 1976, p. 148).

A closer examination of this argument reveals it to be of questionable validity. The possession of schematic rule does not necessary imply that the speaker will produce different types of sentences with the help of this rule simultaneously. Let us assume, for example, that a child does possess a schematic rule for producing word combinations expressing the relation of ingestion to ingested food or drink; it is still possible that in a certain week or fortnight she will not be very interested in talking about many different kinds of food consumption, hence generating in this period only one or two different word combinations expressing the relevant semantic relation. Nor is it logically impossible that children generate their sentences with item-specific formulae, but one of these serves to facilitate the production of similar ones on an item-to-item basis, resulting in a concentration of similar items emerging within a short period of time. *Pace* Schlesinger, the form of internalized rules (schematic, item-specific) and the temporal parameters of starting to use the same type of syntax with different lexical items are independent issues, and one does not illuminate the other.

9   Another experimental study using older children (4 year olds) also failed to show significant effect of semantics on generalization of syntactic patterns to nonce verbs (Pinker *et al.*, 1987, p. 236). In this study, children were trained with the passive of some nonce verbs, then tested on their willingness to generalize the passive to other nonce verbs of a different semantic class. There was no significant difference between generalization to novel action verbs or to stative verbs, the children willing to generalize the unmodelled passive to both types of verbs.

10 The differentiation between core and oblique grammatical relations is equivalent to the distinction between complements and adjuncts. In grammatical theories acknowledging a layered structure to the clause such as Role and Reference Grammar (Foley and Van Valin, 1984) or Relational Grammar (Perlmutter and Postal, 1974), the number of core arguments of a verb is determined by its valency and it is a direct corollary of its lexical semantics. Core grammatical relations, such as the subject, direct object, and indirect object in accusative/nominative languages and the absolutive and ergative in ergative languages, are said to be abstract structural relationships that do not have precise correlations with semantics, pragmatics, or any other aspect of the complements' meaning (Andrews, 1985). Formally, core relations tend to be direct (unmarked for case) rather than prepositional, but this is not an absolute universal and there are many languages in which core relations are also case-marked. In languages where core arguments are mostly unmarked, such as in English, oblique dependents of the verb tend to adjuncts and not core arguments, but some obliques are nevertheless idiosyncratic core complements of verbs, such as the object of *rely on* and so forth, mentioned in Section 3.1.

11 Levin (1985) divides the English transitive verb lexicon into about 20 groups of verbs classified according to major differences in the semantic roles of the subject and direct object arguments. Among these, about eight are represented in children's early speech. This categorization makes all the distinctions among the semantic roles of the direct object elements that are considered crucial in the linguistics literature. For instance, Levin distinguishes between Affected Objects and Objects of Result (or Effected Objects), the former entities that exist prior to the described action and

are seriously affected by it while the latter do not exist prior to the action but rather, are created by it (Lyons, 1968, p. 439). Similarly, the distinction she makes between Patients and Themes is seen as crucial: Patients are seriously changed by the action in their state or condition, e.g., get crushed or chopped, while Themes are merely moved around but not otherwise affected (Van Valin, 1993, pp. 39–43). There are category systems with narrower thematic categories than hers, for instance, Dixon (1991) proposed that transitive verbs form at least 72 different, semantically distinct subgroups. However, Levin's classes appear to represent the minimal level of detail necessary to tap the syntactically relevant semantic differences among direct objects, and, importantly, her system includes all the distinctions among types of Hebrew direct objects mentioned by Berman (1978) and by Glinert (1989).

12   The first six different verbs for each child in the VO pattern in the order they were produced are to be found in the appendix of Ninio (2005a).

5

The growth of syntax

5.1 **The language web**

In the previous chapters we consolidated a view of syntactic development as a process consisting of the learning of lexical items together with their semantic valency and its syntactic expression in multiword utterances. As this type of knowledge is lexical-specific, it is probably self-evident that it is learned from the linguistic environment of the child, namely, from the parents and other adults whom the child hears using his native language. However, the precise role of the environment in syntactic development is an open question. Some authors believe that children develop their syntactic knowledge as autonomous agents, almost completely independent of the linguistic environment; their development is like the reinvention of syntax rather than the adoption of adults' knowledge (Lock, 1980; Pinker, 1994; Gleitman and Newport, 1995). The adult's role is restricted to the provision of some minimal amount of evidence on the type of language the child is surrounded with and with exemplars of words of the language; the child's own mind does the rest. The child—in a very old simile—is like a linguist, forming hypotheses about the language she is learning and its rules, checking them on the linguistic input. The linguistic input—the language spoken to the child and around her—and the context in which this language is packaged for the child, are seen as mostly irrelevant for the course of learning, with the child's own learning processes providing the pace and the ordering. As long as the linguistic environment is not too pathological and it provides the minimal data necessary for the child's hypothesis-testing needs, its precise features are largely immaterial as such for the learning process. In this conceptualization, language is already 'inside' the child, and the role of the acquisition process is merely to make the dormant information available and precision-set, until it is a good replica of the language spoken by others around the child.

Others see children learning syntax by a process of internalization that is crucially dependent on the linguistic input and its features. The environment is seen as an independent force impacting on the child's mind; the child, a passive learning machine reacting to the stimuli provided by the environment by various information-processing reactions such as memory storage, distributional analysis, induction of regularities, and so on. These processes are sensitive to quantitative features of the input, so that the order of acquisition is mostly determined by the items' input frequency. In such impact-type conceptualization of the relationship between the child and the environment, the child has basically very little choice in what he or she will learn, and especially, when. The child is at the mercy of the objective amount of stimulation he or she receives from the input, or the objective distributional patterns existing in it, so much that even the qualitative features of the input (such as relative complexity of different items) are of secondary importance, if any, for determining the course of acquisition. Representative studies with an underlying impact-conception of syntactic learning are, for example, Allen (1997), Gomez and Gerken (1999), Seidenberg and MacDonald (1999), and Theakston et al. (2004; and see also the references listed in Note 16 of Chapter 1). In this view the rules of language are perceived as existing somewhere 'outside', in some objective space, and the child is seen as gradually internalizing them, until his or her cognitive system contains a good replica of the language 'out there'. The child might be an active agent constructing his own knowledge, but he has little choice over the construction process; that is basically under the control of the input. Such approaches have neo-behaviouristic features, as they emphasize the quantitative and deterministic factors of the learning process and, at the same time, downplay the role of social interaction in the acquisition process.

The argument between the two approaches has long reached an impasse. However, there is a third possibility not yet tried out to which we shall turn now. The source of this novel model is Complexity Theory—a discipline that explores the behaviour and characteristics of complex systems.[1] Language undoubtedly qualifies as a complex system,[2] and it pays off to approach its acquisition with methods and viewpoints originating in Complexity Theory.

In the following chapter, we shall develop a conceptualization of the relationship between children and their linguistic environment emerging from Complexity Theory. We shall start by establishing that language is a complex network, consisting of linguistic items (such as words with their semantic and syntactic valency) as well as speakers who produce words and sentences when they speak. Next, we shall examine the relationship between children and the linguistic network consisting of language items and their adult speakers, and arrive at a conclusion that differs from previous conceptualizations. According to our model, children do not reinvent the linguistic network, nor do they internalize it. Instead, when children begin to produce words of their own, they link into the linguistic network, becoming part of the system. Indeed, children acquiring language are just like new users linking into the World-Wide Web (WWW): by linking into the Web, users become part of it. As we shall see, this conceptualization provides new answers to old questions such as what determines the order of acquisition.

5.1.1 The language environment as a complex system

Let us imagine the language environment from the point of view of young children faced with the task of learning to speak. The children are confronted with an intricate and multilayered complex network. It consists of linguistic units of many different types and sizes, be it words, sentences, phonemes, morphemes, intonation patterns, stress patterns, and more, with diverse relationships among them.[3] It also consists of speakers, linked to the linguistic units by the act of producing them. It is a dynamic, evolving, ever-changing network. The experience of the children must be very similar to that of new users of the WWW, facing the huge network for the first time and trying to figure out how to get a hold on it.

5.1.2 Networks

It is customary to represent a complex system graphically as a network. A *network* (or *net*) is a graphic notation for representing a system of interconnected entities. It is a directed graph consisting of nodes (also called vertices), which represent the entities, and links (edges, arcs, pointers or connections), which represent relations between the entities (Bondy and Murty, 1976). Less formally, a network is made up of two or more nodes and of links connecting each node to some other nodes, showing that the nodes are related in some way. The nodes might be taken to represent any kind of entity that participates in some relationship, be these words, sets of individuals, or proteins. The nature of the relation is specified by the label on the link and by the direction of the arrow depicting the link. For example, we might picture a person's internalized lexicon as a graph, with nodes representing individual words and labelled links connecting them. Figure 5.1 presents a hypothetical network.

The number of links of a given node is called its *degree*. For directed graphs each node has both an *in-degree* and an *out-degree*. The node's *in-degree* is the number of directional links having the node as their target, and the node's *out-degree* is the number of directional links leaving the node and targeting some other node. As we shall see, the statistical distribution of degrees is a central feature of natural networks.

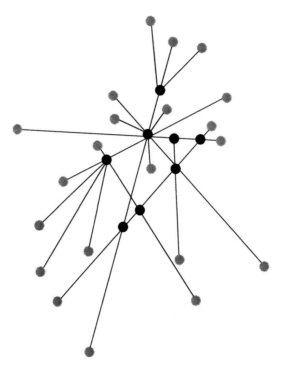

Fig. 5.1 Schematic illustration of a network with two kinds of nodes.

5.1.3 **Skewed frequency distributions in complex systems**

Naturally occurring complex networks possess some generic features, regard-less of what are the items making up the network. Most importantly, they share their *global statistical features*, namely, various quantitative characteristic of the whole system (Watts and Strogatz, 1998; Barabási and Albert, 1999). One of the most important global statistical feature of complex networks—and possibly their defining attribute—is that the number of links connected to a given node is non-random, in fact it is extremely unevenly distributed. A few nodes have a very large number of links, whereas most nodes have only a very few. The distribution of the node connectivities can be best described by a power-law function, or, in some cases, by an exponential function, never by a Gaussian normal distribution. The difference is that unlike a bell-shaped normal distribution, a power-law distribution does not have a maximum at its average value. Rather, in some cases its lowest item is its most frequent one, and the frequencies decrease rather steeply.

Figure 5.2 presents a schematic graph of a power-law distribution, rather similar to the ones actually describing the distribution of in-degrees of large networks. It is clear that the distribution is not symmetrical around its mean.

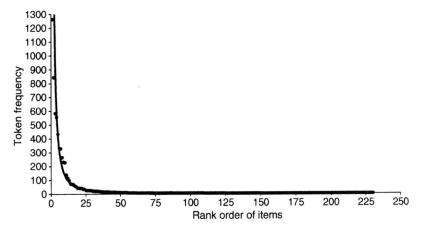

Fig. 5.2 Zipf curve: rank-frequency distribution.

Another difference between the normal distribution and the power-law one is that the latter has a so-called 'fat tail'. If a normal distribution at some early point reaches zero frequency because the phenomenon has an absolute limit and cut-off point (for instance, there are simply no humans who are taller than 4 metres), a power-law distribution seems to reach out to infinity with non-negligible frequencies, namely, with an above-zero likelihood of extreme values. Apparently, complex networks evolve to possess such a skewed distribution of their connectivities.

The extremely skewed distribution of links or degrees in a network means that no node can be taken to represent the scale of the system (like the mean value can in a symmetrical, bell-shaped, normal distribution). In principle, such a distribution has infinite variance and has no stable mean. Barabási and Albert (1999) dubbed networks having a power-law distribution of degrees 'Scale-Free Networks', to connect them to phenomena possessing a fractal geometry (such as ferns or coastlines) that have no definitive scale; fractals follow a power law as they reduce in size by a fixed ratio. In addition, many other natural phenomena, as diverse as the population of cities (Zipf, 1972[1949]) and the amplitude of earthquakes (Gutenberg and Richter, 1944), are scale-free, namely, exhibit power-law distributions, which is taken as an indication that they are the produce of some complex system. In current usage, people talk about networks being scale-free; this is a synonym to their obeying a power-law.[4,5]

Studies have shown that networks formed by words—connected by various different linguistic relationships—exhibit the global statistical features characteristic of complex networks. Syntactic, semantic, and phonological networks were found to be scale-free (Ferrer i Cancho and Solé, 2001; Steyvers and Tenenbaum, 2005; Vitevitch, 2005).

In addition, the best-known treatment of the scale-free statistical feature of the language network, namely, Zipf's law, maps words' frequency of use. We shall elaborate on this subject in the next section.

5.1.4 Zipf's law

It is a very old finding, and one that has the status of a universal law, that if we take a very large text and rank the words in order of their frequency of use, we get a severely skewed distribution, with a few very frequent items and very many infrequent ones. Formally, when the frequency of words is plotted as a function of their rank-order in the vocabulary, the resultant graph follows a regime close to power-law. Figure 5.2 presents a Zipf curve plotting the token frequency of words in a large speech corpus, ordered from the most frequent to the least frequent. The details of this graph will be given in Section 5.3.1 where it is repeated as Figure 5.4.

The law connecting rank and frequency in a power-law function is the Zipf–Mandelbrot law (Zipf, 1965[1935]; Mandelbrot, 1966).[6,7] This law actually applies to most large sets of items that form a complex system, but it was very early on established regarding the behaviour of words used in a text. As we can see in Figure 5.2, word-tokens are distributed non-linearly, with the bulk of the tokens contributed by a few extremely frequent words, followed by a very long tail of rare words.

In order to derive a Zipf curve from a network, we need in this network to represent two kinds of entities: words and speakers. Each word is represented by one kind of node, and each speaker (or speech event), by a node of another kind. Ignoring inter-word relations and only concentrating on directional links between speakers and words they produce, we get the words' frequency of use as the *in-degree* of word nodes.

The graph we have defined is a so-called *bipartite network* (Newman, 2003).[8] In a bipartite graph there are two types of nodes, with links running only between unlike types. In our case, the nodes are linguistic items and speakers; the links are unidirectional, representing the act of production of a certain linguistic item by a speaker. The bipartite graph abstracts out the speaker-item connectivity from the total network, ignoring the inter-item relations as well as the relations among speakers. There are of course many more types of connectivities in the total language network, and most importantly relations of similarity on the basis of shared meaning, sound, and so forth among the language items (see Note 3). In the present analysis we are abstracting one kind of relation—that of speakers to items they produce—out of the complex totality in order to study it in isolation. Figure 5.3 presents a hypothetical bipartite network of words and speakers.

Modelling language as a complex system consisting of both speakers and the words they produce puts in high relief the similarity between language use and surfing in the WWW. A surfer of the WWW is a user of the Web, but, at the same time, he or she is also a component of the Web: it is impossible to use the WWW without linking to it and hence becoming part of the network. Similarly, language is a joint produce of all the people speaking it; emitting some utterance is both using and creating language.

5.1.5 Preferential attachment

In fact, we know quite a lot about the behaviour of new users *vis à vis* the Web. They appear to follow a principle called 'Preferential Attachment' (Barabási and Albert, 1999; Newman, 2003) and link their homepages to pages that are already highly connected, in preference to pages with few or no connections. However, we should not confuse the principle of Preferential Attachment with a gross frequency effect, as the former only works conditional on the users' focus of interest. Indeed, this principle acts rather like the Google search engine's original PageRank algorithm (Brin and Page, 1998): the starting point is always the content users are looking for, and only then do considerations of relative popularity enter into the choice of the preferred websites. A site describing Britney Spears' wardrobe may be among the most popular sites in the year 2005 in terms of absolute number of visits, but Google will not offer it as a first choice to a user looking for information on reasonable apartments for rent in New York City. It may offer the homepage of Craigslist instead, based on its immense relative popularity among apartment seekers. In other words, Web-users' behaviour is first of all guided by the principle of

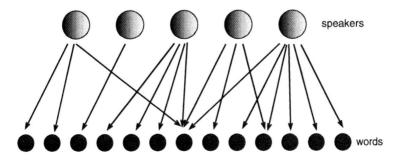

Fig. 5.3 Schematic illustration of a bipartite network of speakers and words.

goal-directedness, and only then, by the principle of preferentially seeking out the most popular site relevant to their concerns.

Preferential Attachment was offered by Barabási and Albert as the process by which the global statistical structure of the Web evolved and by which new users of the Web recreate the same global structure. It is well-established that the links on the WWW (as well as most other complex networks) are not distributed normally in a bell-shaped, symmetrical, Gaussian distribution but rather they are skewed, and obey a power law. According to this model of growth, new users prefer to link to well-established pages on the Web, in fact their choices mirror the already-existing statistical structure of the Web. If new users continue existing trends, the addition of new nodes and new links to the Web does not change the Web's global statistical features. Namely, new nodes that continue to honour the linking preferences of existing nodes in fact behave in a way indistinguishable from the latter.

5.2 Implication for acquisition: learning means linking to the network

Complexity Theory offers a novel conceptualization of language development. Language is a huge complex network, composed of speakers and linguistic items they produce. A young child learning to produce some linguistic item becomes thereby part of the network, establishing himself as yet another speaker node. Children do not reinvent language, nor do they internalize it; they link to it.

In the democratic perspective of complexity, children starting to produce a particular linguistic pattern are like new nodes linking into any complex network, very similar to new users linking into the WWW. The Web is a large network of links and nodes that a new user joins by establishing a node of his own and generating hyperlinks to one or more existing nodes. In the case of linguistic networks, links between speakers and linguistic items are created by the speaker producing a particular linguistic item. The very same analysis applies when we consider the acquisition of the vocabulary, the acquisition of stress patterns, and the acquisition of syntactic constructions. The only difference is that each time a different part of the multifaceted and multilayered complex network is involved.

Syntactic development involves linking to a lexical network. According to our theory, children acquire a lexicalist grammar in which information about the syntactic behaviour of individual predicates (e.g., verbs) is stored in their lexical entry, in the form of valency information. To simplify the discussion, let us assume that syntactic valency of individual verbs is stored in the form of slot-and-frame formulae such as '*eat* X', with X representing some term referring to the semantic object of '*eat*', which is a-thing-to-be-eaten. X can be a word such as '*bananas*' but as syntax is word-based and recursive, the X position can also be filled by a determiner such as '*some*' or '*the*', subsequently getting a dependent of its own such as '*bananas*'. For details of the Merge/ Dependency method of specifying syntactic structure, see Chomsky (1995) or Hudson (1990).

When we want to focus on the acquisition of some particular syntactic construction such as the verb–object (VO) construction, it is useful to talk about a syntactic sub-network which is specific to this construction. The relevant network consists, as usual, of speakers and linguistic items. The speakers are all those adults who produced a VO sentence within the child's hearing. The linguistic items are the verbs that have served in their utterances as the Heads of the VO combinations. We can represent by a node each separate speech event in which somebody uttered a VO sentence, or we can represent each different speaker as a single node, as long as he or she produced at least one VO sentence in the presence of the child.

When the child produces her very first utterance expressing the VO com-bination, such as the typical '*want bottle*', the formal representation of the event is the generation of a new speaker node for the child within the virtual VO network alongside the adults and the other children manning the network, with a link to the word node of '*want*'. Further sentences with different verbs produced by the child generate new links from the child node to other verb elements of the network. Gradually, the child comes to connect to all the different verbs heading VO combinations, fleshing out his own internalized syntactic lexicon.

The bipartite network conceptualization allows a new modelling of the order in which different item-specific formulae are acquired. The order of learning translates to the choice of the linguistic nodes to which the child node links. On this issue, there is a clear prediction based on Complexity Theory. As we saw in Section 5.1.5, according to the theory new nodes linking to an existing network make local decisions as to which existing nodes to link to, in such a way that they maintain the global scale-free structure of the network as they found it. Apparently, they are guided by the principle of Preferential Attachment, preferring already-well connected nodes to less-popular ones (Barabási and Albert, 1999; Newman, 2003).

There is an extremely radical and non-trivial aspect to this conception. Complexity Theory (or at least some versions of it) treats all complex net-works as analogous, and all nodes of the same network as equal. When we say with Complexity Theory that the choice of new items to be acquired by children is being governed by the same principle of Preferential Attachment as the choice of items to use in conversation by adult speakers, we construe the learning situation as one of free choice among available items, equivalent to a competent speaker's choice among items already known to him or her. In effect we say that children make an informed and well-motivated decision what part of the linguistic network to link to next, at any given moment.

The field is accustomed to view the question of the order of acquisition of linguistic items as a different issue from the question what an adult prefers to say, whether in a particular situation or abstracted over different contexts. However, strictly speaking we are asking the exact same question about the child, too, when we deal with the order of acquisition of the child's productive language. We are asking a question not so much about what a child will learn next but about what the child will say next—as our goal is to predict the order of active production of utterances. It is possible that an enquiry into the development of comprehension (as in Golinkoff et al., 1987 or Bavin and Growcott, 1999) would not result in the same answers,[9] and certainly it is inappropriate to apply to it the same conceptualization that we derived from Complexity Theory for production, where a link is defined as the overt expression of an utterance (see also Naigles, 2004). In the strict sense of the word, children are engaged in the same behaviour as adults are when they produce a meaningful utterance in a communicative context. It should not come as a surprise to us that this behaviour is a choice behaviour, similar in its motives and priorities to adults' preferences as to what to say. It is absolutely true that before they can produce the relevant utterance, children need to invest effort into learning to say it, and adults, presumably, already have the relevant piece of knowledge in storage and all they need is retrieve it at any particular moment. However, we do not have any direct information on the learning process and we are attempting to predict not what children will learn next (that happens in the hidden depths of their minds) but what children will say next, out of the relevant repertoire of items. And saying something turns the children into the equals of the adults around them, precisely as Complexity Theory leads us to view them.

In order to make an informed choice among a set of alternatives to learn, children do not need to already *know* these linguistic items but need only to know *of* them. Given that children learn new forms for the expression of some semantic content or communicative intent, in this model we see them scrutinizing adults' speech for ways to express what they wish to say. If, for instance, they want to learn to express a request for an object by a relatively elaborate two-word combination, they might well pass over a rarely-heard expression such as '*hand* (someone) X' and elect to learn a form often used by adults such as '*want* X' instead. However, frequency by itself is meaningless in this learning situation. As with the Google search machine, children will not learn '*want* X' as an expression of refusal, even if it is very frequently heard in absolute terms.

In other words, it is possible to evoke the processes of *semantic matching* (Anderson, 1976) or *pragmatic matching* (Ninio and Wheeler, 1984; Ninio, 1986) in order to explain how do children know which verbs to learn next before already knowing them. Children make their choice on the basis of the content they want to express; they certainly know what they want to say. If they cannot express it to their satisfaction, they turn to the linguistic environment and search for ways to say it. We have to assume that children have a minimal sensitivity for the relative user-frequency of different expressions in their environment and that this guides them in picking the more popular of the available alternatives.

As it was made clear in Section 5.1.5, the principle of Preferential Attachment is not a gross frequency effect as the new participants link to a node (including very popular nodes) only on condition that the link serves their interests. Without being exact copies of the most popular links of the net, such local decisions replicate the spirit of choices made by old nodes of the network (in our case, adult speakers), and therefore the new nodes preserve the statistical features of the network that existed when they joined it.

We can test this theoretical model in quite a direct way, which, as far as I know, has not been attempted before in the complexity literature. This test translates the term *self-organization* to a clear process of continuing to build an existing network with the same power-law features as before. If we take a group of young children just starting to produce some type of linguistic structure and track the gradual development of the syntactic network that they construct as a group, we should find that they literally recreate the global statistical features of the adult network constructed of the same type of linguistic items that they are said to (virtually) link into. We expect some partial overlap of the items they produce with the items most frequently produced by the adults, but by no means a complete overlap, as the children are supposed to be guided by the same principles as the adults and that means following their own separate interests and not some deterministic frequency effect. What we expect to find in the children's evolving network is the very same global statistical features of the adult network they are thereby joining and which they are now supposed to preserve and maintain. In other words, we expect to find that the young children's evolving network will possess the scale-free power-law structure of the adults' network. This structure embodies the very essence of the freedom of choice and self-dictated diversity that characterizes all complex networks, and, in our model of development, also characterizes children's acquisition of syntax.

Our prediction is that just like a new user of the WWW, children exercise choice over which items to learn and produce, in which order, following the universal principle of Preferential Attachment. Following this principle should result in links with a probability proportional to the relative frequency with which previous speakers in the linguistic environment (namely, the mothers) produced combinations with the different verbs. However, Preferential Attachment is a probabilistic rather than a deterministic principle; it is possible that children will choose to link to another node than the next most frequent item, if this suits their momentary preferences better.

The use of Preferential Attachment by a group of child-speakers newly learning some syntactic pattern should generate a child network with the global scale-free statistical features of the mother network right at the beginning of acquisition. We claim children behave just like other speakers of the same pattern, continuing to build the same network as their elders in the linguistic environment. In fact, the differentiation between linguistic environment and child is artificial; once the child starts to produce some type of linguistic item, he or she becomes part of the same complex system as previous speakers producing the same language element.

In summary, according to Complexity Theory children learning to produce some syntactic formula join the network of speakers already producing the same kind of syntax. They exercise a choice over which items to learn to produce according to their needs and interests, and they have a good ear for the best items with the most utility for these needs. If they go for relatively frequent items, it is for the same reasons that an adult (or Google's PageRank) would choose them—because frequency indicates usefulness. In fact, we are testing the hypothesis that children's choice of items to learn is analogous to adults' choice of items to use. This against the alternative hypothesis that children do not choose the items they learn but are passively influenced by such features as input frequency (Theakston *et al.*, 2004).

5.3 Developmental evidence: children recreate the global features of the maternal network

5.3.1 Maternal form-class is scale-free

First, we identified the global statistical features of maternal speech, focusing on a single syntactic construction, the verb–indirect object (VI) combination in Hebrew. Previous studies showed that maternal input has a skewed distribution, so that some verbs account for a very high percentage of all utterance tokens in various syntactic patterns. For example, Goldberg *et al.* (2004) analysed English-speaking mothers' utterance tokens in a large corpus and concluded that one specific verb accounts for a large percentage of utterance tokens in different argument structure constructions, among them the subject–verb–oblique intransitive and the subject–verb–object–object2 ditransitive frames. Similar skewed distributions in English maternal speech samples were reported by Naigles and Hoff-Ginsberg (1995), Sethuraman and Goodman (2004), and Theakston *et al.* (2004), and for Hebrew maternal samples by Ninio (1999a,b).

These studies, however, did not go beyond estimating the relative frequency of a few items from the total distribution. Now we want to map the whole range of items used by mothers when speaking to young children in one specific syntactic construction, and test the hypothesis that the distribution is power-law. This will provide the global statistical structure of the syntactic network children are expected to link to, when they begin producing the relevant syntactic construction.

The data are Hebrew-speaking mothers' utterances expressing the verb–indirect object (VI) construction. This construction consists of the addition of an indirect object with the preposition *le-* ('to') to a verb or adjective, for example, *ten le-ima* 'give to Mommy'. Adjectives were included in the corpus because their syntax with an indirect object is indistinguishable from that of verbs. In the following, 'verb' will be short for 'verb or adjective'. Like the English 'to', the Hebrew *le-* has a homophone used as an adverb of direction; sentences with the adverbial use were not included in the corpus. The sentences included in the corpus could and sometimes did contain other elements besides the verb and the indirect object, such as the subject, direct object, or some adjunct.

Data were obtained from the pooled spoken corpus of 48 Hebrew-speaking mothers addressing young children in 81 hours of free interaction videotaped at home observations (Ninio, 1984). The children were between 10 and 32 months old, mean age about 22 months. This corpus was considered to give a representative sample of speech heard by Hebrew-speaking children at the relevant age group. There are more than 56 000 multiword utterances of all kinds in the pooled multiword corpus. The corpus was searched by hand for sentences in which there was a verb or adjective followed by an indirect object with a *le-* preposition. Overall, there were 6956 utterances of this kind, employing 230 different verbs and adjectives.

Figure 5.4 presents the rank-frequency distribution of all the verbs appearing with an indirect object in the pooled corpus. The statistics plotted are number of utterance tokens per verb, namely, the *in-degree* of the different verbs, when each speech event is counted separately. This figure replicates Figure 5.2, which was used to demonstrate a Zipf curve for words.

The line indicates the closest Zipf-like power-law curve fit to the data. We can observe the very clear power-law distribution of the 230 verbs; the fit of the power-law curve is excellent ($R^2 = 0.98$, namely, a 98% fit). It can be concluded that the use frequency of verbs participating in the indirect-object construction has a typical Zipf distribution.

A second possible statistic is the number of different speakers using each verb in the relevant construction. This measure defines the relative popularity of each verb not in terms of how often it is used but, rather, by how common is its use in a group of speakers. Given that different populations of speakers (adults, children) may differ in how verbose they are (i.e., in their loquaciousness), this latter measure might serve better for comparing different populations than token frequency. Figure 5.5 presents the rank-frequency distribution of the different verbs in terms of number of speakers of 48 mothers producing at least one sentence with the verb.

The line indicates the closest Zipf-like power-law curve fit to the data. We can see that the number of mothers' distribution also has a typical power-law or Zipf-curve shape. The fit of the power-law curve is very good over most of the range ($R^2 = 0.93$, namely, a 93% fit).

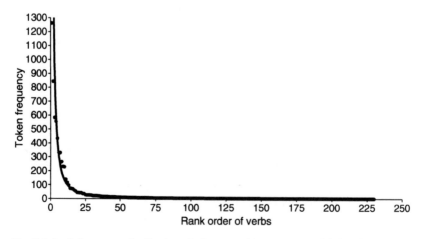

Fig. 5.4 Rank-frequency distribution of all maternal VI sentences with fitted power-law curve.

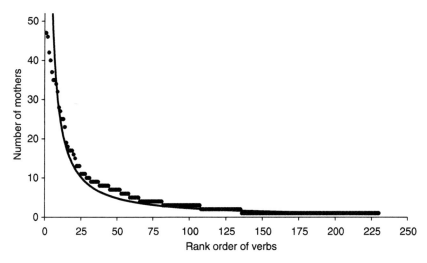

Fig. 5.5 Rank-frequency Zipf curve of number of mothers producing VI sentences with each verb, as a function of the verb's rank.

There is another way to present the same statistical feature and that is the Pareto presentation. Mathematically the two are transformations of each other, but graphically they turn the axes around. I will present them here because much of the literature uses Pareto graphs and it is worthwhile to be familiar with them. On the X axis we plot the token frequency of items ordered by rank, and it increases as we get higher values; on the Y axis we plot the cumulative probability of an item having equal or larger frequency than X. For the lowest value, the probability is 100%, and it decreases as the frequencies get higher. Figure 5.6 presents the Pareto cumulative probability distribution of number of mothers producing at least one sentence with each verb, using logarithmic scales.

The cumulative probabilities also distribute under a power-law function, but Figure 5.6 presents them on a log-log plot, in which the power-law distribution shows up as a straight line. As we can see, the relationship is almost linear on the log-log plot, except for a higher slope at the fat tail of the distribution. The Pareto presentation gives a slope of $b = -1.21$, equivalent to a power-law exponent or *gamma*[10] value of -2.21. The fit of the line is $R^2 = 0.93$ (as in the Zipf presentation). It can be concluded that the use frequency of verbs participating in the indirect-object construction, measured by the spread of the different verbs across different mothers in a sample, has a typical power-law distribution.

As we defined it in Section 5.1.4, the bipartite graph representing the linguistic environment for the acquisition of the VI construction has mothers

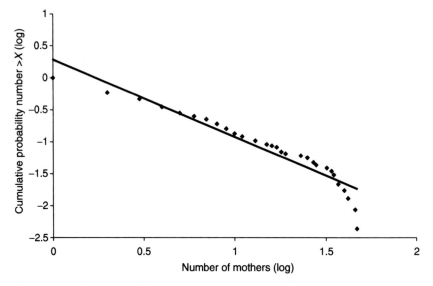

Fig. 5.6 Cumulative probability of maternal VI sentences said by X or more mothers on log-log axes.

as speaker nodes. The linguistic nodes are the different verbs participating in VI combinations in a large corpus of maternal speech. Figures 5.4–5.6 demonstrate that the *in-degrees* of the linguistic nodes follow a power-law, whether we compute them by number of utterance tokens or number of speakers. It appears that despite the extremely small size of this syntax-specific network, consisting only of 230 different verbs nodes and 48 different speaker nodes, it, too, possesses the typical power-law distribution of complex networks. Indeed, the *gamma* value of −2.21 is surprisingly consistent with the typical power-law exponent of the degree distribution of very large-scale-free networks previously studied, which is between −2.1 and −4.0 (Barabási and Albert, 1999; Strogatz, 2001).

The set of verbs participating in the VI pattern is what in linguistics is called a form-class, a subgroup of the total lexicon with similar grammatical behaviour (Bloomfield, 1935, p. 265).[11] This is the first time it has been demonstrated that the use-frequency distribution of a form-class in speech follows a power-law. Zipf (1972[1949]) and others mapped the rank-frequency distribution of all words appearing in written corpora, but they did not repeat the analysis with words consisting specific parts of the lexicon (and certainly not with spoken corpora). Our results suggest that small subgroups of the verb vocabulary—which are a priori quite homogeneous as they are selected by possessing identical syntax—also present a scale-free distribution. It is not trivial that form-classes, too, possess a very skewed power-law distribution. It implies that form-classes may have a structure resembling (fractal-like) the structure of the complete vocabulary. This could be the result of processes of self-organization informally described by linguists such as Dixon (1971), by which form-classes organize around a central kernel vocabulary of generic verbs. In complexity terms we would identify these kernel items with the hubs of the complex network (Barabási, 2002). This subject is beyond the scope of the present book and will have to wait for another opportunity to be explored further.[12]

The maternal network represents the linguistic environment of children acquiring the syntax of indirect objects. In the following, we shall compare children's emerging syntactic network for the same grammatical relation with the mothers' network, and test the hypothesis that children recreate the global statistical features of the input network without necessarily adopting the very same items as the mothers.

5.3.2 Children recreate the global features of the maternal network

To test our developmental hypothesis, we repeated the rank-frequency analysis of verbs in the indirect-object combination with a group of 14 young children as speakers (Ninio, 2005a). The children were unrelated to the mothers studied above. We made separate analyses for the distribution of the first two verbs acquired by the sample, the first three verbs, the first four verbs and so on, up to the first 10 different verbs they produced in this construction. There were a total of 11 different verbs with which the children of the sample produced their first 10 VI sentences. Figure 5.7 presents the rank-frequency distribution of the different verbs, in terms of number of children out of 14 producing at least one sentence with the verb, namely, the *in-degree* of the verbs. The statistics plotted are number of children-speakers for the first two, first three, four, five, six, seven, eight, nine, and first 10 different verbs used by the children in the VI pattern. (The set of the very first verbs had only three different values and was not plotted, as three points are too few to fit a particular curve.) The lines indicate the closest Zipf-like power-law curve fitted to each set of the data.

Figure 5.7 shows that the rank-frequency distribution follows a power-law, and that the slopes are unchanging with increasing number of different items produced.

As we saw in Figure 5.6, there is another way to present the same distribution and that is the Pareto presentation. Figure 5.8 presents the Pareto cumulative probability distribution of number of children producing at least

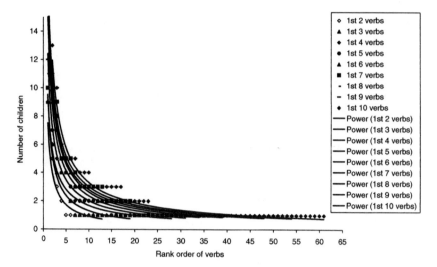

Fig. 5.7 Distribution of number of children by rank order of verbs, for the first 2, 3, 4, 5, 6, 7, 8, 9, and 10 different verbs in VI sentences.

one VI sentence with each verb, for the first two, first three, four, five, six, seven, eight, nine, and first 10 verbs for the children. The figure presents all nine fitted lines on a shared log-log scale.

The estimated power-law exponents are, respectively, -2.11, -2.27, -2.47, -2.40, -2.42, -2.26, -2.48, -2.47, and -2.35. As we can see in Figure 5.8, there is no systematic change with the added number of verbs. In all cases, the fit of the power-law curve is excellent, with $R^2 = 0.96$ or above.

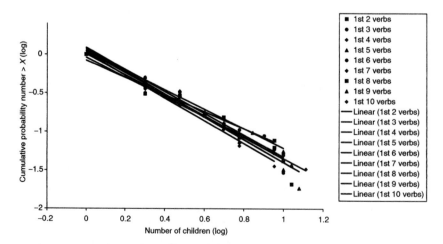

Fig. 5.8 Cumulative probability of number of children being larger than some value, for the first 2, 3, 4, 5, 6, 7, 8, 9, and 10 VI sentences on log-log axes.

Pareto log-log presentation in Figure 5.8 of the nine fitted lines demonstrates that the children's group immediately recreates the power-law distribution of the mother network of the same construction, and that the exponent does not change with development. The frequency distribution of the very first two verbs produced by a group of children in this syntactic construction already has a power-law distribution, with an estimated exponent of -2.11, almost identical to the exponent of the maternal network, which is -2.21. As we predicted, the scale-free characteristic of the children's syntactic network is not the result of gradual development; it appears immediately as the children start producing the relevant syntactic combination. This finding is quite surprising; the children's group recreated with a mere 28 utterances the global statistical features of a network consisting of 6954 nodes. Apparently, syntactic knowledge grows in a fractal manner. In a true scale-free manner, the link structure of the language network is the same at every stage, regardless of the size of the system. Such a process of propagation well suits language, the archetypical complex system.

5.3.3 Replication in another syntactic pattern

To double-check the generality of the findings, the same analysis was performed on a second syntactic construction, the combination of a verb with a direct object (VO). Data were obtained from a study of 20 Hebrew-speaking young children's six earliest sentences with different verbs (Ninio, 2005b). Figure 5.9 presents the rank-frequency distribution of the different verbs, in terms of number of child-speakers for the first 2, first 3, 4, 5, and first six different verbs used by the children in the VO pattern. The lines indicate the closest Zipf-like power-law curve fitted to each set of the data.

Figure 5.10 presents the Pareto cumulative probability distribution of number of children producing a VO sentence with each verb, for the first two, first three, four, five, and first six verbs for the children. The figure presents all five fitted lines on a shared log-log scale.

As we can see in Figures 5.9 and 5.10, the results obtained from the analysis of the VO pattern were similar to those obtained from the VI construction. The estimated power-law exponents are, respectively, -2.14, -2.20, -2.22, -2.22, and -2.22, and there is no systematic change with the added number of verbs. In all cases, the fit of the power-law curve is excellent, with $R^2 = 0.96$ or above. An estimate of the *in-degree* distributions of the maternal network of this syntactic pattern gave a power-law exponent of -2.17. Figure 5.10 shows that in this case, too, the log-log linear lines collapsed to a line closely similar to the maternal one, namely, the very first verbs already had a power-law

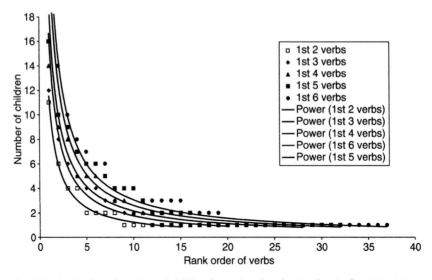

Fig. 5.9 Distribution of number of children by rank order of verbs, for the first 2, 3, 4, 5, and 6 different verbs in VO sentences.

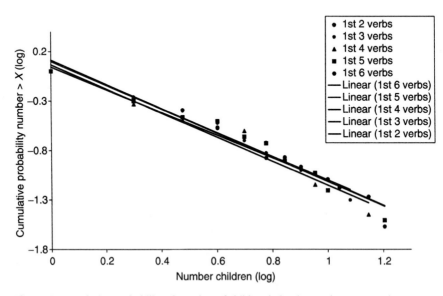

Fig. 5.10 Cumulative probability of number of children being larger than some value X, for the first 2, 3, 4, 5, and 6 VO sentences with a different verb, on log-log axes.

distribution in this sample (with an exponent of -2.14), and the power-law exponent did not change while the children gradually increased their production of the construction to six different verbs.

5.3.4 Children do not copy the input by relative frequency

A deterministic explanation to the similarity between maternal and child networks would be that children follow the relative frequency of items in maternal use and produced the items in the order representing their relative frequency of use by adults. We tested the feasibility of this process by comparing children's first 10 verbs in the VI pattern with mothers' most frequent 10 verbs. Because we did not have information about the children's own mothers' speech, we randomly selected 14 mothers of our maternal sample whose children were at the 12–28 months' age range, identified the 10 most frequent verbs produced by them in this syntactic pattern, and checked if these items give the same distribution as the children's first 10 verbs. The answer is that they do not. Mothers' 10 most frequent verbs closely overlapped[13] so that a mere 31 different verbs accounted for the group's 10 most frequent each (which could have been a maximum of 140 verbs if there were no overlap among the different mothers' verbs). The children's verbs were much less similar to each other's; the group's first 10 consisted of 61 different verbs.

It appears unlikely that children simply copied their network from the mothers' in order of relative frequency, starting with the most frequent maternal items and working their way down to less frequently heard ones. Such a frequency-driven ordering of learning would have created in the children's group a highly similar set of verbs, in fact one that does not have the characteristic power-law distribution but a 'star topology' (Barabási, 2002). If all children started the production of a given syntactic construction with the verb with the highest frequency of use in their linguistic environment, all children would start with the very same verb. There would be no power-law distribution, and in fact no distribution at all, simply one very popular verb serving as the starting verb for everybody. The same with the second verb, and the third and so forth. Even if we allow some variability among families, so that the overall frequency ranking of verbs that different children hear would not be completely identical, it would still be the case that different children's first verbs would be nearly identical to each others', in order of acquisition. At the limit, we would get 10 verbs, each chosen by all 14 children—the distribution would be unitary. It is clear that this is not the case; children's starting verbs have a nicely variable frequency of use in terms of popularity of use among mothers, as well as in terms of token frequency in the speech produced by a large group of mothers. As a result, the group's first 10 verbs spread over 61 different verbs, and the overlap between different children is quite moderate.

The very frequent use of a verb by mothers did make some of the verbs very attractive to children. The Hebrew equivalents of the verbs 'give', 'bring', and 'have', the three most popular with children, were among the 10 most frequent verbs of all the mothers. Such a pronounced preference for frequent verbs has been shown before (Ninio, 1999a; Goldberg et al., 2004) and it is expected under Preferential Attachment. However, extreme frequency in the input is not a sufficient condition for a verb to be learned early in the relevant syntactic construction: other verbs with equally high frequency in the maternal sample were produced by practically none of the children at this early stage, for example, the verbs translating as 'say', 'show', or 'tell' (as in 'tell me'). The reason why they do not learn these verbs very early is probably mostly pragmatic: the verbs they did not produce early are used for eliciting communication (saying, showing, singing) from the other, apparently not a pragmatic function that young children take upon themselves when interacting with their mothers.[14] As we predicted in Section 5.2, relative frequency is relevant for acquisition only if the content is one that the learner is interested in.

High input frequency is not a necessary condition for early production by children, either. More than 60% of the children's first 10 verbs (38 of 61) were not among the 10 most frequent verbs of any of the mothers sampled.[15]

Children skipping over very frequent items in the input and learning less-frequent ones first has been pointed out before (Brown and Hanlon, 1979; Clancy, 1989; Smiley and Huttenlocher, 1995; Wijnen et al., 2001; Rowland et al., 2003; Snedeker and Gleitman, 2004). In some studies there was a systematic preference for less-frequent items over more-frequent ones. One example is given by Wijnen et al. (2001). They looked at the order of acquisition of finite and infinitive forms of the same lexical verbs in Dutch, and found that in the majority of cases, children acquired the infinite forms before their finite counterparts, although the finite forms were always more frequent in the input than the infinites. Another systematic exception to the frequency effect is pointed out by Goodman et al. (2002). They separated the vocabulary into lexical categories and found the surprising finding that categories containing words with higher frequencies are acquired later than those containing words with lower frequencies. A glaring example is closed-class or so-called function words that ever since Zipf (1965[1935]) we know are the most frequent words in the vocabulary; nevertheless, as Goodman et al. found, such words are acquired relatively late. The same finding in the syntactic context[16] implies that the global statistical features of the children's network have probably not been generated by a deterministic process by which children picked verbs in an order following the input frequency. Children learning syntax appear to operate with 'preferential attachment' just like users linking to the WWW. Indeed, they act rather like the Google search engine (Brin and Page, 1998): The starting point is always the content they are looking for, and only then do considerations of relative popularity enter.

This is the reason why only the global statistical features, but not the actual items, of the maternal network are recreated by the group of children at the earliest stage of acquisition. The statistical features emerge right away because what drives the new users is similar to what drives the previous users—the wish to engage freely in contents of their own individual interest. Much of that is shared by other speakers in similar life circumstances but by no means all, even at this very young age.

The complex picture connecting frequency (i.e., *in-degree*) of linguistic items in the speech presented to young children and their adoption or not of the same items might be summarized by concluding that the effect of frequency is under no circumstances a deterministic one—as might be expected from some model of acquisition that treats children as passive learning machines impacted by stimuli. Instead, the frequency effect is probabilistic, and dependent on children's individual foci of interest.[17]

5.4 Conclusions: children join the language network

Application of Complexity Theory to language development sheds new light on the stance of the learner vis-à-vis the linguistic environment. It sees language as a network of speakers and the speech items they produce which children join when they, too, start to produce similar items. Developmental data shows that children act just like Google when it searches the Web: they pick popular items, but only if their content is relevant for them. The results support a view of children as free agents exercising Preferential Attachment when they develop their minds and acquire knowledge in a social environment.

The findings we presented do not support a view of children as passively impacted by the environment and its features. Rather, they offer a view of learners as active agents gradually connecting into a social network composed of other agents and their productions. Complexity Theory offers a robust formalism for dealing with language development and other types of social learning.

Indeed, the conception of children linking into a social network consisting of adults and the social behaviours they produce is strongly reminiscent of a well-known model of development going by the name of Social Learning Theory. The novelty resides merely in the introduction of Complexity Theory as a formalism. In the 1960s and 1970s, at the demise of the deterministic behaviourism, a new, socially oriented, theory of development took hold. This conception lent its terms to the title of several of the more prominent monographs and edited collections of the period, among them *The child's entry into a social world* (Schaffer, 1984), or *The integration of a child into a social world* (Richards, 1974). The similarity to the 'linking' model proposed above is glaringly obvious.[18]

The fundamental theoretical assumption of the reigning *Weltanschauung* was that social interaction with knowledgeable others moves development forward. There were several different versions of the theory, all circling around the same idea. Some of these were:

1. Social Learning Theory emphasizing modelling and imitation (Miller and Dollard, 1941; Bandura, 1962, 1977; Yarrow *et al.*, 1975);

2. Social Cognition Theory emphasizing that a child is enmeshed in the social environment and much cognitive development consists of the child's internalization of the adult's plans of action (Vygotsky, 1962[1934], 1978);

3. studies demonstrating synchronization of behaviours and reciprocity in very young infants and their caretakers—not one side copying the other's behaviour but jointly creating distinct phases of interaction (Stern, 1974, 1977; Brazelton *et al.*, 1974; Bullowa, 1975; Tronick *et al.*, 1979).

4. studies using the construct of interpersonality—emphasizing the emergent space that social interaction creates that is not the private spaces of each individual existing in isolation (Trevarthen, 1977, 1979; Trevarthen and Hubley, 1978);

5. studies naming dyadic interaction as the context and mechanism of cognitive development—emphasizing establishment of meaning by engaging in joint activities (Bruner, 1974, 1975, 1977; Ninio and Bruner, 1978; Schaffer, 1984).

Regarding language acquisition, the main thrust of the Social Learning Theory was that language is acquired as a means of communication, and that it is possible to explain the process of language acquisition as part of a process of acquiring communicative competence. Language was seen as a social skill; the central motivation for acquiring linguistic forms was that they served the child in the achievement of his or her social goals (Bruner, 1974, 1975; Ryan, 1974; Bateson, 1975; Bates, 1976; Snow, 1979; Ninio and Snow, 1988; and see chapters in Feagans *et al.*, 1984). In the best Vygotskian tradition, it was pointed out that the ability to communicate verbally must be learned in the context of interaction between the child and his or her social environment, and that such an intersubjective, culturally determined medium of social exchange as language cannot but be culturally transmitted.

The social-pragmatic view of language acquisition has had a not particularly successful history. As critics (e.g., Atkinson, 1982; Gleitman *et al.*, 1984) rightly pointed out, Social Learning Theory suffered from vagueness, and its inquiry into input and interactive style effects did not add up to a coherent, detailed, and testable model of how language competence is acquired as part of a process of social development.

It is now clear that social-learning or interactive cognitive development can be formulated in the simplest way in complexity terms. We can say that there exists a complex system of human actors and the actions produced by them, and on producing similar acts, the child links into the existing complex network as yet another entity connected to it. Complexity is a 'tough' and mathematically sophisticated formalism; it gives us—maybe for the first time—a robust tool of hypothesis testing, some of which I have applied in this book.

In particular, Complexity Theory provides a new type of statistics to utilize in a study of cognitive development, namely, the global scale-free statistical features of complex networks. In the studies reported in this chapter it was established that the syntactic input of basic constructions such as VO and VI is a scale-free network. In distributional terms that means that the use frequency (or *in-degree*) of the words heading these constructions obeys a power-law. Namely, linguistic input—consisting of speaker nodes and verb nodes—has the typical highly skewed use-frequency distribution of complex networks.

We understand that adults' language nets are scale-free because adults are free to choose what to say, and they prefer to use the most useful, best-working expressions (Barabási and Albert, 1999). We used this fundamental truth to make a strong prediction about children's behaviour when acquiring language in general and syntax in particular. If children learning language indeed behave just like adults and freely choose the best available expressions for their own communicative needs, it is expected that they, too, create a scale-free language network, identical in its parameters to the input network. This, however, does not mean that their network will include exactly the same items as the adults'. As their needs are not identical to those of adults, they will not choose the same expressions, even if these are very frequently said by the adults in their environment. Basically, if we are ready to treat children as the equals of adults in their pragmatic motivations, we are expecting a break with the customary frequency effect, while we are expecting a replication of power-law function best fitting the children's own network.

If we are not ready to treat children as the adults' equals but rather, as more primitive entities being impacted by stimuli from the environment, we embrace an alternative hypothesis according to which children do not exercise choice but, rather, simply copy the adults' speech in some order determined by token frequency or speaker frequency. In this case, theirs will be a different web. As this web is not the result of freedom of choice, it will not be scale free. If all children learn the very same words—because they are the most frequent ones in their linguistic environment—the network they construct will have a 'star topology' (Barabási, 2002), namely, the same few words will be produced by everybody, and the other words will be barely heard. This structure was to be contrasted with the scale-free power-law structure, in which there is great deal of diversity, reflecting the diverse interests and needs of different speakers.

The difference boils down to a question, whose communicative needs dictate the acquisition of language forms by young children. Are these the mothers' communicative needs—determining the frequency of the words they say, and hence determining the 'stimuli' for some behaviouristic 'response' process—or is it the children's communicative needs—in which case they may ignore the frequency of maternal items and learn whatever interests them regardless of how often they hear it in the mothers' speech?

As we saw, the empirical results support the view that children follow their own interests in picking new items to learn and say in interaction. They follow a principle of Preferential Attachment but do not show a gross frequency effect on their choices. The principle of Preferential Attachment is an extremely democratic principle. It implies that a newly added node to an existing network will behave just like all other nodes before it and thus reproduce in its links the statistical structure of the network it joins. A gross frequency effect is not democratic; the entity effected by it is passively impacted by a force it has no control over. In attributing to young children freedom of choice to express their own pragmatic needs by choosing the best available means in their language environment, we honour them with an attribution of sophisticated skills to engage in social learning.

Interestingly, Complexity Theory might well provide the formal vocabulary for talking also about the Power Law of Practice we discussed in Chapter 2.

It has been established in the complexity literature that not only the *in-degree* of nodes distributes with a skewed power-law but also the nodes' *out-degree*. As it has been pointed out by Newman (2003) and others, the explanation of the emergence of power-law distribution by a principle such as

Preferential Attachment does not, logically speaking, apply to *out-degrees*, only to *in-degrees*. Preferential Attachment claims that an already highly linked node—one with a large *in-degree*—will be preferred for further linking by new nodes. This will selectively increase the popular nodes' *in-degree* in a process dubbed 'the rich get richer', creating the skewed power-law distribution. However, the skewed distribution of *out-degrees* is not the result of choice by other nodes, as the statistic of *out-degrees* counts the number of links originating from a single source. In our bipartite network we allowed only one type of connection, links signifying production, whose source is a speaker and whose target is some linguistic unit. Our *in-degrees* belong to the linguistic items, to the words around which certain syntactic formulae are built. Our *out-degrees* belong to individual speakers, and it is a different question why this measure also distributes with a power-law distribution. The proposed growth process is that of practice: the more links a speaker node already generated to different linguistic items, the more likely it is that within a given time period, e.g., within a week, the speaker will produce yet another link to yet another linguistic item. This probability is under a power-law, as we have seen, at least as long as the speaker does not tire out or run out of items to link to.

We might now say that the young speaker learning to produce a new exemplar of a certain kind of syntactic combination (such as a VO combination with yet another transitive verb) accomplishes this learning by linking into two sets of nodes. The choice of the new verb to learn to produce with a direct object involves linking into the adult VO network at some node that the child has not yet linked into. It is expected that the chosen node will have a relatively large *in-degree*, namely, many adults will have used it for the communicative intent the child wants now to learn to express. This linking is one of an informed selection among the different available alternatives.

In addition, the learning of the novel pattern involves the child's own already-linked-to network, composed of the items this child has already produced in the relevant pattern. This virtual linking is one of drawing on stored knowledge, a metaphor for the process of transfer-assisted acquisition. Namely, learning involves two kinds of links. First, children link into the network of speakers, connecting to items produced by others as yet another speaker producing the same. Second, children also link into their own productions, touching base with what they already know.

According to the Power Law of Practice, the more links the child has already make in the past, the easier and faster it will be to link to yet another node. In complexity terms, the more *out-degrees* the child node possesses, the faster will a new link be added to this node. We might say that the linguistic items feed the child node with stored information to use in generating a new link to yet another item, reversing the direction of the existing links that went from child to the linguistic items she has produced. Either way, the number of existing directional links possessed by a source node predicts the probability of the addition of yet another link to the same node. According to this proposal, transfer of learning (aka the Power Law of Practice) is a possible process accounting for the skewed distribution of *out-degrees* in complex networks, not otherwise accounted for by models of growth assuming Preferential Attachment. Interestingly, in the literature covering the WWW it is seldom asked what is the contribution of the information users actually get from the homepages they link to, to the shaping of the WWW. This human developmental study hints that the answer can be found in learning theory: The more information users get from the Web, the more adept they become at using the Web, including but not restricted to becoming more adept at establishing useful hyperlinks to other homepages.

We have come a full cycle, connecting the universal cognitive principle of the effect of learning and transfer to Complexity Theory. I would like to conclude this chapter by proposing that Complexity Theory be employed as a theoretical framework for language acquisition in general, and the acquisition of syntax, in particular. Language is, indeed, a complex system, and so is the process of its growth. Complexity Theory is a powerful tool for thinking about the intricacies of language development, one that can embrace the multitude of interlocking phenomena that language use and language learning involve.

Notes

1   Complex systems are treated by a special brand of science, Complexity Theory, a discipline concerned with complexity phenomena regardless of the specific domain in which they occur (for a review, see Barabási, 2002). Although many different definitions of complex systems have been proposed, three defining characteristics stand out:

  a   *Intricacy*: complex systems consist of a large number of connected components, typically many different kinds linked by multiple relationships, interfaces, or interactions, forming an intricate structure.

  b   *Emergent properties*: a complex system is a system whose properties emerge from the interaction of its component parts, none of which by itself possesses the relevant properties.

  c   *Growth*: complex systems are systems that constantly grow and evolve in a dynamic process. The parts of the system are said to self-organize into larger-scale structures of increasing complexity.

Examples of complex systems are the immune system, neural networks, protein-interaction networks and metabolic networks in biology; crystals and weather systems in physics; Internet routers and the WWW in communications.

2 It is a well-known assertion that language is a system (Wittgenstein, 1978[1953]; de Saussure, 1983[1922]). The argument for treating language as a system is the dependence of meaning or 'value' of individual words on other words, whether words that occur as their alternatives in sentences, or words that occur together with them, building the structure of sentences. De Saussure formalized this system dependence by defining the two kinds of relationships between words as paradigmatic relations, generating meaning in the lexicon of the language, and syntagmatic relations, generating sentences. Because of containing multiple units and multiple relations among them, language qualifies, in modern terminology, as a complex system.

3 Given the multifaceted nature of language, it is customary to study its structure separately for different types of linguistic units and different kinds of relations between units. This is particularly so in the case of the lexicon which is, in graph-theoretical terms, a complex network of words linked by various types of links. As words possess many different features, the relationship between the words in any particular network set up for study depends on the researchers' focus of interest. The lexicon as a phonological network is discussed by Vitevitch (2005), and see also Charles-Luce and Luce (1990, 1995), Luce and Pisoni (1998), Hollich *et al.* (2002), and Storkel (2002). Quillian (1967, 1968), Collins and Quillian (1969), Lindsay and Norman (1977), Brugman and Lakoff (1988), Vickery and Vickery (1987), and Steyvers and Tenenbaum (2005) discuss the lexicon as a semantic network in which words are organized by similarity of meaning in clusters of synonyms. Others define the links among words in a semantic network on other basis than strict similarity; for example, instance relations such as hyponymy have also been utilized for constructing nets (Ceccato, 1961). Syntax is treated as a network by Ferrer i Cancho and Solé (2001), based on an analysis of English texts. In this study, word nodes are linked if they appear next to each other, or one word apart from each other, in sentences, so that a verb would be connected, for instance, to a noun or pronoun and not to another verb similar to it in syntactic behaviour. In another study (Ferrer *et al.*, 2003), corpora of Rumanian, Czech, and German texts were analysed for actual Dependency relations, subjected to a network analysis.

4   Other examples of complex networks with power-law connectivity dis-
    tributions are the Internet backbone, metabolic reactions, telephone calls,
    protein interactions, scientific collaboration, citations between scientific
    papers, human sexual contacts, the WWW, and more. For reviews see
    Strogatz (2001) and Barabási and Bonabeau (2003).

5   Two other global statistical features of complex networks are small-world
    behaviour, namely, the famous 'six degrees of separation' phenomenon,
    namely, a small average path length connecting any two nodes of the
    system; and a high clustering coefficient, namely, a high probability that
    two associates of a given node will also be associates of each other (Watts
    and Strogatz, 1998; Strogatz, 2001; Newman, 2003).

6   Although Zipf's work is much better known, in actuality the first to
    explore the skewed distribution of words in texts was Estoup (1916).

7   Zipf (1972[1949]) reported on several distributions derived from natural
    language that follow power laws; for example, he plotted the number of
    meanings of words and the length of words against their rank of use
    frequency.

8   Many social networks are well-represented by bipartite graphs. There are
    affiliation networks of individuals and the groups they belong to, the links
    between them representing group membership such as people serving on
    boards of directors (Davis and Greve, 1997). Another type of bipartite
    social network are preference networks that have nodes representing indi-
    viduals and the objects of their preference, such as books, films, or music
    files, with a directional link connecting each individual to the objects they
    like (Iamnitchi *et al.*, 2004). Our speaker-language network belongs to
    a third type representing producers and produce, for instance, scientists
    collaborating on research articles (Newman, 2001), or a network describ-
    ing cellular biochemistry where one type of node is for chemicals, and
    another one is for reactions they participate in (Holme and Huss, 2003).

9   Goodman *et al.* (2002) indeed found that within particular lexical categor-
    ies, input frequency was correlated with how early a word appeared in
    children's productive vocabulary, but frequency was not significantly cor-
    related with order of acquisition in children's comprehension vocabulary.

10 The exponent of the power-law function is often symbolized by the Greek
    letter *gamma*.

11 On the definition of form-classes and word-classes see also Hockett
    (1958, p. 162), Robins (1964, p. 229), Crystal (1967), and Lyons (1968,
    pp. 164–165).

12 Kernel vocabulary and its possible role in syntactic development has been treated by Clark (1978, 1996), Goldberg (1995, 1999), Ninio (1999a,b), Thordardottir and Weismer (2001), Goldberg *et al.* (2004), and Sethuraman and Goodman (2004).

13 A considerable degree of overlap among different mothers has been reported before by, for instance, Huttenlocher *et al.* (1991) and by Serratrice *et al.* (2003). In addition, Vihman *et al.* (1994) showed that mothers' content words are more similar to each other's than their children's are.

14 See Ninio and Snow (1996, pp. 103–105, 112–127) on pragmatic differences and other reasons for children diverging from mothers' distribution of expressed communicative intents.

15 Attempts to establish a frequency effect are very problematic for statistical reasons, given the extremely skewed power-law distribution of both maternal and child use-frequency data. The statistical methods used such as Pearson correlations and other regression analyses, *t*-tests, analyses of variance, and so forth require that the variables involved distribute normally; a power-law distribution in fact makes these statistical procedures inapplicable (see also Andriani and McKelvey, 2004). Using rank correlations evokes another problem: because there are very many infrequent items sharing the same absolute use-frequency, the majority of the items may get the same rank, putting into a questionable light the statistical procedure. Researchers often attempt to remedy the skewedness by various measures, including truncating the 'fat tail' of the distribution, i.e., excluding from statistical treatment all frequencies below a certain value (e.g., Goodman *et al.*, 2002; Cameron-Faulkner *et al.*, 2003; Serratrice *et al.*, 2003). This procedure may reduce the skewedness but it does not redress the problem that the data do not have the required normal distribution. On the special statistical problems raised by the skewed shape of word distributions, see also Baayen (2001).

16 Ninio (1999a) described the case of Travis (Tomasello, 1992) who did not begin to use the verb *want* at all until 6 months after she started VO combinations, preferring to express her requests with other verbs such as '*get*', '*bring*', and so on. Tomasello does not give statistics for the distribution of the use of verbs in the parents' speech, but from his descriptions it seems that the parents did use this verb very frequently, as it is mentioned in very many of the parental-model examples he gives, for instance, 'Do you want some more?' (p. 290); 'Do you want to ____ again?' (p. 298); 'Do you want to do it?' (p. 298); 'Do you want to come with me?' (p. 299), 'Do you want to do it too?' (p. 299), 'Do you want to do it yourself?'

(p. 302); 'Do you want that back?' (p. 307), and so on. It is hard to believe that the parents used '*get*' or '*bring*' more often than they used '*want*', and especially any of the more specific obtaining verbs Travis used before she used '*want*' such as '*find*', '*catch*', '*buy*', or '*hold*'. It appears that a child might find a solution to some pragmatic need in other than the most frequently heard expression and stay with it for a very long period without bothering to learn the expression with the highest input frequency.

17 In a study investigating the relation between children's single-word utterances and maternal single-word utterances expressing similar communicative intents, Ninio (1992) found a very strong input frequency effect *within* each type of communicative intent that young children expressed in single-word utterances at the age of 18 months. In this study, the speech of Hebrew-speaking dyads was collected in videotaped unstructured home sessions. The speech of 48 mothers and 24 children were analysed. Single-word utterances were coded for the speaker's communicative intent (e.g., 'Make a statement discussing an established joint focus of attention') and for the relationship of the expression to the underlying intent, namely, the realization rules mapping the intent to the single-word expression. For realization rules modelled by mothers with the greatest relative frequency for their specific intent, namely, rules ranked first among all the rules for their respective intents in the pooled corpus of 48 mothers, the average proportion of children following that rule was 72.6%. For rules ranked second, the mean proportion of children following them dropped to 19.7%; and rules ranked third, 9.6%. The average proportion of children following a rule for rules ranked four or more was only 2.6%. It appears that the most frequently modelled rule for each kind of communicative intent has by far the highest chance of being adopted by children for their own single-word utterances expressing that intent, and the probability sharply decreases for the relatively less frequently modelled rules.

18 The interactionist tradition in language acquisition is still very much alive, and see for example Deckner *et al.* (2006) and reviews by Chapman's (2000) and Hoff (2006). Indeed, the best informal description of children linking into the adults' cognitive network has been coined quite recently by Nelson *et al.* (2003), in whose apt phrase, children are said to be 'entering a community of minds'.

References

Abbot-Smith, K. and Behrens, H. (2002). Acquisition of the German passive: a 'construction conspiracy' account. Paper presented at the Joint meeting of the 9th International Congress of the International Association of the Study of Child Language and the 23rd Annual Symposium on Research in Child Language Disorders (IASCL/SRCLD), Madison, WI.

Abbot-Smith, K., Lieven, E. V. M. and Tomasello, M. (2004). Training 2;6-year-olds to produce the transitive construction: the role of frequency, semantic similarity and shared syntactic distribution. *Developmental Science*, 7, 48–55.

Abbot-Smith, K. and Behrens, H. (in press). How known constructions influence the acquisition of new constructions: the German periphrastic passive and future constructions. *Cognitive Science, 30.*

Abney, S. (1987). The English noun phrase in its sentential aspects. Unpublished Ph.D. thesis, MIT, Cambridge, MA.

Ades, A. E. and Steedman, M. J. (1982). On the order of words. *Linguistics and Philosophy*, 4, 517–558.

Aho, A. V., Sethi, R. and Ullman, J. D. (1986). *Compilers: principles, techniques, and tools*. Reading, MA: Addison-Wesley.

Allen, J. (1997). Probabilistic constraints in language acquisition. In A. Sorace, C. Heycock and R. Shillcock (eds), *Proceedings of the GALA '97 Conference on Language Acquisition* (pp. 300–305). Edinburgh: Edinburgh University Human Communications Research Centre.

Allerton, D. J. (1978). Generating indirect objects in English. *Journal of Linguistics*, 14, 21–33.

Allerton, D. J. (1982). *Valency and the English verb*. London: Academic Press.

Altmann, G. T. M., Dienes, Z. and Goode, A. (1995). Modality independence of implicitly learned grammatical knowledge. *Journal of Experimental Psychology: Learning. Memory and Cognition*, 21, 899–912.

Anderson, J. R. (1976). *Language, memory, and thought*. Hillsdale, NJ: Lawrence Erlbaum.

Anderson, J. R. (1982). Acquisition of cognitive skill. *Psychological Review*, 89, 396–406.

Anderson, J. R. (1993). *Rules of the mind*. Hillsdale, NJ: Lawrence Erlbaum.

Anderson, J. R. and Lebiere, C. (1998). *The atomic components of thought.* Mahwah, NJ: Lawrence Erlbaum.

Anderson, J. R. and Schooler, L. J. (1991). Reflections of the environment in memory. *Psychological Science,* 2, 396–408.

Anderson, S. R. (1977). Comments on the paper by Wasow (The Role of the Theme in Lexical Rules). In P. Culicover, T. Wasow and A. Akmajian. (eds), *Formal syntax* (pp. 361–377). New York: Academic Press.

Andrews, A. (1985). The major functions of the noun phrase. In T. Shopen (ed.), *Language typology and syntactic description,* Vol. 1: *Clause structure* (pp. 62–154). Cambridge: Cambridge University Press.

Andriani, P. and McKelvey, B. (2004). Power law phenomena in organizations. Paper presented at the Fifth International Conference on Complex Systems (ICCS2004), Boston, MA.

Arkin, H. and Colton, R. R. (1950). *Tables for statisticians.* New York: Barnes and Noble.

Askedal, J. O. (1991). Charles S. Peirce's work on relatives and modern Valency Grammar. *Cruzeiro Semiotico,* 15, 69–82.

Atkinson, M. (1982). *Explanations in the study of child language development.* Cambridge: Cambridge University Press.

Atkinson, R. C., Bower, G. H. and Crothers, E. J. (1965). *An introduction to mathematical learning theory.* New York: John Wiley.

Baayen, R. H. (2001). *Word frequency distributions.* Dordrecht: Kluwer.

Baker, C. L. (1979). Syntactic theory and the projection problem. *Linguistic Inquiry,* 10, 533–581.

Baker, M. (1988). *Incorporation: a theory of grammatical function changing.* Chicago, IL: University of Chicago Press.

Baker, M. (1997). Thematic roles and syntactic structures. In L. Haegeman (ed.), *Elements of grammar* (pp. 73–137). Dordrecht: Kluwer.

Baltin, M. R. (1989). Heads and projections. In M. R. Baltin and A. S. Kroch (eds), *Alternative conceptions of phrase structure* (pp. 1–16). Chicago, IL: University of Chicago Press.

Bandura, A. (1962). Social learning through imitation. In M. Jones (ed.), *Nebraska symposium on motivation* (pp. 211–269). Lincoln, NE: University of Nebraska Press.

Bandura, A. (1977). *Social learning theory.* Englewood Cliffs, NJ: Prentice-Hall.

Bar-Hillel, Y. (1953). A quasi-arithmetical notation for syntactic description. *Language,* 29, 47–58.

Barabási, A.-L. (2002). *Linked: the new science of networks.* Cambridge, MA: Perseus.

Barabási, A.-L. and Albert, R. (1999). Emergence of scaling in random networks. *Science,* **286**, 509–512.

Barabási, A.-L. and Bonabeau, E. (2003). Scale-free networks. *Scientific American,* **288**, 60–69.

Barsalou, L. W. (1983). Ad hoc categories. *Memory and Cognition,* 11, 211–227.

Barsalou, L. W. (1990). On the indistinguishability of exemplar memory and abstraction in category representation. In T. K. Srull and R. S. Wyer (eds), *Advances in social cognition,* Vol. 3 (pp. 61–88). Hillsdale, NJ: Lawrence Erlbaum.

Barsalou, L. W. (1991). Deriving categories to achieve goals. In G. H. Bower (ed.), *The psychology of learning and motivation: advances in research and theory,* Vol. 27 (pp. 1–64). San Diego, CA: Academic Press. [Reprinted in A. Ram and D. Leake (eds) (1995). *Goal-driven learning* (pp. 121–176). Cambridge, MA: MIT Press/Bradford Books.]

Bates, E. (1976). *Language and context: studies in the acquisition of pragmatics.* New York: Academic Press.

Bates, E. and Carnevale, G. F. (1993). New directions in research on language development. *Developmental Review,* 13, 436–70.

Bates, E. and Goodman, J. C. (1999). Grammar form the lexicon. In B. MacWhinney (ed.), *The emergence of language* (pp. 197–212). Hillsdale, NJ: Lawrence Erlbaum.

Bates, E., Dale, P. S. and Thal, D. (1995). Individual differences and their implications for theories of language development. In P. Fletcher and B. MacWhinney (eds), *Handbook of child language* (pp. 96–151). Oxford: Basil Blackwell.

Bateson, M. C. (1975). Mother-infant exchanges: the epigenesis of conversational interaction. In D. Aaronson and R. W. Rieber (eds), *Developmental psycholinguistics and communication disorders* (pp. 101–113). New York: the New York Academy of Sciences.

Bavin, E. L. and Growcott, C. (1999). Infants of 24–30 months understand verb frames. In M. Perkins and S. Howard (eds), *New directions in language development and disorders* (pp. 169–177). New York: Kluwer.

Bennett, P. (1995). *A course in Generalized Phrase Structure Grammar.* London: University College London Press.

Berman, R. A. (1978). *Modern Hebrew structure.* Tel Aviv: University Publishing Projects.

Berman, R. A. (1982a). Verb-pattern alternation: the interface of morphology, syntax, and semantics in Hebrew child language. *Journal of Child Language,* 9, 169–91.

Berman, R. A. (1982b). Dative marking of the affectee role: data from modern Hebrew. *Hebrew Annual Review,* 6, 35–59.

Berman, R. A. (1986). A step-by-step model of language learning. In I. Levin (ed.), *Stage and structure: reporting the debate* (pp. 191–219). Norwood, NJ: Ablex.

Berman, R. A. (1988). Word class distinctions in developing grammars. In Y. Levy, I. M. Schlesinger and M. D. S. Braine (eds), *Categories and processes in language acquisition* (pp. 45–72). Hillsdale, NJ: Lawrence Erlbaum.

Berman, R. A. and Armon-Lotem, S. (1997). How grammatical are early verbs? In C. Martinot (ed.), *Actes du colloque international sur l'acquisition de la syntaxe en langue maternelle et en langue étrangère.* Les Annales Littéraires de Université de Franche-Comté, Besançon, France, 631, 17–59.

Berman, R. A. and Dromi, E. (1984). On marking time without aspect in child language. *Papers and Reports on Child Language Development,* 23, 23–32.

Bjork, R. A. and Richardson-Klavhen, A. (1989). On the puzzling relationship between environment, context and human memory. In C. Izawa (ed.), *Current issues in cognitive processes: the Tulane Flowerree Symposium on Cognition.* Hillsdale, NJ: Lawrence Erlbaum.

Blades, M. and Cooke, Z. (1994). Young children's ability to understand a model as a spatial representation. *Journal of Genetic Psychology,* 155, 201–218.

Blake, F. R. (1930). A semantic analysis of case. In J. T. Hatfield and W. Leopold (eds), *Curme volume of linguistic studies,* Language Monographs, 7 (pp. 34–49). Baltimore, MD: Waverly Press.

Bloom, L. (1970). *Language development: form and function in emerging grammars.* Cambridge, MA: MIT Press.

Bloom, L. and Lahey, M. (1978). *Language development and language disorders.* New York: John Wiley.

Bloom, L., Lightbown, P. and Hood, L. (1975). Structure and variation in child language. *Monographs of the Society for Research in Child Development,* 40, 160.

Bloom, L., Lifter, K. and Hafitz, J. (1980). Semantics of verbs and the development of verb inflections in child language. *Language,* 56, 386–412.

Bloom, L., Merkin, W. and Wootten, J. (1982). Wh-questions: Linguistic factors that contribute to the sequence of acquisition. *Child Development,* 53, 1084–1092.

Bloom, L., Tackeff, J. and Lahey, M. (1983). Learning *to* in complement constructions. *Journal of Child Language,* 10, 391–406.

Bloom, L., Rispoli, M., Gartner, B. and Hafitz, J. (1989). Acquisition of complementation. *Journal of Child Language,* 16, 101–120.

Bloom, P. (1990). Syntactic distinctions in child language. *Journal of Child Language,* 17, 343–55.

Bloomfield, L. (1935). *Language.* London: George Allen and Unwin.

Blume, K. (1998). A contrastive analysis of interaction verbs with dative complements. *Linguistics,* 36, 253–280.

Bolinger, D. (1975). *Aspects of language* (2nd edn). New York: Harcourt Brace Jovanovich.

Bondy, J. A. and Murty, U. S. R. (1976). *Graph theory with applications.* New York: North Holland.

Borer, H. and Grodzinsky, Y. (1986). Syntactic cliticization and lexical cliticization: the case of Hebrew dative clitics. In H. Borer (ed.), *Syntax and semantics,* Vol. 19: *The syntax of pronominal clitics* (pp. 175–218). New York: Academic Press.

Bouchard, D. (1991). From conceptual structure to syntactic structure. In K. Leffel and D. Bouchard (eds), *Views on phrase structure.* Dordrecht: Kluwer.

Bowerman, M. (1973a). Early syntactic development: a cross-linguistic study with special reference to Finnish. Cambridge: Cambridge University Press.

Bowerman, M. (1973b). Structural relations in children's utterances: syntactic or semantic? In T. M. Moore (ed.), *Cognitive development and the acquisition of language* (pp. 197–213). New York: Academic Press.

Bowerman, M. (1976). Semantic factors in the acquisition of rules for word use and sentence construction. In D. Morehead and A. Morehead (eds), *Directions in normal and deficient child language.* Baltimore, MD: University Park Press.

Bowerman, M. (1978). Words and sentences: Uniformity, individual variation, and shifts over time in patterns of acquisition. In F. D. Minifie and L. L. Lloyd (eds), *Communicative and cognitive abilities—early behavioral assessment* (pp. 355–371). Baltimore, MD: University Park Press.

Bowerman, M. (1982). Reorganizational processes in lexical and syntactic development. In E. Wanner and L. R. Gleitman (Eds), *Language acquisition: the state of the art* (pp. 319–346). Cambridge: Cambridge University Press.

Bowerman, M. (1990). Mapping thematic roles onto syntactic functions: are children helped by innate linking rules? *Linguistics*, **28**, 1253–89.

Braine, M. D. S. (1963). The ontogeny of English phrase structure: the first phase. *Language*, **39**, 1–13.

Braine, M. D. S. (1976). Children's first word combinations. *Monographs of the Society for Research in Child Development*, **41**, 164.

Braine, M. D. S. and Brooks, P. J. (1995). Verb argument structure and the problem of avoiding an overgeneral grammar. In M. Tomasello and W. E. Merriman (eds), *Beyond names for things* (pp. 353–376). Hillsdale, NJ: Lawrence Erlbaum.

Bransford, J. D., Brown, A. L. and Cocking, R. R. (eds) (1999). *How people learn: Brain, mind, experience, and school.* New York: National Research Council, National Academy of Sciences.

Brazelton, B. T., Koslowski, B. and Main, M. (1974). The origins of reciprocity: the early mother-infant interaction. In M. Lewis and L. A. Rosenblum (eds), *The effect of the infant on its caregiver* (pp. 49–76). Wiley, New York.

Bresnan, J. (1970). On complementizers: toward a syntactic theory of complement types. *Foundations of Language*, **6**, 297–321.

Bresnan, J. (1978). A realistic transformational grammar. In M. Halle, J. Bresnan and G. A. Miller (eds), *Linguistic theory and psychological reality* (pp. 1–59). Cambridge, MA: MIT Press.

Bresnan, J. (2001). *Lexical-Functional Syntax.* Oxford: Basil Blackwell.

Bresnan, J. and Kaplan, R. (1982). Introduction: grammars as mental representations of language. In J. Bresnan and R. Kaplan (eds), *The mental representation of grammatical relations* (pp. xvii–lii). Cambridge, MA: MIT Press.

Brewer, R. (1994). *The science of ecology*, 2nd edn. Philadelphia, PA: Saunders College Publishing.

Brin, S. and Page, L. (1998). The anatomy of a large-scale hypertextual web search engine. *Proceedings of the 7th World Wide Web Conference (WWW7)/Computer Networks*, **30**(1–7), 107–117.

Brooks, P. J. and Tomasello, M. (1999). Young children learn to produce passives with nonce verbs. *Developmental Psychology*, **35**, 29–44.

Brown, A. L. and Kane, M. J. (1988). Preschool children can learn to transfer: learning to learn and learning from example. *Cognitive Psychology*, **20**, 493–523.

Brown, B. L. and Leonard, L. B. (1986). Lexical influences on children's early positional patterns. *Journal of Child Language*, 13, 219–29.

Brown, R. (1973). *A first language: the early stages*. Cambridge, MA: Harvard University Press.

Brown, R. and Bellugi, U. (1964). Three processes in the child's acquisition of syntax. *Harvard Educational Review*, 34, 133–151.

Brown, R. and Fraser, C. (1963). The acquisition of syntax. In C. N. Cofer and B. S. Musgrave (eds), *Verbal behavior and learning: problems and processes* (pp. 158–197). New York: McGraw-Hill.

Brown, R. and Hanlon, C. (1979). Derivational complexity and order of acquistion in child speech. In J. R. Hayes (ed.), *Cognition and development of language* (pp. 11–53). New York: John Wiley.

Brugman, C. and Lakoff, G. (1988). Cognitive topology and lexical networks. In S. I. Small, G. W. Cottrell and M. K. Tanenhaus (eds), *Lexical ambiguity resolution* (pp. 477–508). San Francisco, CA: Morgan Kaufmann.

Bruner, J. S. (1974). The organization of early skilled action. In M. R. M. Richards (ed.), *The integration of a child into a social world* (pp. 167–184). Cambridge: Cambridge University Press.

Bruner, J. S. (1975). From communication to language. *Cognition*, 3, 255–287.

Bruner, J. S. (1977). Early social interaction and language acquisition. In H. R. Schaffer (ed.), *Studies in mother-infant interaction* (pp. 271–289). New York: Academic Press.

Bryan, W. L. and Harter, N. (1897). Studies in the physiology and psychology of the telegraphic language. *Psychological Review*, 4, 27–53.

Bullowa, M. (1975). When infant and adult communicate, how do they synchronize their behaviors? In A. Kendon, R. M. Harris and M. R. Key (eds), *The organization of behavior in face-to-face interaction* (pp. 95–126). Chicago, IL: Mouton Publishers.

Burch, R. (1992). Valental aspects of Peircean algebraic logic. *Computers and Mathematics with Applications*, 23, 665–677.

Bybee, J. L. (2001). *Phonology and language use*. Cambridge: Cambridge University Press.

Byrnes, J. P. (1996). *Cognitive development and learning in instructional contexts*. Boston: Allyn and Bacon.

Cameron-Faulkner, T., Lieven, E. V. M. and Tomasello, M. (2003). A construction based analysis of child directed speech. *Cognitive Science*, 27, 843–873.

Campbell, A. L. and Tomasello, M. (2001). The acquisition of English dative constructions. *Applied Psycholinguistics, 22*, 253–267.

Campbell, R. N. (1976). Propositions and early utterances. In G. Drachman (ed.), *Salzburger Beitrage zur Linguistik*, Vol. II (pp. 247–259). Tubingen: Gunther Narr.

Caplan, L. J. and Schooler, C. (1999). On the use of analogy in text-based memory and comprehension: the interaction between complexity of within-domain encoding and between-domain processing. *Journal of the Learning Sciences, 8*, 41–70.

Carnap, R. (1947). *Meaning and necessity.* Chicago, IL: University of Chicago Press.

Cartwright, T. A. and Brent, M. R. (1997). Syntactic categorization in early language acquisition: formalizing the role of distributional analysis. *Cognition, 63*, 121–170.

Ceccato, S. (1961). *Linguistic analysis and programming for mechanical translation.* New York: Gordon and Breach.

Chapman, R. S. (2000). Children's language learning: an interactionist perspective. *Journal of Child Psychology and Psychiatry and Allied Disciplines, 41*, 33–54.

Charles-Luce, J. and Luce, P. A. (1990). Similarity neighbourhoods of words in young children's lexicons. *Journal of Child Language, 17*, 205–215.

Charles-Luce, J. and Luce, P. A. (1995). An examination of similarity neighbourhoods in young children's receptive vocabularies. *Journal of Child Language, 22*, 727–735.

Chen, Z. and Daehler, M. W. (1992). Intention and outcome: key components of causal structure facilitating mapping in children's analogical transfer. *Journal of Experimental Child Psychology, 53*, 237–257.

Chen, Z. and Klahr, D. (1999). All other things being equal: children's acquisition and transfer the Control of Variables strategy, *Child Development, 70*, 1098–1120.

Chiat, S. (1981). Context-specificity and generalization in the acquisition of pronominal distinctions. *Journal of Child Language, 8*, 75–91.

Chiat, S. (1982). If I were you and you were me: the analysis of pronouns in a pronoun-reversing child. *Journal of Child Language, 9*, 359–79.

Childers, J. B. and Tomasello, M. (2001). The role of pronouns in young children's acquisition of the English transitive construction. *Developmental Psychology, 37*, 730–748

Chomsky, N. (1957). *Syntactic structures.* The Hague: Mouton.

Chomsky, N. (1965). *Aspects of the theory of syntax.* Cambridge, MA: MIT Press.

Chomsky, N. (1970). Remarks on nominalization. In R. Jacobs and P. Rosenbaum (eds), *Readings in transformational grammar* (pp. 184–221). Waltham, MA: Blaisdell Publishing

Chomsky, N. (1971). *Problems of knowledge and freedom.* New York: Pantheon Books.

Chomsky, N. (1975). *Reflections on language.* New York: Random House.

Chomsky, N. (1981). *Lectures on government and binding.* Dordrecht: Foris.

Chomsky, N. (1986). *Knowledge of language: its nature, origin and use.* New York: Praeger.

Chomsky, N. (1995). *The Minimalist Program.* Cambridge, MA: MIT Press.

Chomsky, N. (2001). Derivation by phase. In M. Kenstowicz (ed.), *Ken Hale: a life in language* (pp. 1–52). Cambridge, MA: MIT Press.

Chomsky, N. (2004). Three factors in language design. Unpublished manuscript. MIT, Cambridge, MA.

Chomsky, N., Belletti, A. and Rizzi, L. (2002). *On the nature of language.* Cambridge: Cambridge University Press.

Christiansen, M. H. and Kirby, S. (eds). (2003). *Language evolution: the states of the art.* Oxford: Oxford University Press.

Church, A. (1932/1933). A set of postulates for the foundation of logic. *Annals of Mathematics, Second series,* 33, 346–366 and 34, 839–864.

Clahsen, H. (1990). Constraints on parameter setting: a grammatical analysis of some acquisition stages in German child language. *Language Acquisition,* 1, 361–391.

Clahsen, H., Eisenbeiss, S. and Penke, M. (1996). Lexical learning in early syntactic development. In H. Clahsen (ed.), *Generative perspectives on language acquisition* (pp. 129–159). Amsterdam: John Benjamins.

Clancy, P. M. (1989). Form and function in the acquisition of Korean wh-questions. *Journal of Child Language,* 16, 323–47.

Clancy, P. M. (1995). Subject and object in Korean acquisition: Surface expression and case-marking. In S. Kuno, I-H. Lee, J. Whitman, J. Maling, Y-S, Kang and Y-J. Kim (eds), *Harvard studies in Korean Linguistics* (pp. 3–17). Cambridge, MA: Harvard University Press.

Clark, E. V. (1978). Discovering what words can do. *Papers from the Parasession on the Lexicon, CLS* 14 (pp. 34–57). Chicago, IL: University of Chicago Press.

Clark, E. V. (1996), Early verbs, event types, and inflections. In C. E. Johnson and J. H. V. Gilbert (eds), *Children's language,* Vol. 9 (pp. 61–73). Mahwah, NJ: Lawrence Erlbaum.

Cohen, J., Dunbar, D. K. and McClelland, J. L. (1990). On the control of automatic processes: a parallel distributed processing account of the Stroop effect. *Psychological Review,* 97, 332–361.

Collins, M. J. (1996). A new statistical parser based on bigram lexical dependencies. In *Proceedings of the 34th Meeting of the Association for Computational Linguistics* (pp. 184–191). Santa Cruz: ACL.

Collins, M. J. and Quillian, M. R. (1969). Retrieval time from semantic memory. *Journal of Verbal Learning and Verbal Behavior,* 8, 240–247.

Cormack, A. (1999). Without specifiers. In D. Adger, S. Pintzuk, B. Plunkett and G. Tsoulas (eds), *Specifiers: minimalist approaches* (pp. 46–68). Oxford: Oxford University Press.

Cormack, A. and Smith, N. (2001). Don't move! *University College London Working Papers in Linguistics,* 13, 215–241.

Covington, M. A. (1990). Parsing discontinuous constituents in dependency grammar. *Computational Linguistics,* 16, 234–236.

Covington, M. A. (1994). *An empirically motivated reinterpretation of Dependency Grammar.* (Research Report AI-1994-01). University of Georgia, Athens GE.

Croft, W. (2001). *Radical Construction Grammar: syntactic theory in typological perspective.* Oxford: Oxford University Press.

Crossman, E. R. F. W. (1959). A theory of the acquisition of a speed-skill. *Ergonomics,* 2, 153–166.

Crystal, D. (1967). Word classes in English. *Lingua,* 17, 24–56.

Curry, H. B. and Feys, R. (1958). *Combinatory logic,* Vol. 1. Amsterdam: North Holland.

Dabrowska, E. (2000). From formula to schema: the acquisition of English questions. *Cognitive Linguistics,* 11, 83–102.

Dabrowska, E. and Lieven, E. V. M. (2005). Towards a lexically specific grammar of children's question constructions. *Cognitive Linguistics,* 16, 437–474.

Davis, A. and Koenig, J.-P. (2000). Linking as constraints on word classes in a hierarchical lexicon. *Language,* 76, 56–91.

Davis, G. F. and Greve, H. R. (1997). Corporate elite networks and governance changes in the 1980s. *American Journal of Sociology,* 103, 1–37.

Deckner, D. F., Adamson, L. B. and Bakeman, R. (2006). Child and maternal contributions to shared reading: effects on language and literacy development. *Journal of Applied Developmental Psychology,* 27, 31–41.

Delaney, P. F., Reder, L. M., Staszewski, J. J. and Ritter, F. E. (1998). The strategy specific nature of improvement: the power law applies by strategy within task. *Psychological Science*, 9, 1–8.

Deuchar, M. (1999). Are function words non-language-specific in early bilingual two-word utterances? *Bilingualism: Language and Cognition*, 2, 23–34.

Deuchar, M. and Quay, S. (2000). *Bilingual acquisition: theoretical implications of a case study*. Oxford: Oxford University Press.

Dezso, L. (1982). *Studies in syntactic typology and contrastive grammar*. The Hague: Mouton.

Dixon, R. M. W. (1971). A method of semantic description. In D. D. Steinberg and L. A. Jakobovits (eds), *Semantics: an interdisciplinary reader in philosophy, linguistics and psychology* (pp. 436–471). Cambridge: Cambridge University Press.

Dixon, R. M. W. (1982). The semantics of giving. In R. M. W. Dixon (ed.), *Where have all the adjectives gone? And other essays in semantics and syntax* (pp. 117–139). Berlin: Mouton.

Dixon, R. M. W. (1991). *A new approach to English grammar, on semantic principles*. Oxford: Oxford University Press.

Dowty, D. R. (1982). Grammatical relations and Montague Grammar. In P. Jacobson and G. K. Pollum (eds), *The nature of syntactic representation* (pp. 79–130). Dordrecht: Reidel.

Dowty, D. R. (1989). On the semantic content of the notion of 'thematic role'. In G. Chierchia, B. Partee and R. Turner (eds), *Properties, types, and meaning*, Vol. 2 (pp. 69–129). Dordrecht: Kluwer.

Dowty, D. R. (1991). Thematic proto-roles and argument selection. *Language*, 67, 547–619.

Dowty, D. R. (2000). 'The garden swarms with bees' and the fallacy of 'argument alternation'. In Y. Ravin and C. Leacock (eds), *Polysemy: theoretical and computational approaches* (pp. 111–28). New York: Oxford University Press.

Dromi, E. (1986). The one-word period as a stage in language development: quantitative and qualitative accounts. In I. Levin (ed.), *Stage and structure: reopening the debate* (pp. 220–245). Norwood, NJ: Ablex.

Dromi, E. (1987). *Early lexical development*. Cambridge: Cambridge University Press.

Duane, J. T. (1964). Learning curve approach to reliability monitoring. *IEEE Transactions on Aerospace*, 2, 563–566.

Elbers, L. (1990). The synchronic relation between two- and three-word sentences. Paper presented at the Fifth International Congress for the Study of Child Language, Budapest, Hungary.

Elman, J. L., Bates, E., Johnson, M. H., Karmiloff-Smith, A., Parisi, D. and Plunkett, K. (1996). *Rethinking innateness.* Cambridge, MA: MIT Press.

Epstein, S. D. (1999). Un-principled syntax: the derivation of syntactic relations. In S. D. Epstein and N. Hornstein, (eds), *Working minimalism* (pp. 317–345). Cambridge: MIT Press.

Epstein, S. D., Groat, E. M., Kawashima, R. and Kitahara, H. (1998). *A derivational approach to syntactic relations.* Oxford: Oxford University Press.

Ervin-Tripp, S. M. (1966). Language development. In L. W. Hoffman and M. L. Hoffman (eds), *Review of child development research,* Vol. 2 (pp. 55–105). New York: Russell Sage Foundation.

Estoup, J. B. (1916). *Gammes stenographiques.* Paris: Gauthier Villars.

Ewing, G. (1982). Word-order invariance and variability in five children's three-word utterances: a limited-scope analysis. In C. E. Johnson and C. L. Thew (eds), *Proceedings of the Second International Congress for the Study of Child Language,* Vol. 1 (pp. 151–165).Washington, DC: University Press of America.

Feagans, L., Garvey, G. J. and Golinkoff, R. M. (eds). (1984). *The origins and growth of communication.* Norwood, NJ: Ablex.

Fenson, L., Dale, P. S., Reznick, J. S., Bates, E., Thal, D. J. and Pethick, S. J. (1994). Variability in early communicative development. *Monographs of the Society for Research in Child Development,* 59, 242.

Ferrer i Cancho, R. and Solé, R. V. (2001). Two regimes in the frequency of words and the origins of complex lexicons: Zipf's law revisited. *Journal of Quantitative Linguistics,* 8, 165–173.

Ferrer i Cancho, R., Solé, R. V. and Kohler, R. (2003). Universality in syntactic dependency networks. *SFI Working Paper* no. 03-06-042.

Filip, H. (1996). Psychological predicates and the syntax-semantics interface. In A. Goldberg (ed.), *Conceptual structure, discourse, and language* (pp. 131–147). Stanford: CSLI Publications.

Fillmore, C. (1968). The case for case. In E. Bach and T. Harms (eds), *Universals in linguistic theory* (pp. 1–88). New York: Holt, Rinehart and Winston.

Finch, S. P. and Chater, N. (1992). Bootstrapping syntactic categories. In *Proceedings of the 14th Annual Conference of the Cognitive Science Society of America.* Hillsdale, NJ: Lawrence Erlbaum.

Finch, S. P. and Chater, N. (1994). Distributional bootstrapping: from word class to proto-sentences. In *Proceedings of the 16th Annual Meeting of the Cognitive Science Society of America*. Hillsdale, NJ: Lawrence Erlbaum.

Fisher, C., Gleitman, H. and Gleitman, L. R. (1991). On the semantic content of subcategorization frames. *Cognitive Psychology*, 23, 331–392.

Fitts P. M. and Posner, M. I. (1967). *Human performance*. Belmont, CA: Brooks/Cole.

Foley, W. A. and Van Valin, R. D. Jr. (1984). *Functional syntax and universal grammar*. Cambridge: Cambridge University Press.

Forner, M. (1979). The mother as LAD: Interaction between order and frequency of parental input and child production. In F. R. Eckman and A. J. Hastings (eds), *Studies in first and second language acquisition* (pp. 17–44). Rowley, MA: Newbury House.

Francis, H. (1969). Structure in the speech of a 21/2-year old. *British Journal of Educational Psychology*, 39, 291–302.

Fraser, N. M. (1993). Dependency parsing. Unpublished Ph.D. thesis, University College London, London.

Fraser, N. M. (1994). Dependency Grammar. In R. Asher (ed.), *Encyclopedia of Language and Linguistics* (pp. 860–864). Oxford: Pergamon Press.

Frege, G. (1967). Begriffsschrift, a formula language, modelled upon that of arithmetic, for pure thought (S. Bauer-Mengelberg, Trans.). In J. van Heijenoort (ed.), *From Frege to Godel: a source book in mathematical logic, 1879–1931* (pp. 1–82). Cambridge, MA: Harvard University Press. (Original work published 1879.)

Frege, G. (1970). Function and concept (P. Geach, Trans.). In P. Geach and M. Black (eds), *Translations from the philosophical writing of Gottlob Frege* (pp. 21–41). Oxford: Basil Blackwell. (Original work published 1891.)

Gaifman, H. (1965). Dependency systems and phrase-structure systems. *Information and Control*, 8, 304–337.

Ganger, J. and Brent, M. R. (2004). Reexamining the vocabulary spurt. *Developmental Psychology*, 40, 621–632.

van Geert, P. (1991). A dynamic systems model of cognitive and language growth. *Psychological Review*, 98, 3–53.

Gentner, D. (1978). On relational meaning: the acquisition of verb meaning. *Child Development*, 49, 988–998.

Gentner, D. (1983). Structure-mapping: a theoretical framework for analogy. *Cognitive Science*, 7, 155–170.

Gentner, D. (1989). The mechanisms of analogical learning. In S. Vosniadou and A. Ortony (eds), *Similarity, analogy, and thought* (pp. 199–241). Cambridge: Cambridge University Press.

Gentner, D. and Markman, A. B. (1997). Structure mapping in analogy and similarity. *American Psychologist*, 52, 45–56.

Gentner, D. and Medina, J. (1998). Similarity and the development of rules. *Cognition*, 65, 263–297.

Gentner, D. and Rattermann, M. J. (1991). Language and the career of similarity. In S. A. Gelman and J. P. Bymes (eds), *Perspectives on language and thought: Interrelations in development* (pp. 225–277). New York: Cambridge University Press.

Gentner, D. and Toupin, C. (1986). Systematicity and surface similarity in the development of analogy. *Cognitive Science*, 10, 277–300.

Gentner, D., Loewenstein, J. and Thompson, L. (2003). Learning and transfer: a general role for analogical encoding. *Journal of Educational Psychology*, 95, 393–408.

Gick, M. L. and Holyoak, K. J. (1983). Schema induction and analogical transfer. *Cognitive Psychology*, 15, 1–38.

Givón, T. (1997). Introduction. In Givón, T. (ed.), *Grammatical relations: a functionalist perspective* (pp. 1–30). Amsterdam: John Benjamins.

Gleitman, L. R. (1990). The structural sources of verb learning. *Language Acquisition*, 1, 3–35.

Gleitman, L. R. and Newport, E. L. (1995). The invention of language by children: environmental and biological influences on the acquisition of language. In L. R. Gleitman and M. Liberman (eds), *An invitation to cognitive science*, Vol. 1: *Language* (pp. 1–24). Cambridge, MA: MIT Press.

Gleitman, L. R., Newport, E. L. and Gleitman, H. (1984). The current status of the Motherese hypothesis. *Journal of Child Language*, 11, 43–79.

Glinert, L. (1989). *The grammar of Modern Hebrew*. Cambridge: Cambridge University Press.

Goldberg, A. E. (1995). *Constructions: a Gonstruction Grammar approach to argument structure*. Chicago, IL: University of Chicago Press.

Goldberg, A. E. (1999). The emergence of argument structure semantics. In B. MacWhinney (ed.), *The emergence of language* (pp. 197–213). Hillsdale, NJ: Lawrence Erlbaum.

Goldberg, A. E. (2005). *Constructions at work: the nature of generalization in language*. Oxford University Press.

Goldberg, A. E., Casenhiser, D. M. and Sethuraman, N. (2004). Learning argument structure generalizations. *Cognitive Linguistics,* 15, 289–316.

Golinkoff, R. M., Hirsh-Pasek, K., Cauley, K. and Gordon, L. (1987). The eyes have it: lexical and syntactic comprehension in a new paradigm. *Journal of Child Language,* 14, 23–45.

Gomez, R. L. and Gerken, L. (1999). Artificial grammar learning by 1-year-olds leads to specific and abstract knowledge. *Cognition,* 70, 109–135.

Goodman, J. C., Dale, P. S. and Li, P. (2002). The relationship between parental frequency and the order of acquisition in lexical development. Poster presented at the Joint meeting of the 9th International Congress of the International Association of the Study of Child Language and the 23rd Annual Symposium on Research in Child Language Disorders (IASCL/ SRCLD), Madison, WI.

Goodman, N. (1972). Seven strictures on similarity. In N. Goodman (ed.), *Problems and projects* (pp. 437–447). New York: Bobbs-Merrill.

Goswami, U. (1991). Analogical reasoning: what develops? A review of research and theory. *Child Development,* 62, 1–22.

Goswami, U. (1992). *Analogical reasoning in children.* Hillsdale, NJ: Lawrence Erlbaum.

Goswami, U. (1996). Analogical reasoning and cognitive development. In H. W. Reese (ed.), *Advances in child development and behavior* (pp. 92–135). New York: Academic Press.

Goswami, U. and Brown, A. L. (1989). Melting chocolate and melting snowmen: analogical reasoning and causal relations. *Cognition,* 35, 69–95.

Green, G. M. (1997). Modelling grammar growth: Universal grammar without innate principles or parameters. Paper presented at GALA97 Conference on Language Acquisition, Edinburgh.

Greenfield, P. M. and Smith, J. H. (1976). *The structure of communication in early language development.* New York: Academic Press.

Grimshaw, J. (1990). *Argument structure.* Cambridge, MA: MIT Press.

Gropen, J., Pinker, S., Hollander, M., Goldberg, R. and Wilson, R. (1989). The learnability and acquisition of the dative alternation in English. *Language,* 65, 203–257.

Gupta, P. and Cohen, N. J. (2002). Theoretical and computational analysis of skill learning, repetition priming, and procedural memory. *Psychological Review,* 109, 401–448.

Gutenberg, B. and Richter, R. F. (1944). Frequency of earthquakes in California. *Bulletin of the Seismological Society of America,* 34, 185–188.

Haegeman, L. (1991). *Introduction to Government and Binding Theory.* Oxford: Basil Blackwell.

Hahn, U. and Chater, N. (1998). Similarity and rules: distinct? exhaustive? empirically distinguishable? *Cognition,* **65,** 197–230.

Hale, K. and Keyser, S. J. (1993). On argument structure and the lexical expression of syntactic relations. In K. Hale and S. J. Keyser (ed.), *The view from Building 20* (pp. 53–109). Cambridge, MA: MIT Press.

Hauser, M. D., Chomsky, N. and Fitch, W. T. (2002). The faculty of language: What is it, who has it, and how did it evolve? *Science,* **298,** 1569–1579.

Hayes, D. G. (1964). Dependency theory: a formalism and some observations. *Language,* **40,** 511–525.

Heathcote, A., Brown, S. and Mewhort, D. J. K. (2000).Repealing the power law: the case for an exponential law of practice. *Psychonomic Bulletin and Review,* **7,** 185–207.

Helbig, G. (1992). *Probleme der Valenz-und Kasustheorie: Konzepte der Sprach-und Literaturwissenschaft.* Tubingen: Niemeyer.

Hellwig, P. (1986). Dependency Unification Grammar (DUG). *Proceedings of the 11th International Conference on Computational Linguistics* (pp. 195–198). Bonn.

Heny, F. (1979). Review of N. Chomsky (1975), *The logical structure of linguistic theory.* New York: Plenum. *Synthese,* **40,** 317–352.

Hill, J. C. (1984). Combining two-term relations: evidence in support of flat structure. *Journal of Child Language,* **11,** 673–678.

Hirsh-Pasek, K. and Golinkoff, R. M. (1991). Language comprehension: a new look at some old themes. In N. Krasnegor, D. M. Rumbaugh, R. L. Schiefelbusch and M. Studdert-Kennedy (eds), *Biological and behavioral determinants of language development* (pp. 301–320). Hillsdale, NJ: Erlbaum.

Hirsh-Pasek, K. and Golinkoff, R. M. (1996). *The origins of grammar: evidence from early language comprehension.* MIT Press. Cambridge.

Hockett, C. F. (1958). *A course in modern linguistics.* New York: Macmillan.

Hoff, E. (2006). How social contexts support and shape language development. *Developmental Review,* **26,** 55–88.

Hollich, G., Jusczyk, P. and Luce, P. A. (2002). Lexical neighborhood effects in 17-month-old word learning. *Proceedings of the 26rd Annual Boston University Conference on Language Development* (pp. 314–323). Boston, MA: Cascadilla Press.

Holme, P. and Huss, M. (2003). Discovery and analysis of biochemical subnetwork hierarchies. In R. Gauges, U. Kummer, J. Pahle and U. Rost (eds), *3rd Workshop on Computation of Biochemical Pathways and Genetic Networks, European Media Lab Proceedings* (pp. 3–9). Berlin: Logos.

Hopper, P. J. and Thompson, S. A. (1980). Transitivity in grammar and discourse. *Language,* **56**, 251–299.

Hopper, P. J. and Thompson, S. A. (1984). The discourse basis for lexical categories in universal grammar. *Language,* **60**, 703–752.

Horgan, D. (1980). Nouns: love 'em or leave 'em. In V. Teller and S. I. White (eds), *Studies in child language and multilingualism.* New York: Annals of the New York Academy of Sciences.

Hornby, A. S. (1945). *A guide to patterns and usage in English.* London: Oxford University Press.

Hudson, R. (1984). *Word Grammar.* Oxford: Basil Blackwell.

Hudson, R. (1990). *English Word Grammar.* Oxford: Basil Blackwell.

Hudson, R. (1993). Do we have heads in our minds? In G. G. Corbett, N. Fraser and S. McGlashan (eds), *Heads in grammatical theory* (pp. 266–292). Cambridge: Cambridge University Press.

Hudson, R. (1995). *Word meaning.* London: Routledge.

Hudson, R., Rosta, A., Holmes, J. and Gisborne, N. (1996). Synonyms and syntax. *Journal of Linguistics,* **32**, 439–446.

Hull, C. L. (1943). *Principles of behavior.* New York: Appleton-Century-Crofts.

Hummel, J. E. and Holyoak, K. J. (1997). Distributed representations of structure: a theory of analogical access and mapping. *Psychological Review,* **104**, 427–466.

Husserl, E. (1970). *Logical investigations* (J. N. Findlay, Trans.). London: Routledge and Kegan Paul. (Original work published 1900.)

Huttenlocher, J., Haight, W., Bryk, A., Seltzer, M. and Lyons, T. (1991). Early vocabulary growth: Relation to language input and gender. *Developmental Psychology,* **27**, 236–248.

Hyams, N. (1986). *Language acquisition and the theory of parameters.* Dordrecht: Reidel.

Iamnitchi, A., Ripeanu, M. and Foster, I. (2004). Small-world file-sharing communities. Paper presented at the 23rd Conference of the IEEE Communications Society (InfoCom 2004), Hong Kong.

Ingram, D. (1979a). Early patterns of grammatical development. Paper presented at the conference 'Language behavior in infancy and early childhood', Santa Barbara, CA.

Ingram, D. (1979b). Stages in the development of one-word utterances: transition to semantic relations. In P. L. French (ed.), *The development of meaning* (pp. 256–281). Hiroshima: Bunka Hyoron.

Ingram, D. (1981). Early patterns of grammatical development. In R. Stark (ed.), *Language behavior in infancy and early childhood* (pp. 327–352). New York: Elsevier North Holland.

Ingram, D. (1989). *First language acquisition.* Cambridge: Cambridge University Press.

Ingram, D. and Thompson, W. (1996). Early syntactic acquisition in German: evidence for the modal hypothesis. *Language, 72,* 97–120.

Jackendoff, R. S. (1972). *Semantic interpretation in generative grammar.* Cambridge MA: MIT Press.

Jackendoff, R. S. (1977). *X' syntax: a study of phrase structure.* Cambridge, MA: MIT Press.

Jackendoff, R. S. (1983). *Semantics and cognition.* Cambridge, MA: MIT Press.

Jackendoff, R. S. (1987). The status of thematic relation in linguistic theory. *Linguistic Inquiry, 18,* 369–411.

Jackendoff, R. S. (1990). *Semantic structures.* Cambridge, MA: MIT Press.

Jelinek, E. (1984). Empty categories, case, and configurationality. *Natural Language and Linguistic Theory, 2,* 39–76.

Johnson, C. E. (1980). The ontogenesis of question words in children's language. Paper presented at the Fifth Annual Boston University Conference on Language Development, October 1980.

Johnson, C. E. (2000). What you see is what you get: the importance of transcription for interpreting children's morphosyntactic development. In L. Menn and N. Ratner (eds), *Methods for studying language production* (pp. 181–204). Mahwah, NJ: Lawrence Erlbaum.

Johnson, H. and Johnson, P. (1991). Task Knowledge Structures: psychological basis and integration into system design. *Acta Psychologica, 78,* 3–26.

Kaplan, R. and Bresnan, J. (1982). Lexical-functional Grammar: a formal system for grammatical representation. In J. Bresnan (ed.), *The mental representation of grammatical relations* (pp. 173–281). Cambridge, MA: MIT Press.

Kauschke, C. and Hofmeister, C. (2002). Early lexical development in German: a study on vocabulary growth and vocabulary composition during the second and third year of life. *Journal of Child Language, 29,* 735–757.

Keenan, E. L. (1975). *Formal semantics of natural language.* Cambridge: Cambridge University Press.

Keenan, E. L. (1976). Towards a universal definition of 'subject'. In C. N. Li (ed.), *Subject and topic* (pp. 303–333). New York: Academic Press.

Keren-Portnoy, T. (in press). Facilitation and practice in verb acquisition. *Journal of Child Language.*

Kiekhoefer, K. (2002). The acquisition of the ditransitive construction. Paper presented at the Joint meeting of the 9th International Congress of the International Association of the Study of Child Language and the 23rd Annual Symposium on Research in Child Language Disorders (IASCL/ SRCLD), Madison, WI.

Kirsner, K. and Speelman, C. (1996). Skill acquisition and repetition priming: one principle, many processes. *Journal of Experimental Psychology: Learning, Memory and Cognition,* 22, 1–13.

Klahr, D. (2000). *Exploring science: the cognition and development of discovery processes.* Cambridge, MA: MIT Press.

Klima, E. S. and Bellugi-Klima, U. (1966). Syntactic regularities in the speech of children. In J. Lyons and R. J. Wales (eds), *Psycholinguistics papers* (pp. 183–208). Edinburgh: Edinburgh University Press.

Koenig, J.-P. and Davis, A. (2001). Sublexical modality and the structure of lexical semantic representations. *Linguistics and Philosophy,* 24, 71–124.

Köppe, R. and Meisel, J. M. (1995). Code-switching in bilingual first language acquisition. In L. Milroy and P. Muysken (eds), *One speaker, two languages: cross-disciplinary perspectives on code-switching* (pp. 276–301), Cambridge: Cambridge University Press.

Kramer, A. F., Strayer, D. L. and Buckley, J. (1990). Development and transfer of automatic processing. *Journal of Experimental Psychology: Human Perception and Performance,* 16, 505–522.

Krohne, D. T. (2001). *General ecology.* Pacific Grove, CA: Brooks/Cole.

Kuczaj, S. A. and Brannick, N. (1979). Children's use of the Wh question model auxiliary placement rule. *Journal of Experimental Child Psychology,* 28, 43–67.

Kuczaj, S. A. and Maratsos, M. P. (1983). Initial verbs of yes-no questions: a different kind of grammatical category. *Developmental Psychology,* 19, 440–44.

Lakoff, G. (1987). *Women, fire and dangerous things.* Chicago, IL: University of Chicago Press.

Langacker, R. W. (1987). *Foundations of cognitive grammar, Vol. I.* Stanford: Stanford University Press.

van Langendonck, W. (1987). Word Grammar and child grammar. *Belgian Journal of Linguistics,* 2, 109–132.

van Langendonck, W. (1994). Determiners as heads? *Cognitive Linguistics*, 5, 243–259.

Lebeaux, D. S. (1986). *The interpretation of derived nominals*. In A. M. Farley, P. F. Farley and K.-E. McCullogh (eds), *CLS 22: Papers from the General Session of the Twenty-Second Annual Regional Meeting of the Chicago Linguistic Society* (pp. 231–247). Chicago, IL: Chicago Linguistic Society.

Lebeaux, D. S. (2000). *Language acquisition and the form of the grammar*. Amsterdam: John Benjamins.

Lee, T. H. (2004). Productivity in the early word combinations of Cantonese-speaking children. In S. Feng and S. Zhongwei (eds), *The joy of research—A Festschrift in honor of Professor William S-Y.Wang on his seventieth birthday* (pp. 38–58). Tianjin: Nankai University Press.

Leopold, W. (1939–1949). *Speech development of a bilingual child*. Evanston, IL: Northwestern University Press.

Levin, B. (1985). Introduction. In B. Levin (ed.), *Lexical semantics in review*, Lexicon Project Working Papers 1, Center for Cognitive Science, MIT, Cambridge, MA.

Levin, B. (1993). *English verb classes and alternations*. Chicago, IL: Chicago University Press.

Levin, B. (1999). Objecthood: an event structure perspective. In S. J. Billings, J. P. Boyle and A. M. Griffith (eds.), *CLS 35: The Main Session. Papers from the Thirty-Fifth Annual Regional Meeting of the Chicago Linguistic Society, Vol. 1* (pp. 223–247). Chicago, IL: Chicago Linguistic Society.

Levin, B. and Rappaport Hovav, M. (1995). *Unaccusativity: at the syntax-lexical semantics interface*. Linguistic Inquiry Monograph 26. Cambridge, MA: MIT Press.

Levin, B. and Rappaport Hovav, M. (1996). Lexical semantics and syntactic structure. In S. Lappin (ed.), *The handbook of contemporary semantic theory* (pp. 487–507). Oxford: Basil Blackwell.

Levy, Y. (1988). The nature of early language: evidence from the development of Hebrew morphology. In Y. Levy, I. M. Schlesinger and M. D. S. Braine (eds), *Categories and processes in language acquisition* (pp. 73–98). Hillsdale, NJ: Lawrence Erlbaum.

Levy, Y., Schlesinger, I. M. and Braine, M. D. S. (eds). (1988). *Categories and processes in language acquisition*. Hillsdale, NJ: Lawrence Erlbaum.

Lieven, E. V. M., Pine, J. M. and Baldwin, G. (1997). Lexically-based learning and early grammatical development. *Journal of Child Language*, 24, 187–219.

Lindsay, P. and Norman, D. A. (1977): *Human information processing: an introduction to psychology*, (2nd edn). San Diego, CA: Hartcourt Brace Jovanovich.

Lock, A. J. (1980). *The guided reinvention of language*. London: Academic Press.

Loewenstein, J. and Gentner, D. (2001). Spatial mapping in preschoolers: close comparisons facilitate far mappings. *Journal of Cognition and Development*, 2, 189–219.

Logan, G. D. (1988). Toward an instance theory of automatization. *Psychological Review*, 95, 492–527.

Logan, G. D. (1990). Social cognition gets specific. In T. K. Srull and R. S. Wyer (eds), *Advances in social cognition*, Vol. 3 (pp. 141–151). Hillsdale, NJ: Lawrence Erlbaum.

Logan, G. D. (1992). Shapes of reaction-time distributions and shapes of learning curves: a test of the instance theory of automaticity. *Journal of Experimental Psychology: Learning, Memory, and Cognition*, 18, 883–914.

Luce, P. A. and Pisoni, D. B. (1998). Recognizing spoken words: the neighbourhood activation model. *Ear and Hearing*, 19, 1–36.

Lust, B. (1999). Universal grammar: the strong continuity hypothesis in first language acquisition. In W. C. Ritchie and T. K. Bhatia (eds), *Handbook of child language acquisition* (pp. 111–156). San Diego, CA: Academic Press.

Lyons, J. (1968). *Introduction to theoretical linguistics*. Cambridge: Cambridge University Press.

MacKay, D. (1982). The problems of flexibility, fluency, and speed-accuracy trade-off in skilled behavior. *Psychological Review*, 89, 483–506.

Macnamara, J. (1972). Cognitive basis of language learning in infants. *Psychological Review*, 79, 1–14.

MacWhinney, B. (1975). Pragmatic patterns in child syntax. *Stanford Papers and Reports on Child Language Development*, 10, 153–165.

MacWhinney, B. (1982). Basic syntactic processes. In S. A. Kuczaj (ed.), *Language development:* Vol. 1. *Syntax and semantics* (pp. 73–136). Hillsdale, NJ: Lawrence Erlbaum.

MacWhinney, B. (2004). A multiple process solution to the logical problem of language acquisition. *Journal of Child Language*, 31, 883–914.

Mandelbrot, B. (1966). Information theory and psycholinguistics: a theory of word frequencies. In P. Lazarsfeld and N. Henry (eds), *Readings in mathematical social science* (pp. 350–368). Cambridge, MA: MIT Press.

Maratsos, M. P. (1979). How to get from words to sentences. In D. Aaronson and R. Rieber (eds), *Psycholinguistic research: Implications and applications.* (pp. 285–356). Hillsdale, NJ: Lawrence Erlbaum.

Maratsos, M. P. (1982). The child's construction of grammatical categories. In E. Wanner and L. R. Gleitman (eds), *Language acquisition: the state of the art* (pp. 240–266). Cambridge: Cambridge University Press.

Maratsos, M. P. (1983). Some current issues in the study of the acquisition of grammar. In P. H. Mussen (ed.), *Handbook of child psychology: formerly Carmichael's manual of child psychology,* (4th edn) (pp. 707–786). New York: Wiley.

Marcus, G., Vijayan, S., Bandi Rao, S. and Vishton, P. M. (1999). Rule-learning in seven-month-old infants. *Science,* **283,** 77–80.

Matsumoto, Y. (1996). Interaction of factors in construal: Japanese relative clauses. In M. Shibatani and S. A. Thompson (eds), *Grammatical constructions: their form and meaning* (pp. 103–124). Oxford: Clarendon Press.

Matthews, D. E., Lieven, E. V. M., Theakston, A. L. and Tomasello, M. (2005). The role of frequency in the acquisition of English word order. *Cognitive Development,* **20,** 121–136.

Mazur, J. E. and Hastie, R. (1978). Learning as accumulation: a reexamination of the learning curve. *Psychological Bulletin,* **85,** 1256–1274.

McAndrews, M. P and Moskowitch, M. (1985). Rule-based and exemplar-based classification in artificial grammar learning. *Memory and Cognition,* **13,** 469–475.

McClure, K. and Pine, J. M. (2002). Examining the Verb Island hypothesis. Paper presented at the Joint meeting of the 9th International Congress of the International Association of the Study of Child Language and the 23rd Annual Symposium on Research in Child Language Disorders (IASCL/ SRCLD), Madison, WI.

McCord, M., Bernth, A., Lappin, S. and Zadrozny, W. (1992). Natural language processing within a Slot Grammar framework. *International Journal on Artificial Intelligence Tools,* **1,** 229–277.

McCune, L. and Vihman, M. M. (1999). Relational words and motion events: a universal bootstrap to syntax. Paper presented at the SRCD Biennial Meeting, Albuquerque, NM.

McCune-Nicolich, L. (1981). The cognitive bases of early relational words. *Journal of Child Language,* **8,** 15–36.

McGregor, K. K., Sheng, L. and Smith, B. (2005). The precocious two-year-old: status of the lexicon and links to the grammar. *Journal of Child Language,* **32,** 563–585.

McKay, D. G. (1988). The problem of flexibility, fluency, and speed-accuracy trade-off in skilled behavior. *Psychological Review,* **89**, 483–506.

Medin, D. L. and Schaffer, M. M. (1978). Context Theory and classification learning. *Psychological Review,* **85**, 207–238.

Medin, D. L., Goldstone, R. L. and Gentner, D. (1993). Respects for similarity. *Psychological Review,* **100**, 254–278.

Mel'cuk, I. A. (1979). *Studies in dependency syntax.* Ann Arbor: Karoma.

Mel'cuk, I. A. (1988). *Dependency syntax: theory and practice.* Albany, NY: State University of New York Press.

Miller, N. F. and Dollard, J. (1941). *Social learning and imitation.* New Haven: Yale University Press.

Miller, W. R. and Ervin, S. M. (1964). The development of grammar in child language. *Monographs of the Society for Research in Child Development,* **29**, 92.

Mintz, T. H., Newport, E. L. and Bever, T. G. (2002). The distributional structure of grammatical categories in speech to young children. *Cognitive Science,* **26**, 393–425.

Montague, R. (1974). *Formal philosophy* (R. H. Thomason, ed.). London: Yale University Press.

Moortgat, M. (1988). *Categorial investigations: logical and linguistic aspects of the Lambek Calculus.* Dordrecht: Foris.

Morgan, J., Shi, R. and Allopenna, P. (1996). Perceptual bases of rudimentary grammatical categories: toward a broader conceptualization of bootstrapping. In J. L. Morgan and K. Demuth, (eds), *Signal to syntax: bootstrapping from speech to grammar in early acquisition* (pp. 263–283). Hillsdale, NJ: Lawrence Earlbaum.

Morris, W. C., Cottrell, G. W. and Elman, J. L. (2000). A connectionist simulation of the empirical acquisition of grammatical relations. In S. Wermter and R. Sun (eds), *Hybrid neural symbolic integration* (pp. 175–193). Berlin: Springer-Verlag.

Murphy, G. L. and Medin, D. L. (1985). The role of theories in conceptual coherence. *Psychological Review,* **92**, 289–316.

Naigles, L. R. (1990). Children use syntax to learn verb meanings. *Journal of Child Language,* **17**, 357–374.

Naigles, L. R. (2004). Comprehension matters: a commentary on 'A multiple process solution to the logical problem of language acquisition'. *Journal of Child Language,* **31**, 936–940.

Naigles, L. R. and Hoff-Ginsberg, E. (1995). Input to verb learning: evidence for the plausibility of syntactic bootstrapping. *Developmental Psychology,* **31**, 827–837.

Nelson, K. (1973). Structure and strategy in learning to talk. *Monographs of the Society for Research in Child Development*, 141, 38.

Nelson, K. (1981). Individual differences in language development: implications for development and language. *Developmental Psychology*, 17, 170–87.

Nelson, K., Plesa Skwerer, D., Goldman, S., Henseler, S., Presler, N. and Fried Walkenfeld, F. (2003). Entering a community of minds: an experiential approach to 'Theory of Mind'. *Human Development*, 46, 24–46.

Nerb, J., Ritter, F. E. and Krems, J. (1999). Knowledge level learning and the power law: a Soar model of skill acquisition in scheduling. *Kognitionswissenschaft [Journal of the German Cognitive Science Society]* Special issue on cognitive modeling and cognitive architectures, D. Wallach and H. A. Simon (eds), 20–29.

Newell, A. (1990). *Unified theories of cognition.* Cambridge, MA: Harvard University Press.

Newell, A. and Rosenbloom, P. S. (1981). Mechanisms of skill acquisition and the law of practice. In J. R. Anderson (ed.), *Cognitive skills and their acquisition* (pp. 1–51). Hillsdale, NJ: Lawrence Erlbaum.

Newell, K. M., Liu, Y-T. and Mayer-Kress, G. (2001). Time scales in motor learning and development. *Psychological Review*, 108, 57–82.

Newman, M. E. J. (2001). The structure of scientific collaboration networks. *Proceedings of the National Academy of Sciences of USA*, 98, 404–409.

Newman, M. E. J. (2003). The structure and function of complex networks. *SIAM Review* 45, 167–256.

Newport, E. L. and Aslin, R. N. (2000). Innately constrained learning: Blending old and new approaches to language acquisition. In S. C. Howell, S. A. Fish and T. Keith-Lucas (eds), *Proceedings of the 24th annual Boston University conference on language development.* Somerville, MA: Cascadilla Press.

Ninio, A. (1984). *Functions of speech in mother-infant interaction.* Final Science Report to the United States-Israel Binational Science Foundation (BSF), Jerusalem, Israel.

Ninio, A. (1986). The direct mapping of function to form in children's early language. *Journal of Psycholinguistic Research*, 15, 559 (Abstract).

Ninio, A. (1988). On formal grammatical categories in early child language. In Y. Levy, I. M. Schlesinger and M. D. S. Braine (eds), *Categories and processes in language acquisition* (pp. 99–119). Hillsdale, NJ: Lawrence Erlbaum.

Ninio, A. (1992). The relation of children's single word utterances to single word utterances in the input. *Journal of Child Language*, 19, 87–110.

Ninio, A. (1994). Predicting the order of acquisition of three-word constructions by the complexity of their dependency structure. *First Language*, 14,
119–152.

Ninio, A. (1995). Compiler Grammar: a dependency-oriented minimalist
approach. *Theoretical Linguistics*, 21, 159–195.

Ninio, A. (1996). A proposal for the adoption of dependency grammar as the
framework for the study of language acquisition. In G. Ben Shakhar and
A. Lieblich (eds), *Volume in honor of Shlomo Kugelmass* (pp. 85–103).
Jerusalem: Magnes.

Ninio, A. (1998). Acquiring a dependency grammar: the first three stages in
the acquisition of multiword combinations in Hebrew-speaking children.
In G. Makiello-Jarza, J. Kaiser and M. Smolczynska (eds), *Language acquisition and developmental psychology* (pp. 201–210). Cracow: Universitas.

Ninio, A. (1999a). Pathbreaking verbs in syntactic development and the
question of prototypical transitivity. *Journal of Child Language*, 26,
619–653.

Ninio, A. (1999b). Model learning in syntactic development: intransitive
verbs. *International Journal of Bilingualism*, 3, 111–131.

Ninio, A. (2003). No verb is an island: negative evidence on the Verb Island
hypothesis. *Psychology of Language and Communication*, 7, 3–21.

Ninio, A. (2005a). Testing the role of semantic similarity in syntactic development. *Journal of Child Language*, 32, 35–61.

Ninio, A. (2005b). Accelerated learning without semantic similarity: indirect
objects. *Cognitive Linguistics*, 16, 531–556.

Ninio, A. and Bruner, J. S. (1978). The achievement and antecedents of
labelling. *Journal of Child Language*, 5, 1–15.

Ninio, A. and Snow, C. E. (1988). Language acquisition through language use:
the functional sources of children's early utterances. In Y. Levy, I. Schlesinger and M. D. S. Braine (eds), *Categories and processes in language
acquisition* (pp. 11–30). Hillsdale, NJ: Lawrence Erlbaum.

Ninio, A. and Snow, C. E. (1996). *Pragmatic development*. Boulder, CO:
Westview Press.

Ninio, A. and Wheeler, P. (1984). Functions of speech in mother-infant
interaction. In L. Feagans, G. J. Garvey and R. M. Golinkoff (eds), *The
origins and growth of communication* (pp. 196–207). Norwood, NJ: Ablex.

Nosofsky, R. M. (1984). Choice, similarity, and the context theory of classification. *Journal of Experimental Psychology: Learning, Memory, and Cognition*, 10, 104–114.

Nosofsky, R. M. (1988). Similarity, frequency, and category representation. *Journal of Experimental Psychology: Learning, Memory and Cognition,* 14, 54–65.

Nosofsky, R. M. (1992). Exemplar-based approach to relating categorization, identification, and recognition. In F. G. Ashby (ed.), *Multidimensional models of perception and cognition* (pp. 207–225). Hillsdale, NJ: Lawrence Erlbaum.

Nosofsky, R. M. and Palmeri, T. J. (1997). An exemplar-based random-walk model of speeded classification. *Psychological Review,* 104, 266–300.

Novick, L. R. (1988). Analogical transfer, problem similarity, and expertise. *Journal of Experimental Psychology: Learning, Memory, and Cognition,* 14, 510–520.

Oehrle, R. T. (1994). Term-labelled categorial type systems. *Linguistics and Philosophy,* 17, 633–678.

Ohlsson, S. (1992). The learning curve for writing books: evidence from Professor Asimov. *Psychological Science,* 3, 380–382.

Ono, K. and Budwig, N. (2005). Caregiver input and young children's use of unaccusative intransitives in novel verb experiments. Poster presented at the 30th Annual Boston University Conference on Language Development, Boston, MA.

Osgood, C. E. (1949). The similarity paradox in human learning: a resolution. *Psychological Review,* 56, 132–143.

Osgood, C. E., Suci, C. J. and Tannenbaum, P. H. (1957). *The measurement of meaning.* Urbana, IL: University of Illinois Press.

Paas, F. G. and Van Merrienboer, J. J. (1994). Variability of worked examples and transfer of geometrical problem-solving skills: a cognitive load approach. *Journal of Educational Psychology,* 86, 122–133.

Palmeri, T. J. (1997). Exemplar similarity and the development of automaticity. *Journal of Experimental Psychology: Learning Memory and Cognition,* 23, 324–354.

Payne, T. E. (1997). *Describing morphosyntax: a guide for field linguists.* Cambridge: Cambridge University Press.

Peirce, C. S. (1992). *Reasoning and the logic of things: the Cambridge Conference Lectures of 1898.* Harvard University Press, Cambridge, Massachusetts. (Original work published 1898.)

Perlmutter, D. M. and Postal, P. M. (1974). *Lectures on Relational Grammar.* LSA Linguistic Institute, University of Massachusetts at Amherst.

Perlmutter, D. M and Postal, P. M. (1984). The 1-Advancement Exclusiveness Law. In D. M. Perlmutter and C. G. Rosen (eds), *Studies in Relational Grammar* 2 (pp. 81–125). Chicago, IL: University of Chicago Press.

Perruchet, P. and Pacteau, C. (1990). Synthetic grammar learning: Implicit rule abstraction or explicit fragmentary knowledge? *Journal of Experimental Psychology: General*, 119, 264–275.

Peters, A. M. (1983). *The units of language acquisition*. Cambridge: Cambridge University Press.

Peters, A. M. (1995). Strategies in the acquisition of syntax. In P. Fletcher and B. MacWhinney (eds), *Handbook of language acquisition* (pp. 462–482). Oxford: Basil Blackwell.

Piattelli-Palmarini, M. (1980). *Language and learning: the debate between Jean Piaget and Noam Chomsky*. Cambridge: Harvard University Press.

Pine, J. M. and Lieven, E. V. M. (1993). Reanalyzing rote-learned phrases: individual differences in the transition to multi-word speech. *Journal of Child Language*, 20, 551–571.

Pine, J. M., Lieven, E. V. M. and Rowland, C. F. (1998). Comparing different models of the development of the English verb category. *Linguistics*, 36, 807–830.

Pinker, S. (1984). *Language learnability and language development*. Cambridge, MA: Harvard University Press.

Pinker, S. (1989). *Learnability and cognition: the acquisition of argument structure*. Cambridge, MA: MIT Press.

Pinker, S. (1994). *The language instinct: how the mind creates language*. New York: William Morrow.

Pinker, S. Lebeaux, D. S. and Frost, L. A. (1987). Productivity and constraints in the acquisition of the passive. *Cognition*, 26, 195–267.

Poeppel, D. and Wexler, K. (1993).The full competence hypothesis of clause structure in early German. *Language*, 69, 1–33.

Pollard, C. and Sag, I. A. (1987). *Information-based analysis of language*—Vol. 1: *Fundamentals*. Number 13 in CSLI Lecture Notes. CSLI.

Pollard, C. and Sag, I. A. (1994). *Head-Driven Phrase Structure Grammar*. Chicago, IL: Chicago University Press.

Powers, S. M. (2002). Merge as a basic mechanism of language: evidence from language acquisition. In E. Witruk and A. D. Friederici (eds), *Basic functions of language, reading and reading disability* (pp. 105–117). Dordrecht, Netherlands: Kluwer.

Pustejovsky, J. (1991). The generative lexicon. *Computational Linguistics*, 17, 409–441.

Quillian, M. R. (1967). Word concepts: a theory and simulation of some basic semantic capabilities. *Behavioral Science*, 12, 410–430.

Quillian, M. R. (1968). Semantic memory. In M. Minsky (ed.), *Semantic information processing* (pp. 227–270). Cambridge, MA: MIT Press.

Radford, A. (1990). *Syntactic theory and the acquisition of English syntax.* Oxford: Basil Blackwell.

Radford, A. (1996). Towards a structure-building model of acquisition. In H. Clahsen (ed.), *Generative perspectives on language acquisition* (pp. 43–89). Amsterdam: John Benjamins.

Radford, A. (2000). Children in search of perfection: towards a minimalist model of acquisition. *Essex Research Reports in Linguistics*, 33, 21–32.

Ram, A. and Leake, D. (eds). (1995). *Goal-driven learning.* Cambridge, MA: MIT Press/Bradford Books.

Rambow, O. and Joshi, A. K. (1994). A formal look at dependency grammars and phrase-structure grammars, with special consideration of word-order phenomena. In L. Wanner (ed.), *Current issues in Meaning-Text Theory* (pp. 47–66). London: Pinter.

Rappaport Hovav, M. and Levin, B. (1995). *The elasticity of verb meaning. IATL 2: Proceedings of the Tenth Annual Conference of the Israel Association for Theoretical Linguistics and the Workshop on the Syntax-Semantics Interface.* Bar Ilan University, Ramat Gan, Israel.

Rattermann, M. J. and Gentner, D. (1998). More evidence for a relational shift in the development of analogy: Children's performance on a causal-mapping task. *Cognitive Development*, 13, 453–478.

Redington, M., Chater, N. and Finch, S. P. (1998). Distributional information: a powerful cue for acquiring syntactic categories. *Cognitive Science*, 22, 435–469.

Reeves, L. M. and Weisberg, R. W. (1993). On the concrete nature of human thinking: content and context in analogical transfer. *Educational Psychology*, 13, 245–258.

Reichenbach, H. (1947). *Elements of symbolic logic.* New York: Macmillian.

Richards, M. R. M. (ed.) (1974). *The integration of a child into a social world.* Cambridge University Press.

Rickard, T. C. (1997). Bending the Power law: a CMPL theory of strategy shifts and the automatization of cognitive skills. *Journal of Experimental Psychology: General*, 126, 288–311.

Roberts, K. (1983). Comprehension and production of world order in Stage 1. *Child Development*, **54**, 443–449.

Roberts, W. A. (1972). Free recall of word lists varying in length and rate of presentation: a test of total-time hypotheses. *Journal of Experimental Psychology*, **92**, 365–372.

Robins, R. H. (1964). *General linguistics: an introductory survey*. London: Longmans, Green.

Robinson, J. J. (1970). Dependency structures and transformational rules. *Language*, **46**, 259–285.

Robinson, P. (1986). Constituency or dependency in the units of language acquisition? An approach to describing the learner's analysis of formulae. *Lingvisticae Investigationes, International Journal of French Linguistics and General Linguistics*, **10**, 417–437.

Roeper, T. (1996). The role of merger theory and formal features in acquisition. In H. Clahsen (ed.), *Generative perspectives on language acquisition* (pp. 415–449). Amsterdam: John Benjamins.

Rosenbloom, P. S. and Newell, A. (1987a). Learning by chunking, a production system model of practice. In D. Klahr, P. Langley and R. Neches (eds), *Production system models of learning and development* (pp. 221–286). Cambridge, MA: MIT Press.

Rosenbloom, P. S. and Newell, A. (1987b). An integrated computational model of stimulus-response compatibility and practice. In G. H. Bower (ed.), *The psychology of learning and motivation*, Vol. 21 (pp. 1–52). New York: Academic Press.

Ross, B. H. (1984). Remindings and their effects in learning a cognitive skill. *Cognitive Psychology*, **16**, 371–416.

Ross, J. R. (1972). The category squish: Endstation Hauptwort. In *Papers from the Eighth Regional Meeting, Chicago Linguistic Society* (pp. 316–328). Chicago, IL: Chicago Linguistic Society.

Ross, J. R. (1973). Nouniness. In O. Fujimura (ed.), *Three dimensions of linguistic theory* (pp. 137–258). Tokyo: TEC Co. Ltd.

Rowland, C. F., Pine, J. M., Lieven, E. V. M. and Theakston, A. L. (2003). Determinants of acquisition order in wh-questions: re-evaluating the role of caregiver speech. *Journal of Child Language*, **30**, 609–635.

Ruhland, R., Wijnen, F. and van Geert, P. (1995). An exploration into the application of dynamic systems modelling to language acquisition. In M. Verrips and F. Wijnen (eds), *Approaches to parameter setting. Amsterdam*

Series in Child Language Development, Vol. 4 (pp. 107–134). Amsterdam: Institute of General Linguistics.

Ryan, J. (1974). Early language development: towards a communicational analysis. In M. P. M. Richards (ed.), *The integration of a child into a social world* (pp. 185–213). London: Cambridge University Press.

Saffran, J. R. (2001). The use of predictive dependencies in language learning. *Journal of Memory and Language*, 44, 493–515.

Saffran, J. R. (2002). Constraints on statistical language learning. *Journal of Memory and Language*, 47, 172–196.

Salkoff, M. (1983). Bees are swarming in the garden. *Language*, 59, 288–346.

de Saussure, F. (1983). *Course in general linguistics.* (R. Harris, Trans.) (C. Bally & A. Sechehaye, eds). London: Duckworth. (Original work published 1922.)

Schabes, Y. (1990). Mathematical and computational aspects of lexicalized grammars. Unpublished Ph.D. thesis. (MS-CIS-90–48, LINC LAB179). Computer Science Department, University of Pennsylvania, Philadelphia, PA.

Schaffer, H. R. (1984). *The child's entry into a social world.* London: Academic Press.

Schlesinger, I. M. (1971). The production of utterances and language acquisition. In D. I. Slobin (ed.), *The ontogenesis of grammar: a theoretical symposium* (pp. 63–101). New York: Academic Press.

Schlesinger, I. M. (1974). Relational concepts underlying language. In R. Schiefelbusch and L. Lloyd (eds), *Language perspectives: acquisition, retardation, and intervention* (pp. 129–152). Baltimore, MD: University Park Press.

Seidenberg, M. S. and MacDonald, M. C. (1999). Probabilistic constraints approach to language acquisition and processing. *Cognitive Science*, 23, 569–588.

Serratrice, L., Joseph, K. L. and Conti-Ramsden, G. (2003). The acquisition of past tense in preschool children with specific language impairment and unaffected controls: regular and irregular forms. *Linguistics*, 41–42, 321–349.

Sethuraman, N. and Goodman, J. C. (2004, April). Children's mastery of the transitive construction. Paper presented at the Stanford Child Language Research Forum, Palo Alto, CA.

Sgall, P., Hajičová, E. and Panevová, J. (1986). *The meaning of the sentence in its semantic and pragmatic aspects.* Dordrecht: D. Reidel.

Shieber, S. M. (1986). *An introduction to unification-based approaches to grammar.* (CSLI Lecture Notes, Vol. 4.).Stanford, CA: Center for the Study of Language and Information.

Shrager, J. C., Hogg, T. and Huberman, B. A. (1988). A dynamical theory of the power-law of learning in problem solving. In *Proceedings of the Tenth Annual Conference of the Cognitive Science Society* (pp. 468–474). Hillsdale, NJ: Cognitive Science Society.

Singley, M. K. and Anderson, J. R. (1985). The transfer of text-editing skill. *International Journal of Man Machine Studies,* 22, 403–423.

Singley, M. K. and Anderson, J. R. (1989). *The transfer of cognitive skill.* Cambridge: MA: Harvard University Press.

Sleator, D. and Temperley, D. (1991). Parsing English with a Link Grammar. Carnegie Mellon University Computer Science technical report (CMU-CS-91–196, October 1991).

Slobin, D. I. (1985). Crosslinguistic evidence for the language-making capacity. In D. I. Slobin (ed.), *The crosslinguistic study of language acquisition,* Vol. 2 (pp. 1159–1249). Hillsdale, NJ: Lawrence Erlbaum.

Smiley, P. and Huttenlocher, J. (1995). Conceptual development and the child's early words for events, objects, and persons. In M. Tomasello and W. E. Merriman (eds), *Beyond names for things: young children's acquisition of verbs* (pp. 21–62). Hillsdale, NJ: Lawrence Erlbaum.

Smoczynska, M. (1976). Early syntactic development: pivot look and pivot grammar. *Polish Psychological Bulletin,* 1, 37–43.

Snedeker, J. and Gleitman, L. R. (2004). Why it is hard to label our concepts. In G. Hall and S. Waxman (eds), *Weaving a lexicon* (pp. 257–293). Cambridge, MA: MIT Press.

Snoddy, G. S. (1926). Learning and stability: a psychological analysis of a case of motor learning with clinical applications. *Journal of Applied Psychology,* 10, 1–36.

Snow, C. E. (1979). The role of social interaction in language acquisition. In W. A. Collins (ed.), *Minnesota Symposia on Child Psychology,* Vol. 12 (pp. 157–182). Hillsdale, NJ: Lawrence Erlbaum.

Speas, M. (1990). *Phrase structure in natural language.* Dordrecht: Kluwer.

Starosta, S. (1988). *The case for Lexicase.* London: Pinter.

Steedman, M. J. (1988). Combinators and grammars. In R. T. Oehrle, E. Bach and D. Wheeler (eds), *Categorial grammars and natural language structures* (pp. 417–442). Dordrecht: Reidel.

Steedman, M. J. (2000). *The syntactic process.* Cambridge, MA: MIT Press.

Stern, D. N. (1974). Mother and infant at play: the dyadic interaction involving facial, vocal and gaze behaviors. In M. Lewis and L. A. Rosenblum (eds), *The effect of the infant on its caregiver* (pp. 187–214). New York: Wiley-Interscience.

Stern, D. N. (1977). *The first relationship: infant and mother.* Cambridge, MA: Harvard University Press.

Steyvers, M. and Tenenbaum, J. (2005). The large-scale structure of semantic networks: Statistical analyses and a model of semantic growth. *Cognitive Science,* **29**, 41–78.

Storkel, H. L. (2002). Restructuring similarity neighborhoods in the developing mental lexicon. *Journal of Child Language,* **29**, 251–274.

Stowell, T. (1981). Origins of phrase structure. Unpublished Ph.D. thesis, MIT, Cambridge, MA.

Strogatz, S. H. (2001). Exploring complex networks. *Nature,* **410**, 268–276.

Szagun, G. (2001). Learning different regularities: the acquisition of noun plurals by German-speaking children. *First Language,* **21**, 109–141.

Taylor, J. R. (1989). *Linguistic categorization: prototypes in linguistic theory.* Oxford: Clarendon.

Tesnière, L. (1959). *Elements de syntaxe structurale.* Paris: Klincksieck.

Theakston, A. L., Lieven, E. V. M., Pine, J. M. and Rowland, C. F. (2004). Semantic generality, input frequency and the acquisition of syntax. *Journal of Child Language,* **31**, 61–99.

Thordardottir, E. T. and Weismer, S. E. (2001). High-frequency verbs and verb diversity in the spontaneous speech of school-age children with specific language impairment. International *Journal of Language and Communication Disorders,* **36**, 221–244.

Thorndike, E. L. (1906). *Principles of teaching.* New York: A. G. Seiler.

Thorndike, E. L. (1913). *Educational psychology,* Vols. 1 and 2. New York: Columbia University Press.

Thorndike, E. L. (1931). *Human learning.* New York: Century.

Tomasello, M. (1992). *First verbs: a case study of early grammatical development.* Cambridge: Cambridge University Press.

Tomasello, M. (1998). The return of constructions. *Journal of Child Language,* **25**, 431–447.

Tomasello, M. (2000a). Do young children have adult syntactic competence? *Cognition,* **74**, 209–253.

Tomasello, M. (2000b). First steps toward a usage-based theory of language acquisition. *Cognitive Linguistics,* **11**, 61–82.

Tomasello, M. (2003). *Constructing a language: a usage-based theory of language aquisition.* Cambride, MA: Harvard University Press.

Tomasello, M. and Brooks, P. J. (1998). Young children's earliest transitive and intransitive constructions. *Cognitive Linguistics,* **9,** 379–395.

Tomasello, M. and Brooks, P. J. (1999). Early syntactic development. In M. Barrett (ed.), *The development of language* (pp. 161–190). Hove: Psychology Press.

Trevarthen, C. (1977). Descriptive analyses of infant communicative behaviour. In H. R. Schaffer (ed.), *Studies in mother-infant interaction: the Loch Lamond Symposium* (pp. 227–270). London: Academic Press.

Trevarthen, C. (1979). Communication and co-operation in early infancy: a description of primary intersubjectivity. In M. Bullowa (ed.), *Before speech* (pp. 321–72). Cambridge: Cambridge University Press.

Trevarthen, C. and Hubley, P. (1978). Secondary intersubjectivity: confidence, confiding and acts of meaning in the first year. In A. Lock (ed.), *Action, gesture and symbol* (pp. 183–229). London: Academic Press.

Tronick, E., Als, H. and Adamson, L. B. (1979): Structure of early face-to-face communicative interactions. In M. Bullowa (ed.), *Before speech* (pp. 349–372). Cambridge: Cambridge University Press.

Trueswell, J. and Gleitman, L. R. (2004). Children's eye movements during listening: developmental evidence for a constraint-based theory of sentence processing. In J. M. Henderson and F. Ferreira (eds), *The interface of language, vision, and action: eye movements and the visual world* (pp. 319–346). New York: Psychology Press.

Tutte, W. T. (1984). *Graph theory.* Menlo Park, CA: Addison-Wesley.

Tversky, A. (1977). Features of similarity. *Psychological Review,* **84,** 327–352.

Uziel-Karl, S. (2002). How general is verb argument structure? The developmental history of early verbs in Hebrew. Paper presented at the 18th Meeting of The Israel Association for Theoretical Linguistics (IATL18). Bar Ilan University, Ramat Gan, Israel.

Van Valin, R. D. Jr. (1993). A synopsis of Role and Reference Grammar. In R. D. Van Valin (ed.), *Advances in Role and Reference Grammar* (pp. 1–164). Amsterdam: John Benjamins.

Venneman, T. (1977). Konstituenz und Dependenz in einigen neueren Grammatiktheorien. [Constituency and dependency in a new theory of grammar] *Sprachwissenschaft,* **2,** 259–301.

Vickery, B. C. and Vickery, A. (1987). *Information science—theory and practice.* London: Bowker-Saur.

Vihman, M. M. (1999). The transition to grammar in a bilingual child: positional patterns, model learning, and relational words. *International Journal of Bilingualism*, 3, 267–301.

Vihman, M. M., Kay, E., de Boysson-Bardies, B., Durand, C. and Sundberg, U. (1994). External sources of individual differences? A cross-linguistic analysis of the phonetics of mothers' speech to 1-year-old children. *Developmental Psychology*, 30, 651–662.

de Villiers, J. G. (1980). The process of rule learning in child speech: a new look. In K. E. Nelson (ed.), *Children's language*, Vol. 2 (pp. 1–44). New York: Gardner Press.

de Villiers, J. G. and de Villiers, P. A. (1978). *Language acquisition*. Cambridge, MA: Harvard University Press.

Vitevitch, M. S. (2005). Phonological neighbors in a small world: What can graph theory tell us about word learning? Paper presented to the Complex Systems and Networks Group at Indiana University; avaliable at http://vw.indiana.edu/talks-spring05/vitevitch.ppt.

Vygotsky, L. S. (1962). *Thought and language* (E. Hanfmann and G. Vakar, eds and trans.). Cambridge, MA: MIT Press. (Original work published 1934.)

Vygotsky, L. S. (1978). *Mind in society: the development of higher psychological processes*. (M. Cole, V. John-Steiner, S. Scribner and E. Souberman, eds. and trans.). Cambridge, MA: Harvard University Press.

Watanabe, S. (1969). *Knowing and guessing*. New York: Wiley.

Watts, D. J. and Strogatz, S. H. (1998). Collective dynamics of 'small-world' networks. *Nature*, 393, 440–442.

Wechsler, S. (1995). *The semantic basis of argument structure*. Stanford, CA: CSLI Publications.

Wells, G. (1974). Learning to code experience through language. *Journal of Child Language*, 1, 243–69.

Wijnen, F., Kempen, M. and Gillis, S. (2001). Root infinitives in Dutch early child language: an effect of input? *Journal of Child Language*, 28, 629–660.

Williamon, A. and Valentine, E. (2000). Quantity and quality of musical practice as predictors of performance quality. *British Journal of Psychology*, 91, 353–376.

Williams, E. (1984). Argument structure and morphology. *The Linguistic Review*, 1, 81–114.

Wilson, S. (2003). Lexically specific constructions in the acquisition of inflection in English. *Journal of Child Language*, 30, 1–41.

Wittgenstein, L. (1978). *Philosophical investigations* (G. E. M. Anscombe, trans.). Oxford: Blackwell. (Original work published 1953.)

Yarrow, L. J., Rubenstein, J. and Pedersen, F. (1975). *Infant and environment: early cognitive and motivational development.* New York: Wiley.

Zaenen, A. (1993). Unaccusativity in Dutch: integrating syntax and lexical semantics. In J. Pustejovsky (ed.), *Semantics and the lexicon* (pp. 129–162). Dordrecht: Kluwer.

Zipf, G. K. (1965). *Psycho-biology of language: an introduction to dynamic philology.* Cambridge, MA: MIT Press. (Original work published 1935.)

Zipf, G. K. (1972). *Human behaviour and the principle of least effort: an introduction to human ecology.* New York: Hafner. (Original work published 1949.)

Author Index

Subject Index

A

abstract syntactic rule (abstract
schema; schema) 1–4, 22, 35,
45, 65, 69, 70–3, 77–8, 80–4,
85, 87, 90–1, 97–9, 100, 104,
110, 114
see also Phrase Structure Rules

abstraction 45, 64, 69, 80, 82–3,
85–6, 91–2, 97–8, 100, 105
see also schema formation

accelerating acquisition *see*
acceleration

acceleration 3, 39–42, 45–59,
62–63, 66, 67, 68, 81–2, 89,
103–114

accusative case 90, 94
see also case

accusative-nominative languages 57,
67, 74, 88, 94, 103, 117

action (thematic category) 19–20,
74, 95, 96, 111, 117–8

actor (agent; thematic category) 11,
19, 20, 45, 61, 68, 74, 75, 95,
115

acyclic graph 9, 32
see also graph

Adam (child subject) 19

adjacency (projectivity) 33

adjective 12, 18, 22, 34, 70, 71, 131

adjunct 9, 16, 35, 117, 131

adverb 9, 12, 34, 131

agent *see* actor

agents (free) 5, 119, 120, 141, 143

analogical reasoning 38, 65, 85

analogy 4, 35, 37–9, 45, 61–4, 65, 69,
83–6, 90–1, 92–4, 97, 102

arc *see* link

argument 2, 4, 13–15, 18, 19–23, 26,
29, 32, 37, 62, 69, 73, 74–5,
77, 86, 88, 91, 92, 94, 95,
96–8, 102, 117

arity *see* logical valency

article 18

asymmetry 7–11, 15, 21, 29, 87

autonomy of syntax 90, 95, 98, 99,
114, 119

auxiliary verb 18, 58

B

behavioural features (of grammatical
relations) 94

bilingual development 26–7, 35–6

bipartite graph (bipartite
network) 4–5, 124–7, 133–4,
145, 148

bootstrapping 90, 98

C

canonical syntactic mapping 76

canonical word-order 17, 75, 94

case 94, 117
see also accusative case; dative case;
nominative case

case roles *see* thematic roles

categorization 85, 90, 92, 93, 95, 108,
115, 117

category formation 91, 99, 104,
108–9